MR & MRS X

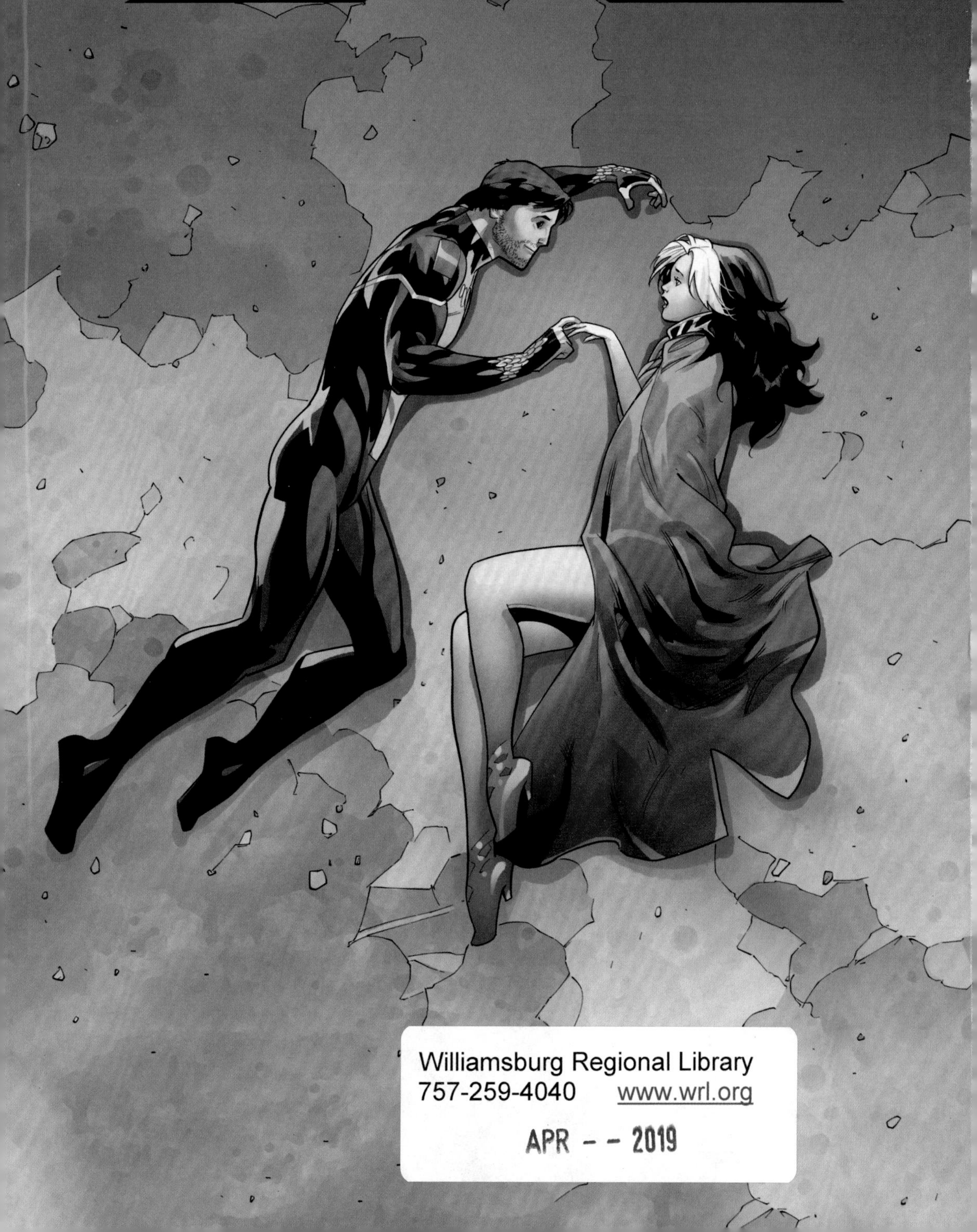

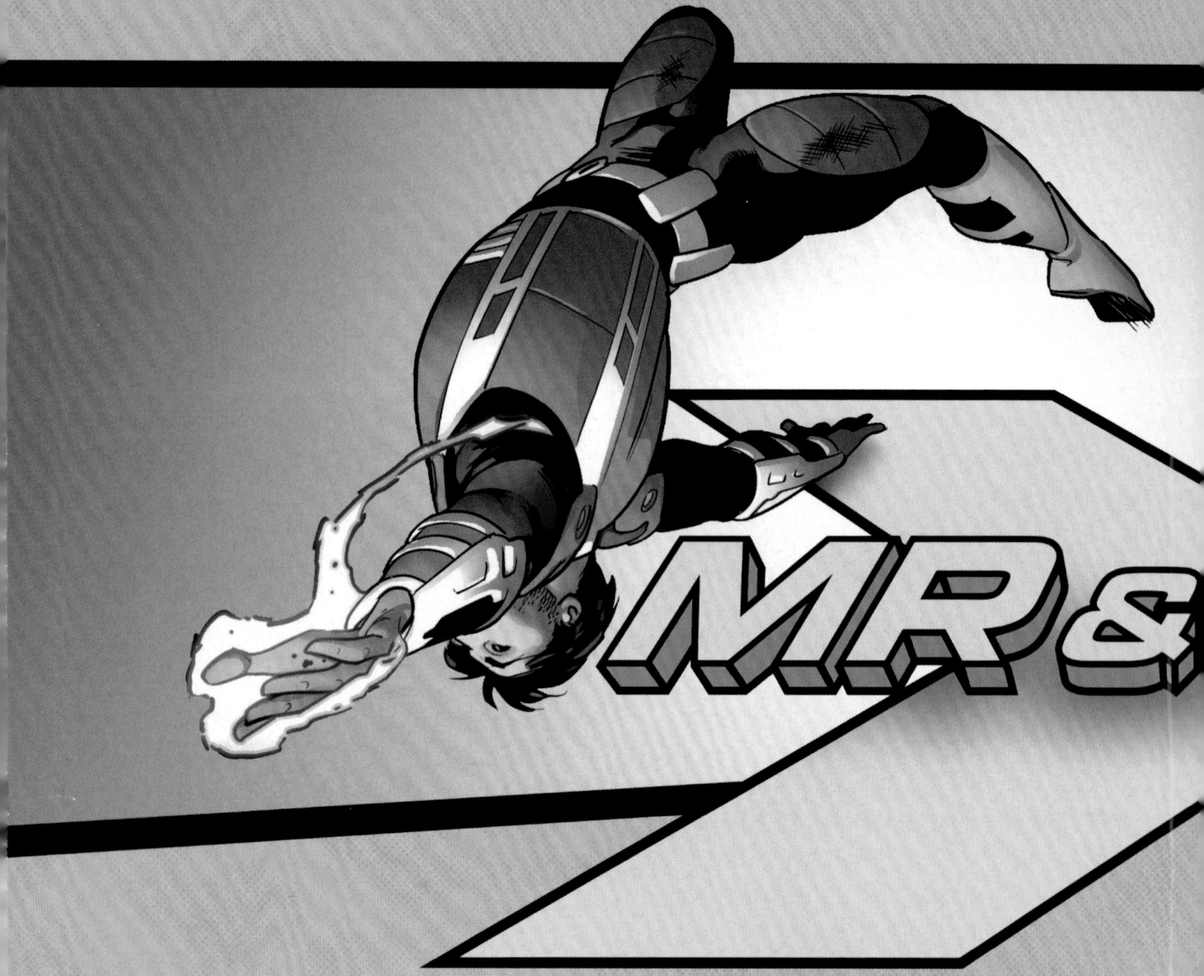
MR &

ANNALISE BISSA & DANNY KHAZEM
ASSISTANT EDITORS

DARREN SHAN — EDITOR

JORDAN D. WHITE — X-MEN GROUP EDITOR

COLLECTION EDITOR **JENNIFER GRÜNWALD** ▪ ASSISTANT EDITOR **CAITLIN O'CONNELL** ▪ ASSOCIATE MANAGING EDITOR **KATERI WOODY**
EDITOR, SPECIAL PROJECTS **MARK D. BEAZLEY** ▪ VP PRODUCTION & SPECIAL PROJECTS **JEFF YOUNGQUIST** ▪ SVP PRINT, SALES & MARKETING **DAVID GABRIEL**
BOOK DESIGNER **JAY BOWEN**

EDITOR IN CHIEF **C.B. CEBULSKI** ▪ CHIEF CREATIVE OFFICER **JOE QUESADA** ▪ PRESIDENT **DAN BUCKLEY** ▪ EXECUTIVE PRODUCER **ALAN FINE**

MR. AND MRS. X VOL. 1: LOVE AND MARRIAGE. Contains material originally published in magazine form as MR. AND MRS. X #1-6. First printing 2019. ISBN 978-1-302-91351-9. Published by MARVEL WORLDWIDE, INC., a subsidiary of MARVEL ENTERTAINMENT, LLC. OFFICE OF PUBLICATION: 135 West 50th Street, New York, NY 10020. **Printed in Canada.** DAN BUCKLEY, President, Marvel Entertainment; JOHN NEE, Publisher; JOE QUESADA, Chief Creative Officer; TOM BREVOORT, SVP of Publishing; DAVID BOGART, SVP of Business Affairs & Operations, Publishing & Partnership; DAVID GABRIEL, SVP of Sales & Marketing, Publishing; JEFF YOUNGQUIST, VP of Production & Special Projects; DAN CARR, Executive Director of Publishing Technology; ALEX MORALES, Director of Publishing Operations; DAN EDINGTON, Managing Editor; SUSAN CRESPI, Production Manager; STAN LEE, Chairman Emeritus. For information regarding advertising in Marvel Comics or on Marvel.com, please contact Vit DeBellis, Custom Solutions & Integrated Advertising Manager, at vdebellis@marvel.com. For Marvel subscription inquiries, please call 888-511-5480. **Manufactured between 1/4/2019 and 2/5/2019 by SOLISCO PRINTERS, SCOTT, QC, CANADA.**

10 9 8 7 6 5 4 3 2 1

M.RS

KELLY THOMPSON
WRITER

OSCAR BAZALDUA & **DAVID LOPEZ**
[#1-5] ARTISTS [#6]

FRANK D'ARMATA & **NAYOUNG KIM**
[#1-5] COLOR ARTISTS [#6]

VC's JOE SABINO & **TRAVIS LANHAM**
[#1, #3-6] LETTERERS [#2]

TERRY DODSON & RACHEL DODSON
COVER ART

1

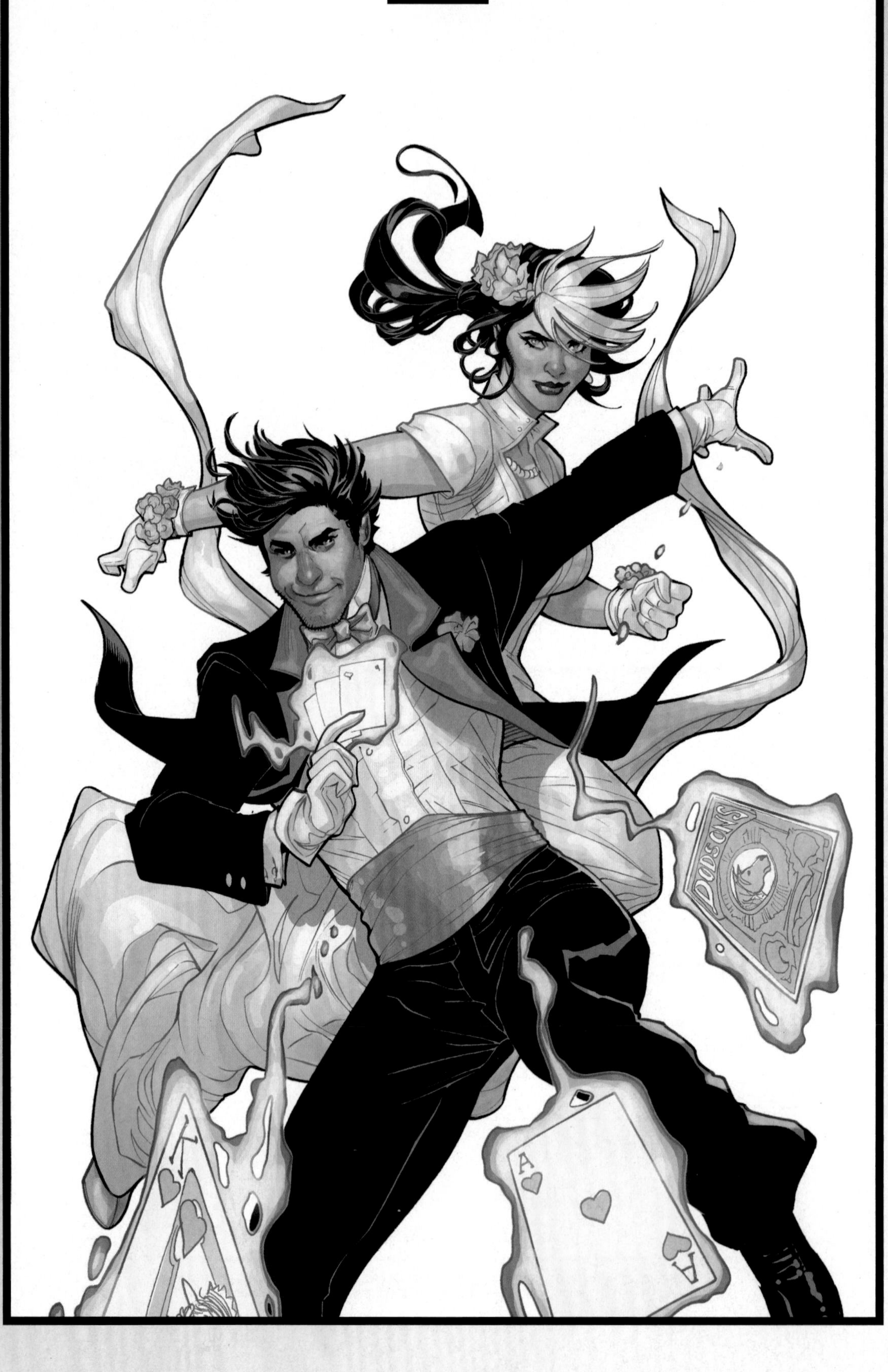
DODSONS

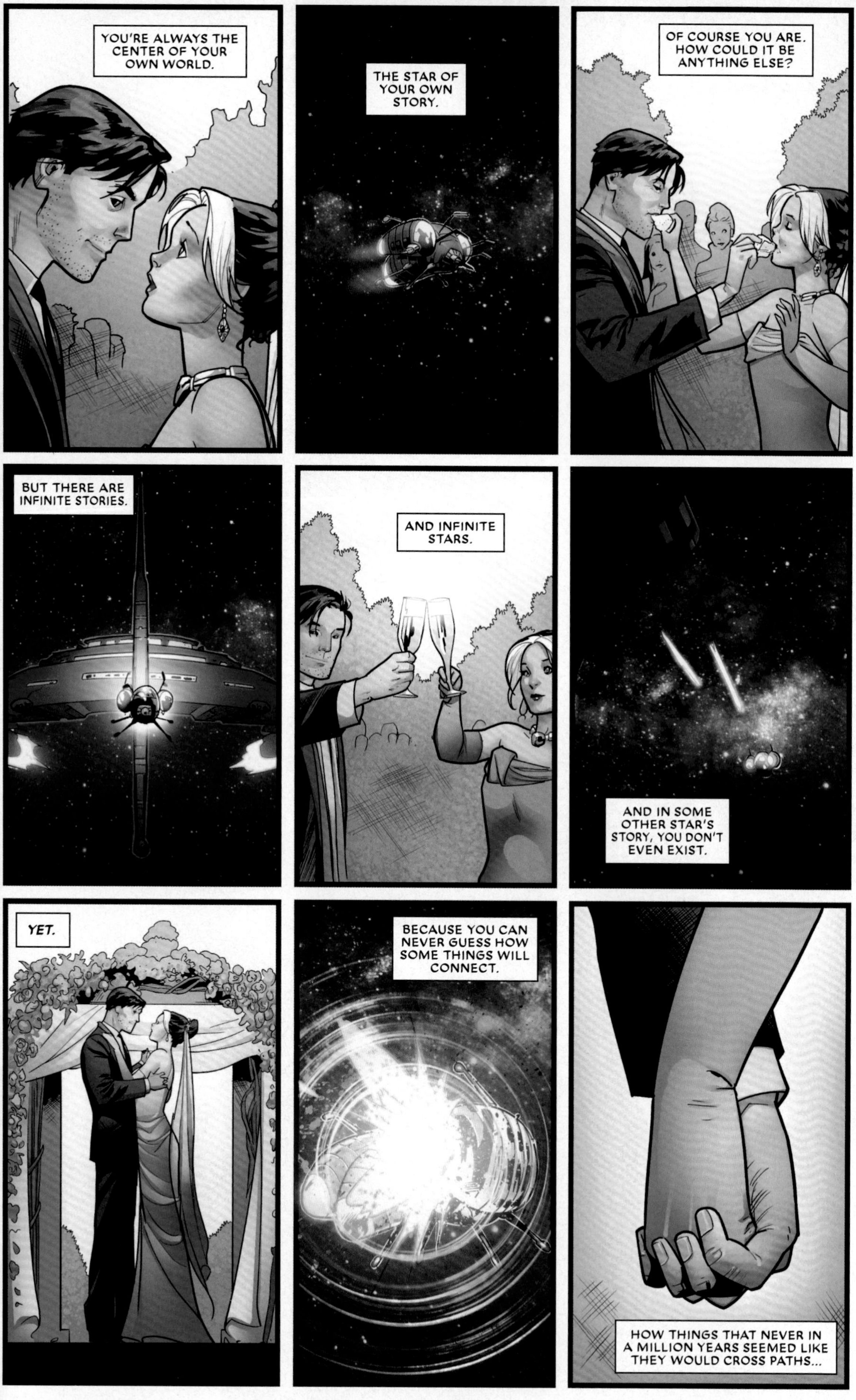
YOU'RE ALWAYS THE CENTER OF YOUR OWN WORLD.
THE STAR OF YOUR OWN STORY.
OF COURSE YOU ARE. HOW COULD IT BE ANYTHING ELSE?
BUT THERE ARE INFINITE STORIES.
AND INFINITE STARS.
AND IN SOME OTHER STAR'S STORY, YOU DON'T EVEN EXIST.
YET.
BECAUSE YOU CAN NEVER GUESS HOW SOME THINGS WILL CONNECT.
HOW THINGS THAT NEVER IN A MILLION YEARS SEEMED LIKE THEY WOULD CROSS PATHS...

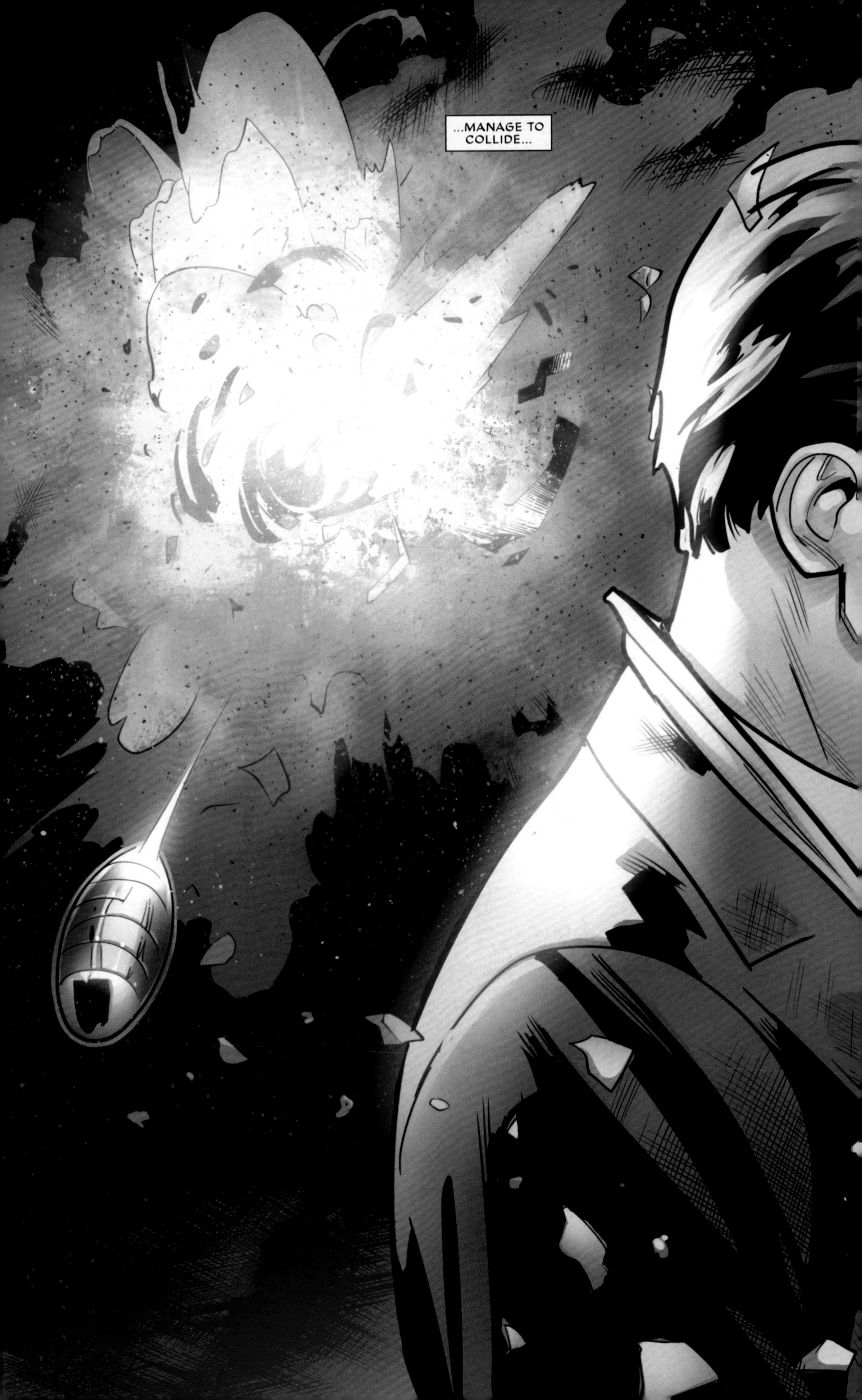
...MANAGE TO COLLIDE...

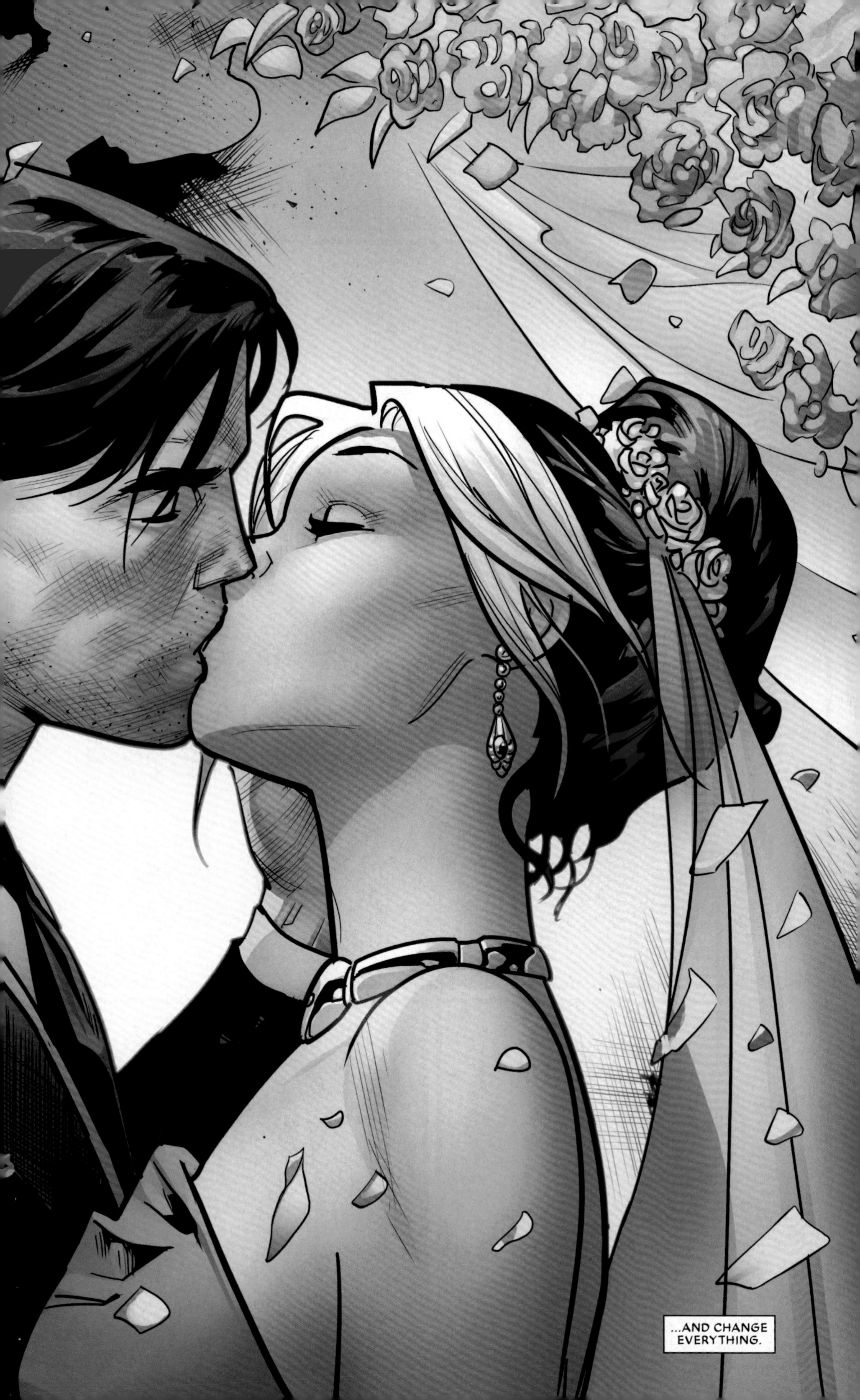
...AND CHANGE EVERYTHING.

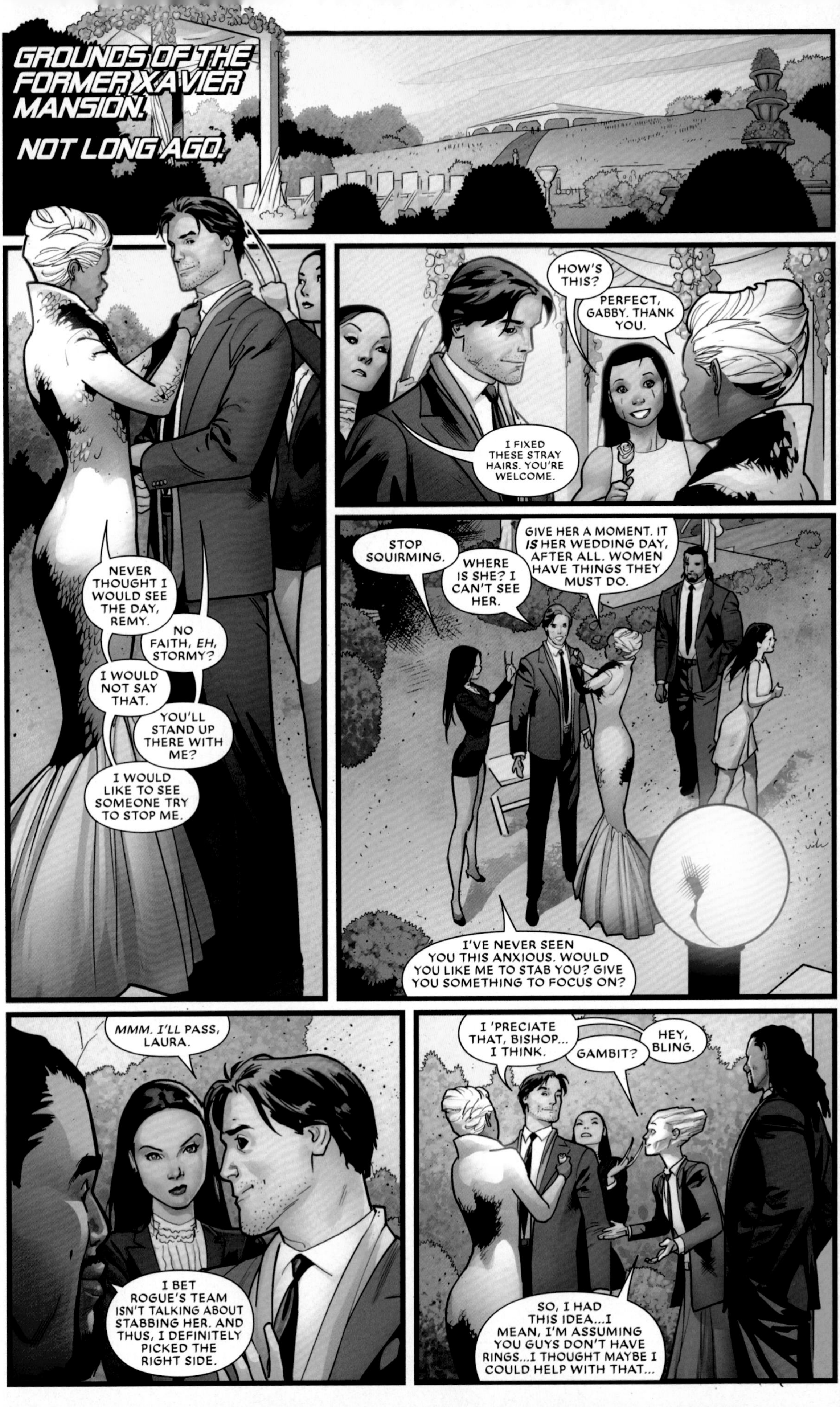
GROUNDS OF THE FORMER XAVIER MANSION.
NOT LONG AGO.
NEVER THOUGHT I WOULD SEE THE DAY, REMY.
NO FAITH, EH, STORMY?
I WOULD NOT SAY THAT.
YOU'LL STAND UP THERE WITH ME?
I WOULD LIKE TO SEE SOMEONE TRY TO STOP ME.
HOW'S THIS?
PERFECT, GABBY. THANK YOU.
I FIXED THESE STRAY HAIRS. YOU'RE WELCOME.
STOP SQUIRMING.
WHERE IS SHE? I CAN'T SEE HER.
GIVE HER A MOMENT. IT IS HER WEDDING DAY, AFTER ALL. WOMEN HAVE THINGS THEY MUST DO.
I'VE NEVER SEEN YOU THIS ANXIOUS. WOULD YOU LIKE ME TO STAB YOU? GIVE YOU SOMETHING TO FOCUS ON?
MMM. I'LL PASS, LAURA.
I BET ROGUE'S TEAM ISN'T TALKING ABOUT STABBING HER. AND THUS, I DEFINITELY PICKED THE RIGHT SIDE.
I 'PRECIATE THAT, BISHOP... I THINK.
HEY, BLING.
GAMBIT?
SO, I HAD THIS IDEA...I MEAN, I'M ASSUMING YOU GUYS DON'T HAVE RINGS...I THOUGHT MAYBE I COULD HELP WITH THAT...

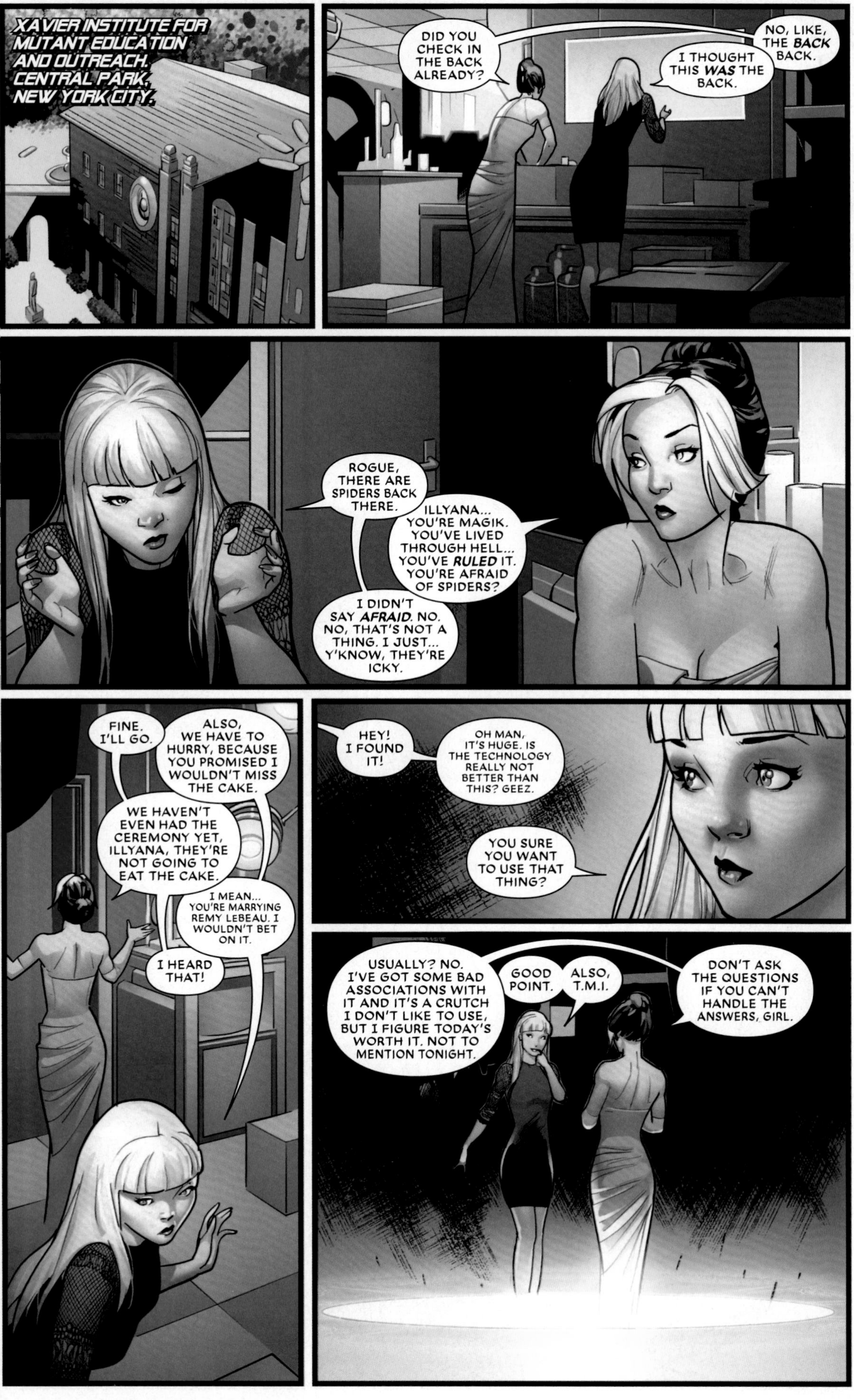
XAVIER INSTITUTE FOR MUTANT EDUCATION AND OUTREACH. CENTRAL PARK, NEW YORK CITY.
DID YOU CHECK IN THE BACK ALREADY?
I THOUGHT THIS WAS THE BACK.
NO, LIKE, THE BACK BACK.
ROGUE, THERE ARE SPIDERS BACK THERE.
ILLYANA... YOU'RE MAGIK. YOU'VE LIVED THROUGH HELL... YOU'VE RULED IT. YOU'RE AFRAID OF SPIDERS?
I DIDN'T SAY AFRAID. NO. NO, THAT'S NOT A THING. I JUST... Y'KNOW, THEY'RE ICKY.
FINE. I'LL GO.
ALSO, WE HAVE TO HURRY, BECAUSE YOU PROMISED I WOULDN'T MISS THE CAKE.
WE HAVEN'T EVEN HAD THE CEREMONY YET, ILLYANA, THEY'RE NOT GOING TO EAT THE CAKE.
I MEAN... YOU'RE MARRYING REMY LEBEAU. I WOULDN'T BET ON IT.
I HEARD THAT!
HEY! I FOUND IT!
OH MAN, IT'S HUGE. IS THE TECHNOLOGY REALLY NOT BETTER THAN THIS? GEEZ.
YOU SURE YOU WANT TO USE THAT THING?
USUALLY? NO. I'VE GOT SOME BAD ASSOCIATIONS WITH IT AND IT'S A CRUTCH I DON'T LIKE TO USE, BUT I FIGURE TODAY'S WORTH IT. NOT TO MENTION TONIGHT.
DON'T ASK THE QUESTIONS IF YOU CAN'T HANDLE THE ANSWERS, GIRL.
GOOD POINT.
ALSO, T.M.I.

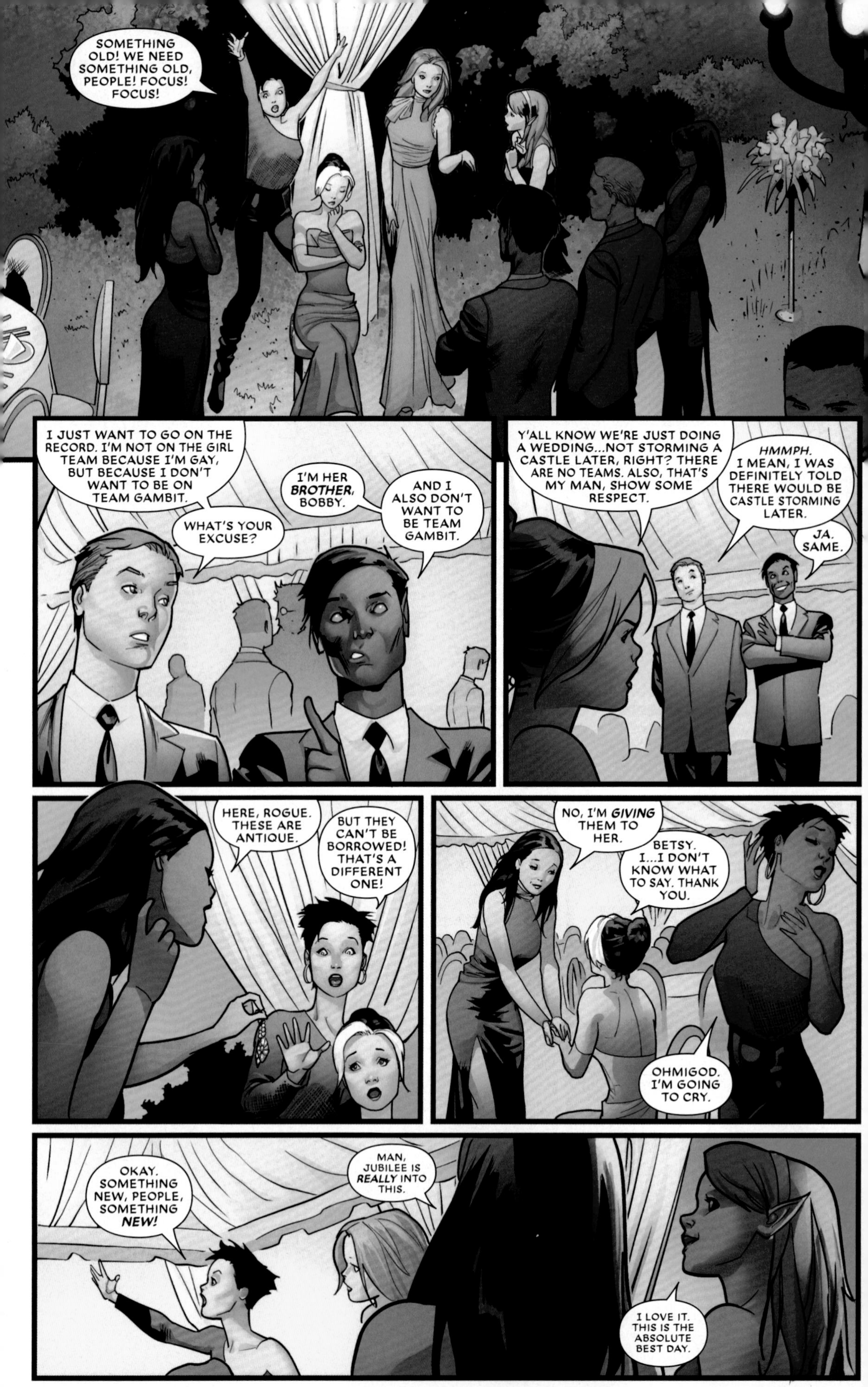
SOMETHING OLD! WE NEED SOMETHING OLD, PEOPLE! FOCUS! FOCUS!
I JUST WANT TO GO ON THE RECORD. I'M NOT ON THE GIRL TEAM BECAUSE I'M GAY, BUT BECAUSE I DON'T WANT TO BE ON TEAM GAMBIT.
WHAT'S YOUR EXCUSE?
I'M HER BROTHER, BOBBY.
AND I ALSO DON'T WANT TO BE TEAM GAMBIT.
Y'ALL KNOW WE'RE JUST DOING A WEDDING...NOT STORMING A CASTLE LATER, RIGHT? THERE ARE NO TEAMS. ALSO, THAT'S MY MAN, SHOW SOME RESPECT.
HMMPH. I MEAN, I WAS DEFINITELY TOLD THERE WOULD BE CASTLE STORMING LATER.
JA. SAME.
HERE, ROGUE. THESE ARE ANTIQUE.
BUT THEY CAN'T BE BORROWED! THAT'S A DIFFERENT ONE!
NO, I'M GIVING THEM TO HER.
BETSY. I...I DON'T KNOW WHAT TO SAY. THANK YOU.
OHMIGOD. I'M GOING TO CRY.
OKAY. SOMETHING NEW, PEOPLE, SOMETHING NEW!
MAN, JUBILEE IS REALLY INTO THIS.
I LOVE IT. THIS IS THE ABSOLUTE BEST DAY.

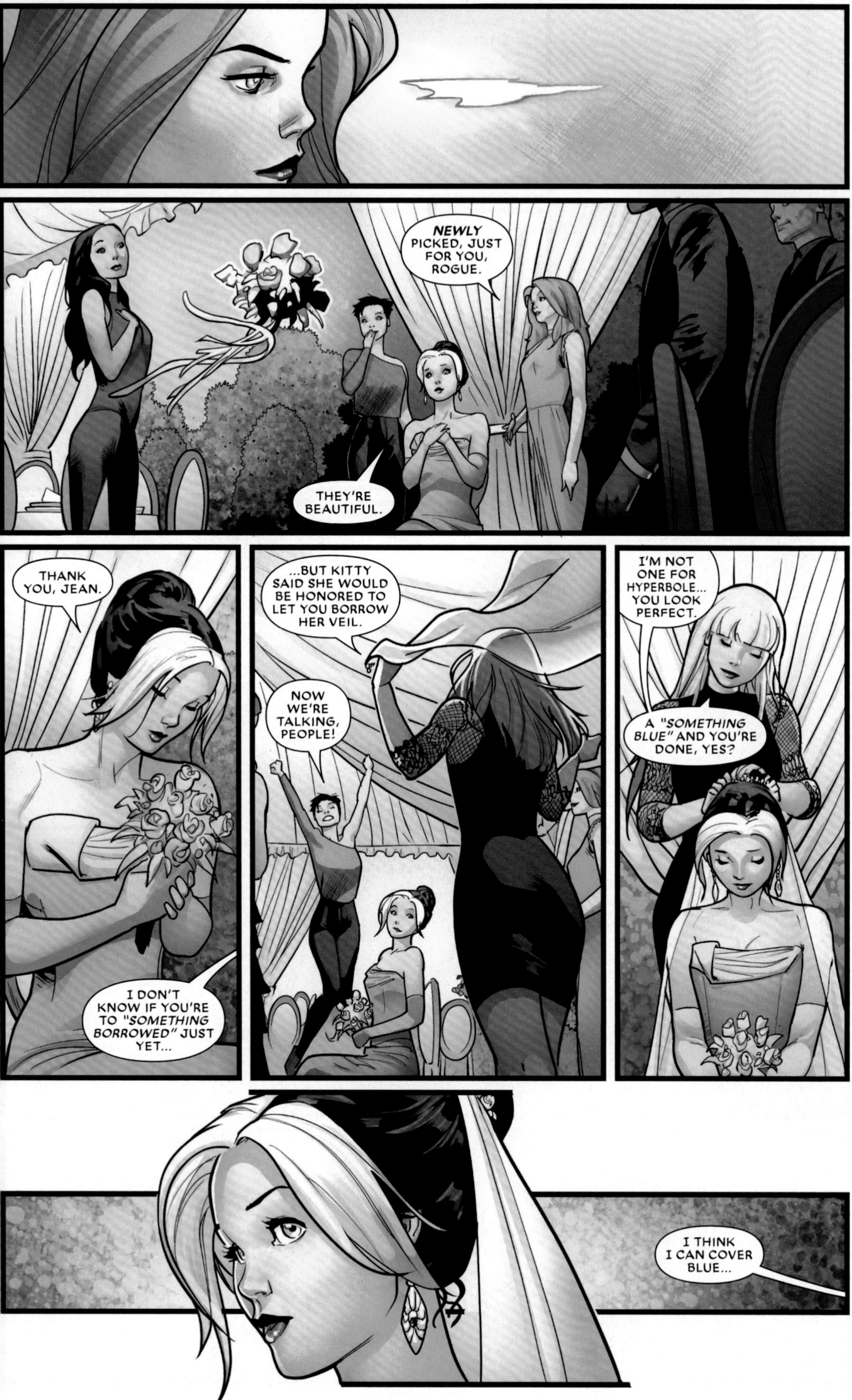
NEWLY PICKED, JUST FOR YOU, ROGUE.
THEY'RE BEAUTIFUL.
THANK YOU, JEAN.
I DON'T KNOW IF YOU'RE TO "SOMETHING BORROWED" JUST YET...
...BUT KITTY SAID SHE WOULD BE HONORED TO LET YOU BORROW HER VEIL.
NOW WE'RE TALKING, PEOPLE!
I'M NOT ONE FOR HYPERBOLE... YOU LOOK PERFECT.
A "SOMETHING BLUE" AND YOU'RE DONE, YES?
I THINK I CAN COVER BLUE...

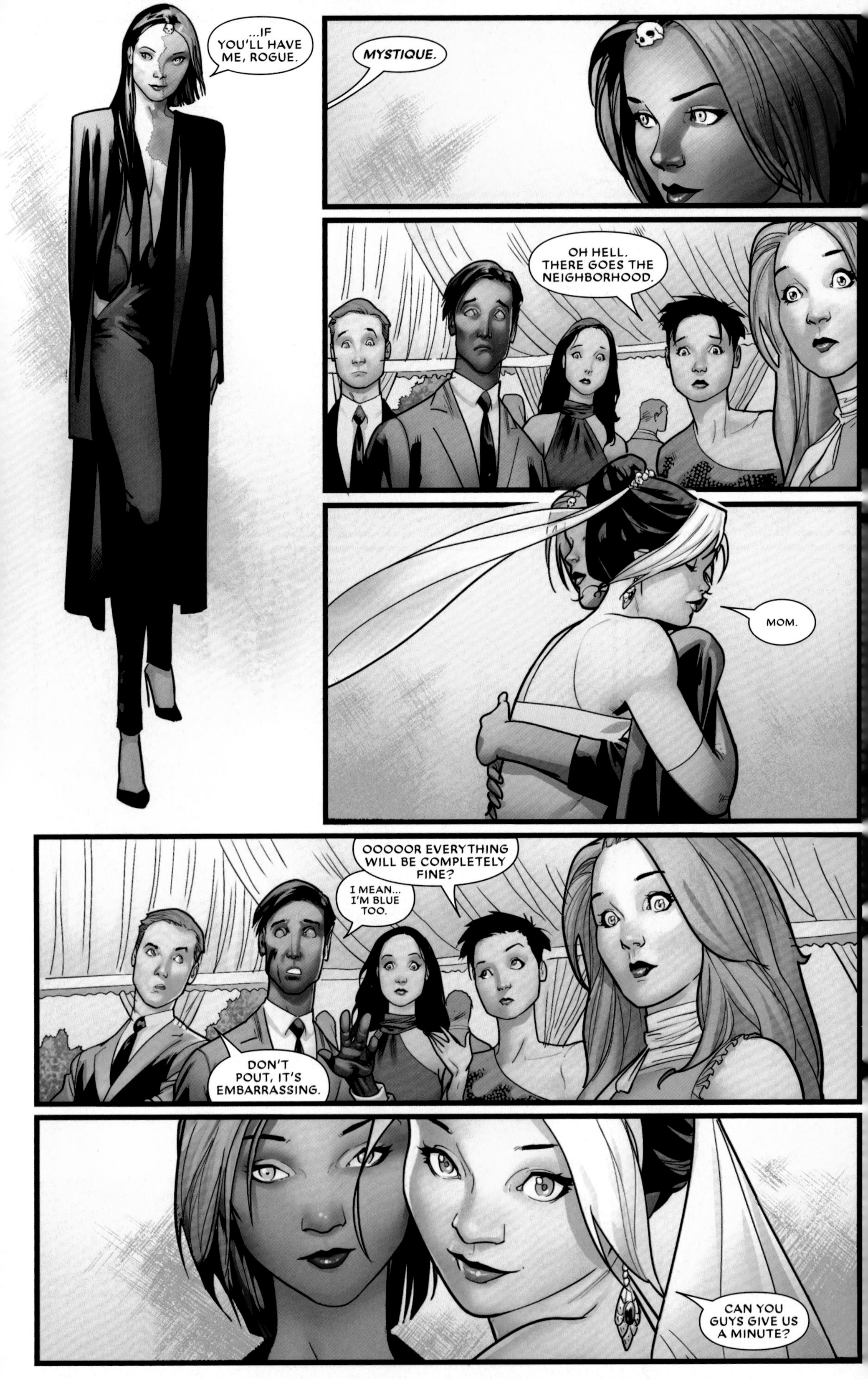
...IF YOU'LL HAVE ME, ROGUE.
MYSTIQUE.
OH HELL. THERE GOES THE NEIGHBORHOOD.
MOM.
OOOOOR EVERYTHING WILL BE COMPLETELY FINE?
I MEAN... I'M BLUE TOO.
DON'T POUT, IT'S EMBARRASSING.
CAN YOU GUYS GIVE US A MINUTE?

SO YOU WERE HERE ALL ALONG? POSING AS ABIGAIL BRAND?

I HAD IT ON GOOD AUTHORITY BRAND WOULDN'T BE ABLE TO MAKE THE TRIP. THOUGHT I'D BORROW HER INVITE. COMPLETELY HARMLESS. I DIDN'T EVEN BRING A PLUS ONE.

RARELY DO YOU DO THINGS I'D CATEGORIZE AS "COMPLETELY HARMLESS." WHY ARE YOU REALLY HERE, MYSTIQUE?

ARE YOU KIDDING? MUTANT "WEDDING OF THE CENTURY" AND YOU THOUGHT I WAS GOING TO MISS IT?

OF COURSE, I DIDN'T REALIZE IT WAS ACTUALLY GOING TO TURN OUT TO BE TRUE.

SO...YOU'RE NOT GOING TO... I DON'T KNOW... KIDNAP ME? BRAINWASH SOMEONE? TURN INTO ME AND STRAND REMY AT THE ALTAR OR TRY TO SLEEP WITH HIM "FOR MY OWN GOOD"? JUST STOP ME WHEN I NAME THE RIGHT ONE.

I...I WANT ONLY THE BEST FOR YOU, ROGUE. I MAY HAVE GONE ABOUT THAT IN... QUESTIONABLE WAYS IN THE PAST, BUT IT'S STILL ALL I'VE EVER WANTED FOR YOU. THE BEST.

YOU WON'T MIND ME BEING A TAD SKEPTICAL.

MIND? I'D BE ASHAMED IF YOU WEREN'T. I RAISED YOU BETTER THAN THAT.

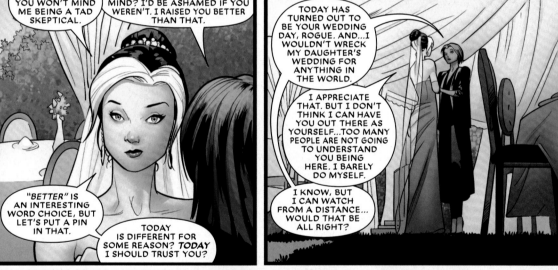

TODAY HAS TURNED OUT TO BE YOUR WEDDING DAY, ROGUE. AND...I WOULDN'T WRECK MY DAUGHTER'S WEDDING FOR ANYTHING IN THE WORLD.

I APPRECIATE THAT. BUT I DON'T THINK I CAN HAVE YOU OUT THERE AS YOURSELF...TOO MANY PEOPLE ARE NOT GOING TO UNDERSTAND YOU BEING HERE. I BARELY DO MYSELF.

I KNOW, BUT I CAN WATCH FROM A DISTANCE... WOULD THAT BE ALL RIGHT?

"BETTER" IS AN INTERESTING WORD CHOICE, BUT LET'S PUT A PIN IN THAT.

TODAY IS DIFFERENT FOR SOME REASON? TODAY I SHOULD TRUST YOU?

THANK YOU, MOM.

ARE YOU ABSOLUTELY CERTAIN I CAN'T INTEREST YOU IN A DIFFERENT GROOM?

SHHHHHHH. DON'T RUIN IT.

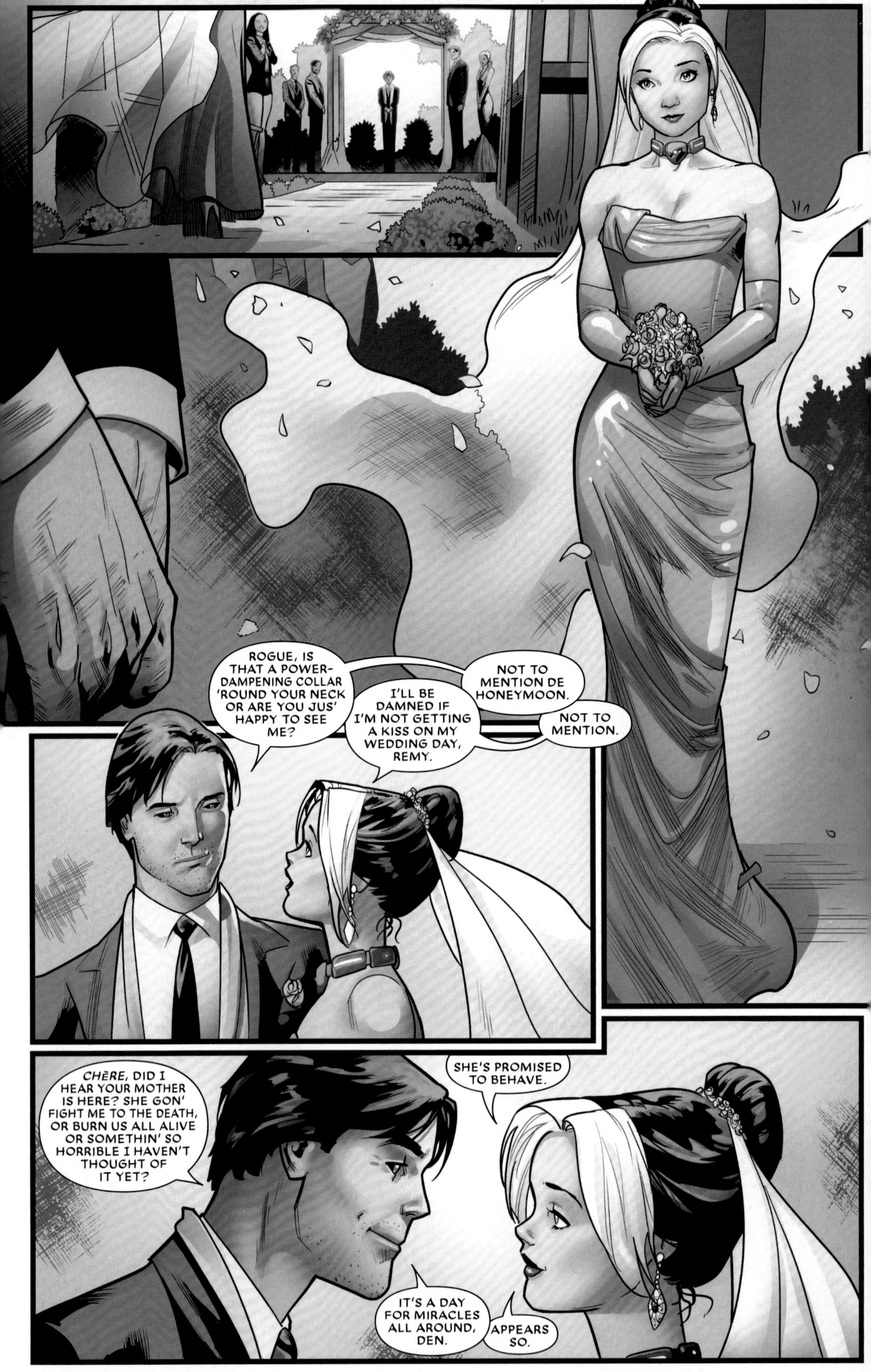

ROGUE, IS THAT A POWER-DAMPENING COLLAR 'ROUND YOUR NECK OR ARE YOU JUS' HAPPY TO SEE ME?
I'LL BE DAMNED IF I'M NOT GETTING A KISS ON MY WEDDING DAY, REMY.
NOT TO MENTION DE HONEYMOON.
NOT TO MENTION.
CHÈRE, DID I HEAR YOUR MOTHER IS HERE? SHE GON' FIGHT ME TO THE DEATH, OR BURN US ALL ALIVE OR SOMETHIN' SO HORRIBLE I HAVEN'T THOUGHT OF IT YET?
SHE'S PROMISED TO BEHAVE.
IT'S A DAY FOR MIRACLES ALL AROUND, DEN.
APPEARS SO.

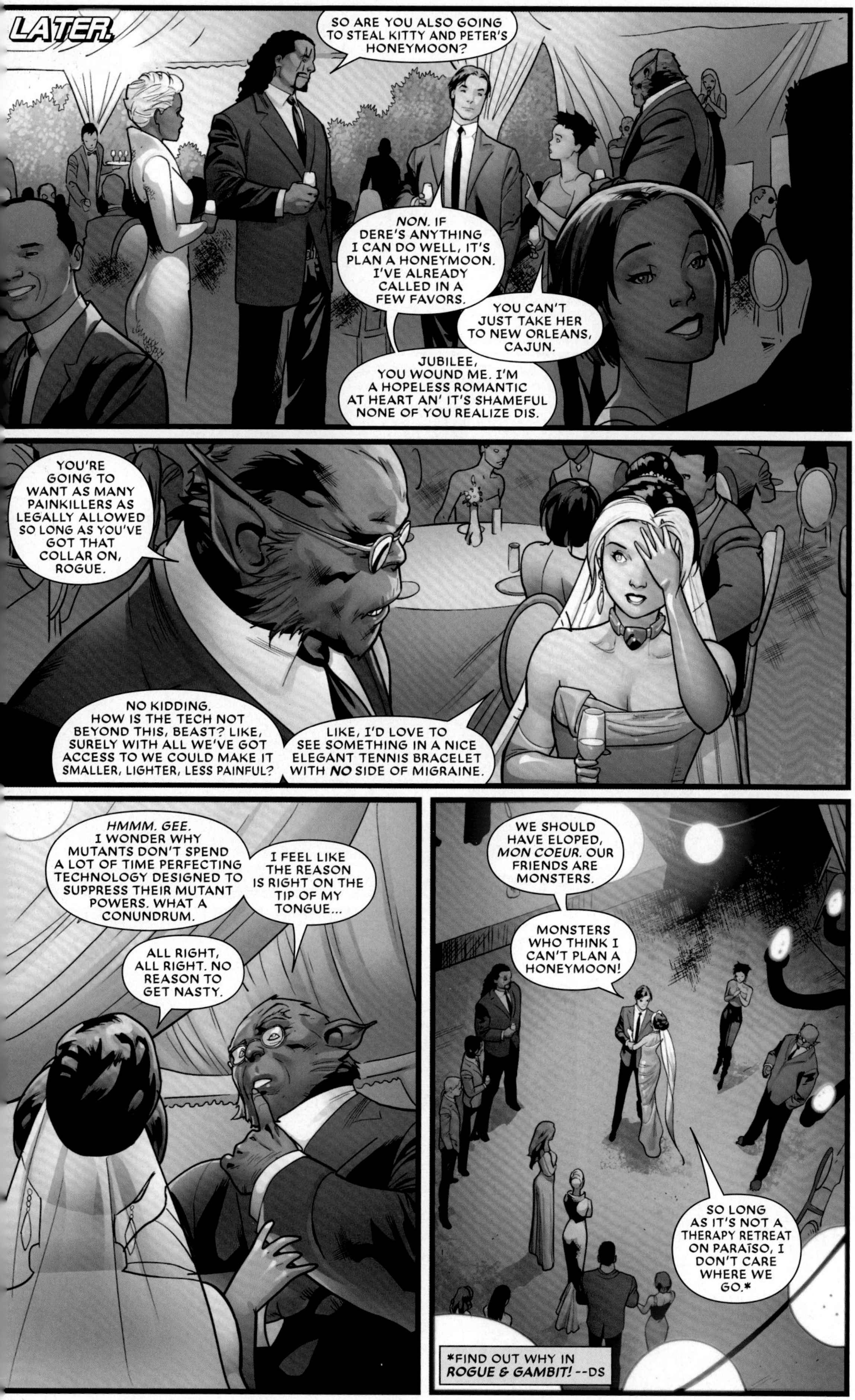
LATER.
SO ARE YOU ALSO GOING TO STEAL KITTY AND PETER'S HONEYMOON?
NON. IF DERE'S ANYTHING I CAN DO WELL, IT'S PLAN A HONEYMOON. I'VE ALREADY CALLED IN A FEW FAVORS.
YOU CAN'T JUST TAKE HER TO NEW ORLEANS, CAJUN.
JUBILEE, YOU WOUND ME. I'M A HOPELESS ROMANTIC AT HEART AN' IT'S SHAMEFUL NONE OF YOU REALIZE DIS.
YOU'RE GOING TO WANT AS MANY PAINKILLERS AS LEGALLY ALLOWED SO LONG AS YOU'VE GOT THAT COLLAR ON, ROGUE.
NO KIDDING. HOW IS THE TECH NOT BEYOND THIS, BEAST? LIKE, SURELY WITH ALL WE'VE GOT ACCESS TO WE COULD MAKE IT SMALLER, LIGHTER, LESS PAINFUL?
LIKE, I'D LOVE TO SEE SOMETHING IN A NICE ELEGANT TENNIS BRACELET WITH NO SIDE OF MIGRAINE.
HMMM. GEE. I WONDER WHY MUTANTS DON'T SPEND A LOT OF TIME PERFECTING TECHNOLOGY DESIGNED TO SUPPRESS THEIR MUTANT POWERS. WHAT A CONUNDRUM.
I FEEL LIKE THE REASON IS RIGHT ON THE TIP OF MY TONGUE...
ALL RIGHT, ALL RIGHT. NO REASON TO GET NASTY.
WE SHOULD HAVE ELOPED, MON COEUR. OUR FRIENDS ARE MONSTERS.
MONSTERS WHO THINK I CAN'T PLAN A HONEYMOON!
SO LONG AS IT'S NOT A THERAPY RETREAT ON PARAÍSO, I DON'T CARE WHERE WE GO.*
*FIND OUT WHY IN ROGUE & GAMBIT! --DS

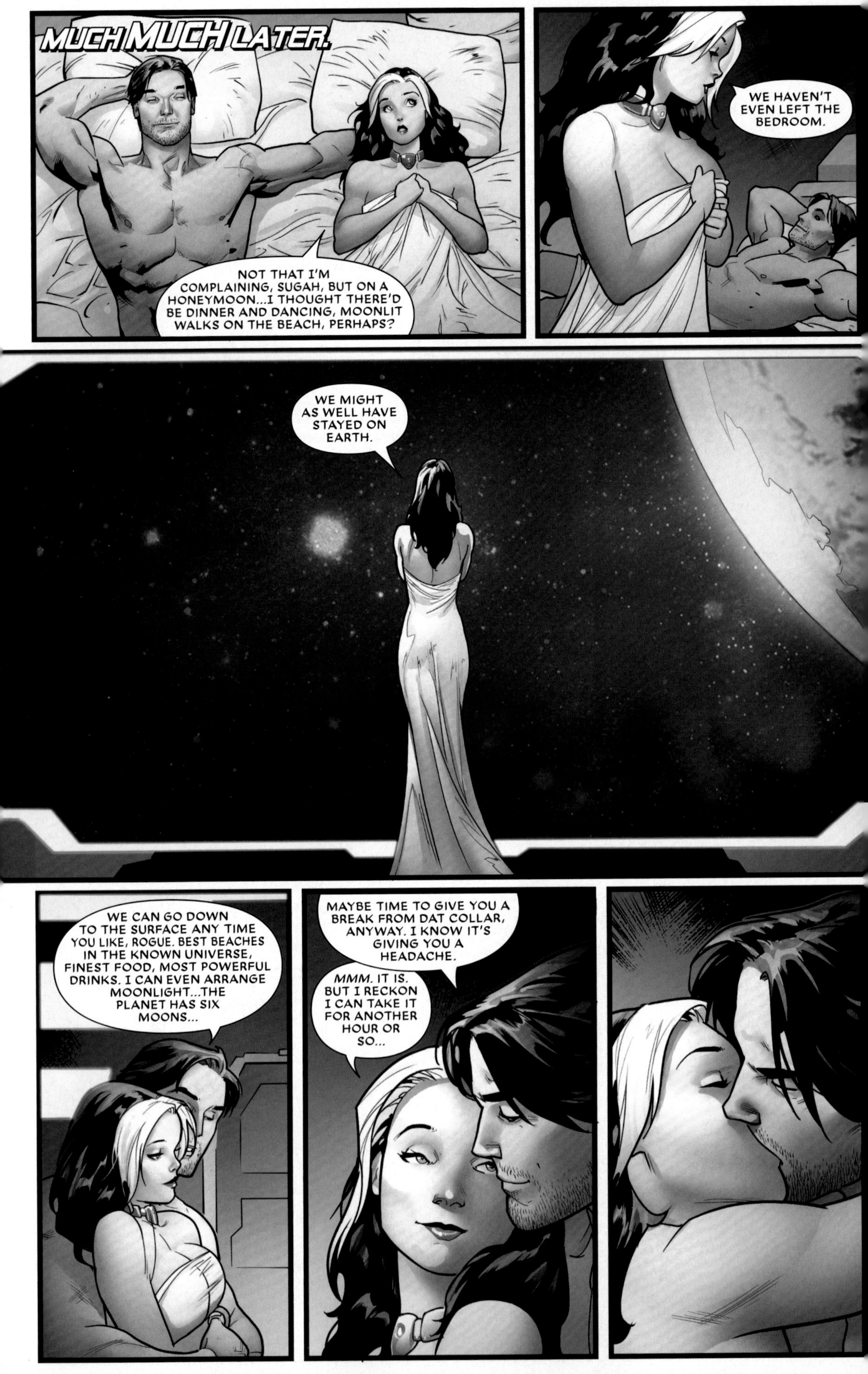
MUCH MUCH LATER.
NOT THAT I'M COMPLAINING, SUGAH, BUT ON A HONEYMOON...I THOUGHT THERE'D BE DINNER AND DANCING, MOONLIT WALKS ON THE BEACH, PERHAPS?
WE HAVEN'T EVEN LEFT THE BEDROOM.
WE MIGHT AS WELL HAVE STAYED ON EARTH.
WE CAN GO DOWN TO THE SURFACE ANY TIME YOU LIKE, ROGUE. BEST BEACHES IN THE KNOWN UNIVERSE, FINEST FOOD, MOST POWERFUL DRINKS. I CAN EVEN ARRANGE MOONLIGHT...THE PLANET HAS SIX MOONS...
MAYBE TIME TO GIVE YOU A BREAK FROM DAT COLLAR, ANYWAY. I KNOW IT'S GIVING YOU A HEADACHE.
MMM. IT IS. BUT I RECKON I CAN TAKE IT FOR ANOTHER HOUR OR SO...

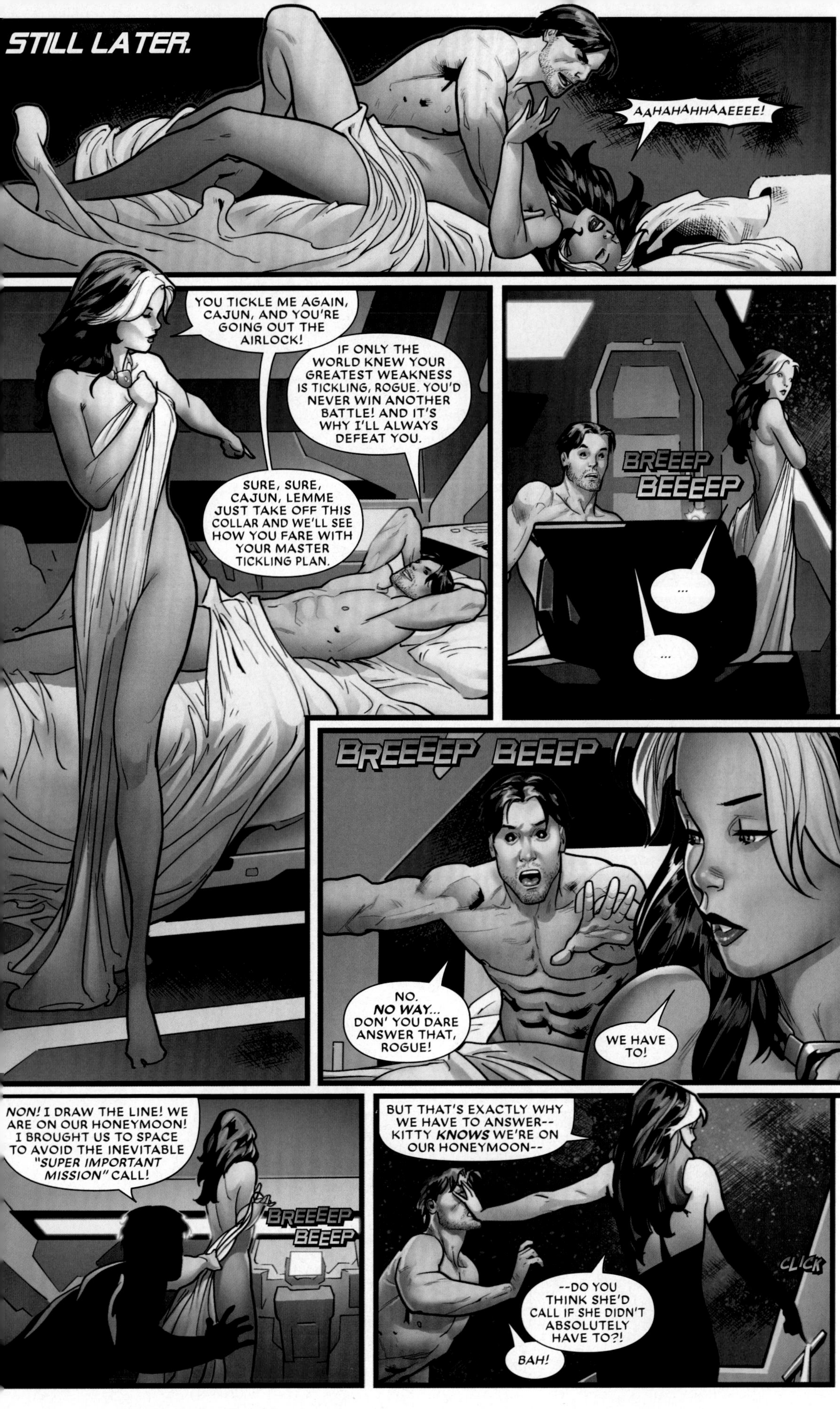
STILL LATER.
AAHAHAHHAAEEEE!
YOU TICKLE ME AGAIN, CAJUN, AND YOU'RE GOING OUT THE AIRLOCK!
IF ONLY THE WORLD KNEW YOUR GREATEST WEAKNESS IS TICKLING, ROGUE. YOU'D NEVER WIN ANOTHER BATTLE! AND IT'S WHY I'LL ALWAYS DEFEAT YOU.
SURE, SURE, CAJUN, LEMME JUST TAKE OFF THIS COLLAR AND WE'LL SEE HOW YOU FARE WITH YOUR MASTER TICKLING PLAN.
BREEEP BEEEEP
...
...
BREEEEP BEEEP
NO. NO WAY... DON' YOU DARE ANSWER THAT, ROGUE!
WE HAVE TO!
NON! I DRAW THE LINE! WE ARE ON OUR HONEYMOON! I BROUGHT US TO SPACE TO AVOID THE INEVITABLE "SUPER IMPORTANT MISSION" CALL!
BREEEEP BEEEP
BUT THAT'S EXACTLY WHY WE HAVE TO ANSWER-- KITTY KNOWS WE'RE ON OUR HONEYMOON--
CLICK
--DO YOU THINK SHE'D CALL IF SHE DIDN'T ABSOLUTELY HAVE TO?!
BAH!

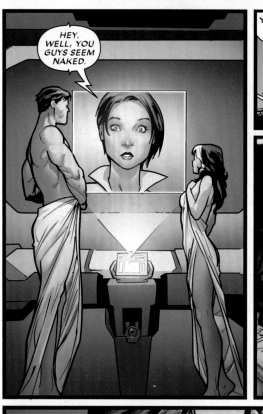

HEY. WELL, YOU GUYS SEEM NAKED.

YOU EXPECTED SOMETHING ELSE, KITTY?

UM. NOT REALLY. I GUESS "HOPED" WOULD BE A BETTER WORD? WOULD THROWING ON SOME PANTS HAVE BEEN TOTALLY UNREASONABLE?

HOW DID YOU EVEN GET THIS NUMBER?

YOU THINK I DON'T KNOW CAROL DANVERS' NUMBER? I KNOW SHE AND ALPHA FLIGHT LOANED YOU THE SHIP.

DAMMIT.

ALL RIGHT. ENOUGH FROM BOTH OF YOU. WHAT'S HAPPENING?

RIGHT. LISTEN, I AM SORRY TO BOTHER YOU GUYS, BUT WE DO HAVE AN EMERGENCY. AND I'M AFRAID IT CAN'T WAIT.

YEAH, BUT WE'RE IN SPACE.

THAT'S SORTA THE PROBLEM. THE EMERGENCY IS IN SPACE. YOU TWO ARE CLOSER THAN ANYONE ELSE BY...A LOT.

WHAT ABOUT MAGIK? PIXIE? LILA CHENEY?

ALL ENGAGED ELSEWHERE I'M AFRAID, OR UNREACHABLE.

SURELY WE'RE NOT THE ONLY OPTION?

YOU'RE THE ONLY OPTION I TRUST, ROGUE. THIS IS... SENSITIVE.

...OKAY.

AH! GAMBIT! THE SHEET! C'MON!

DAMMIT!!!

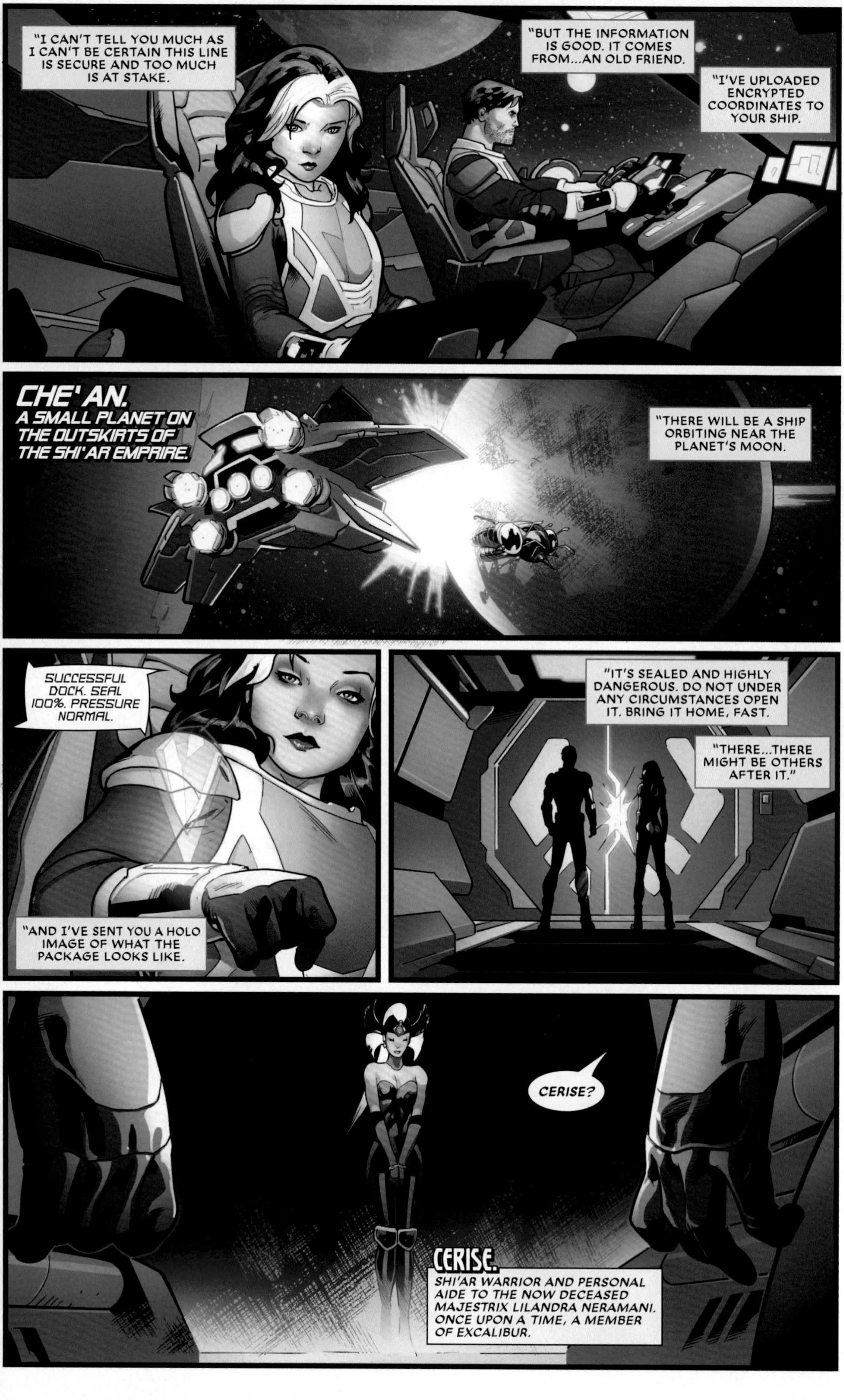
"I CAN'T TELL YOU MUCH AS I CAN'T BE CERTAIN THIS LINE IS SECURE AND TOO MUCH IS AT STAKE.
"BUT THE INFORMATION IS GOOD. IT COMES FROM...AN OLD FRIEND.
"I'VE UPLOADED ENCRYPTED COORDINATES TO YOUR SHIP.
CHE' AN.
A SMALL PLANET ON THE OUTSKIRTS OF THE SHI'AR EMPIRE.
"THERE WILL BE A SHIP ORBITING NEAR THE PLANET'S MOON.
SUCCESSFUL DOCK. SEAL 100%. PRESSURE NORMAL.
"AND I'VE SENT YOU A HOLO IMAGE OF WHAT THE PACKAGE LOOKS LIKE.
"IT'S SEALED AND HIGHLY DANGEROUS. DO NOT UNDER ANY CIRCUMSTANCES OPEN IT. BRING IT HOME, FAST.
"THERE...THERE MIGHT BE OTHERS AFTER IT."
CERISE?
CERISE.
SHI'AR WARRIOR AND PERSONAL AIDE TO THE NOW DECEASED MAJESTRIX LILANDRA NERAMANI. ONCE UPON A TIME, A MEMBER OF EXCALIBUR.

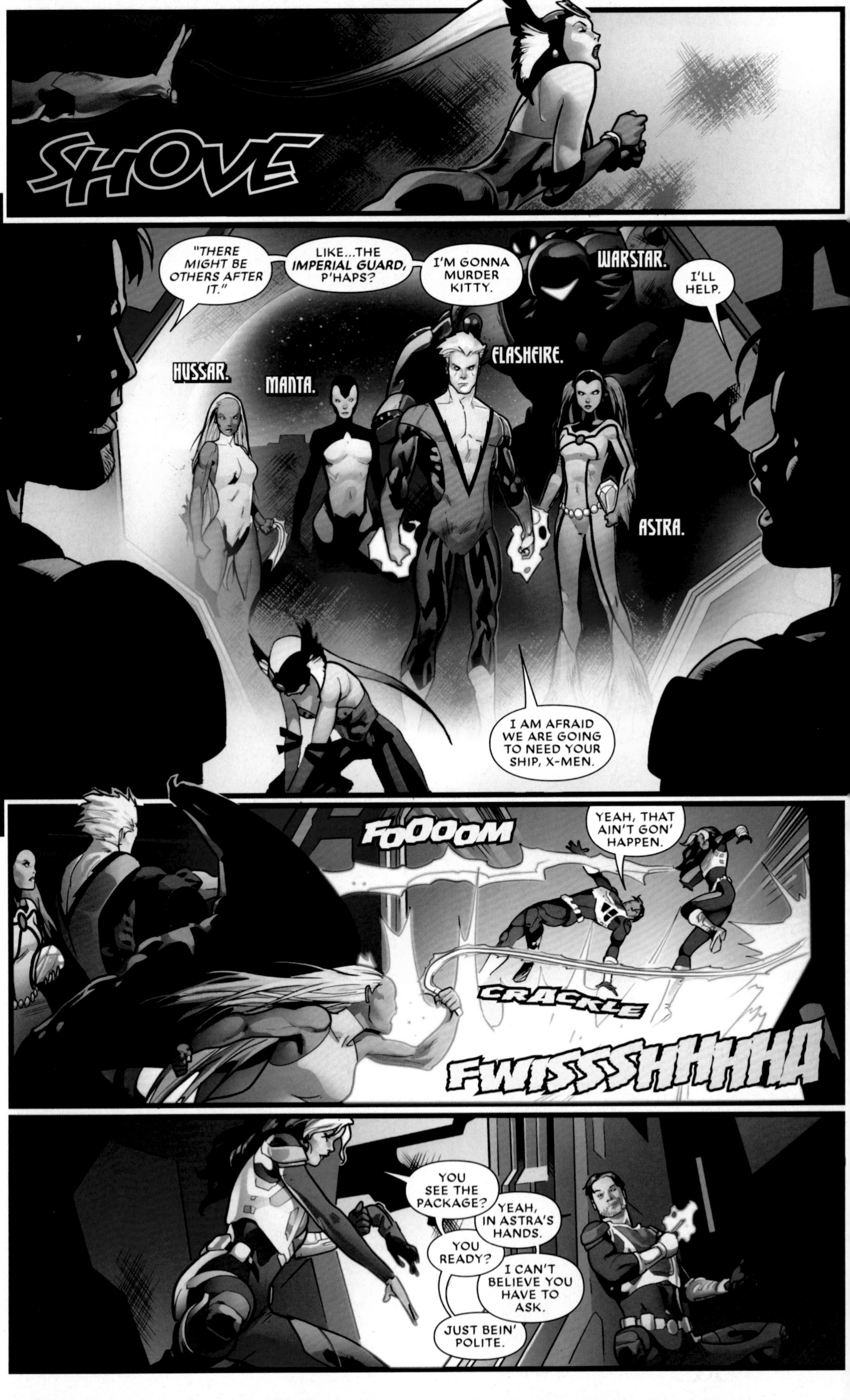
SHOVE
"THERE MIGHT BE OTHERS AFTER IT."
LIKE...THE IMPERIAL GUARD, P'HAPS?
I'M GONNA MURDER KITTY.
WARSTAR.
I'LL HELP.
HUSSAR.
MANTA.
FLASHFIRE.
ASTRA.
I AM AFRAID WE ARE GOING TO NEED YOUR SHIP, X-MEN.
FOOOOM
YEAH, THAT AIN'T GON' HAPPEN.
CRACKLE
FWISSSHHHHA
YOU SEE THE PACKAGE?
YEAH, IN ASTRA'S HANDS.
YOU READY?
I CAN'T BELIEVE YOU HAVE TO ASK.
JUST BEIN' POLITE.

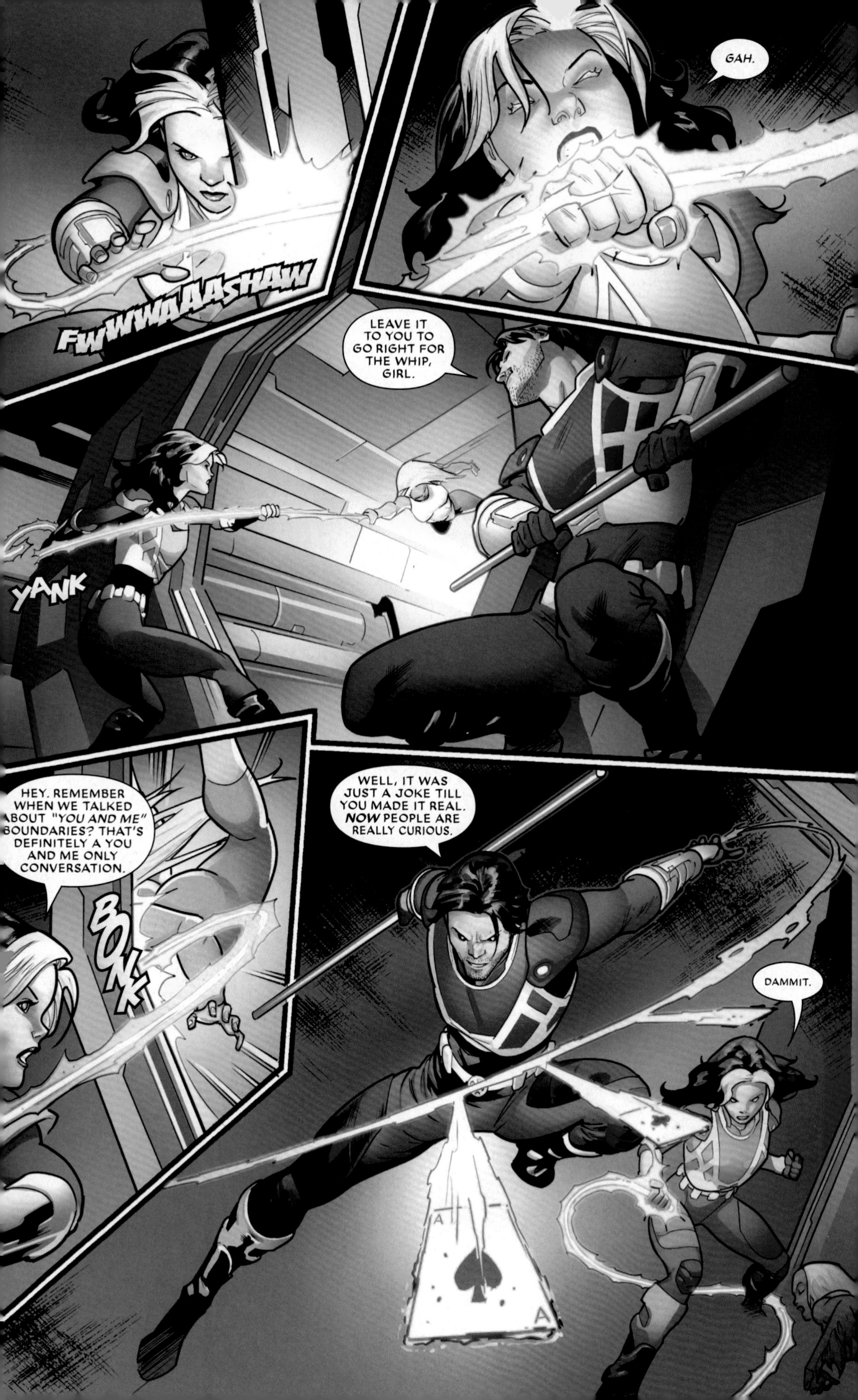
GAH.
FWWWAAASHAW
LEAVE IT TO YOU TO GO RIGHT FOR THE WHIP, GIRL.
YANK
HEY. REMEMBER WHEN WE TALKED ABOUT "YOU AND ME" BOUNDARIES? THAT'S DEFINITELY A YOU AND ME ONLY CONVERSATION.
BONK
WELL, IT WAS JUST A JOKE TILL YOU MADE IT REAL. NOW PEOPLE ARE REALLY CURIOUS.
DAMMIT.

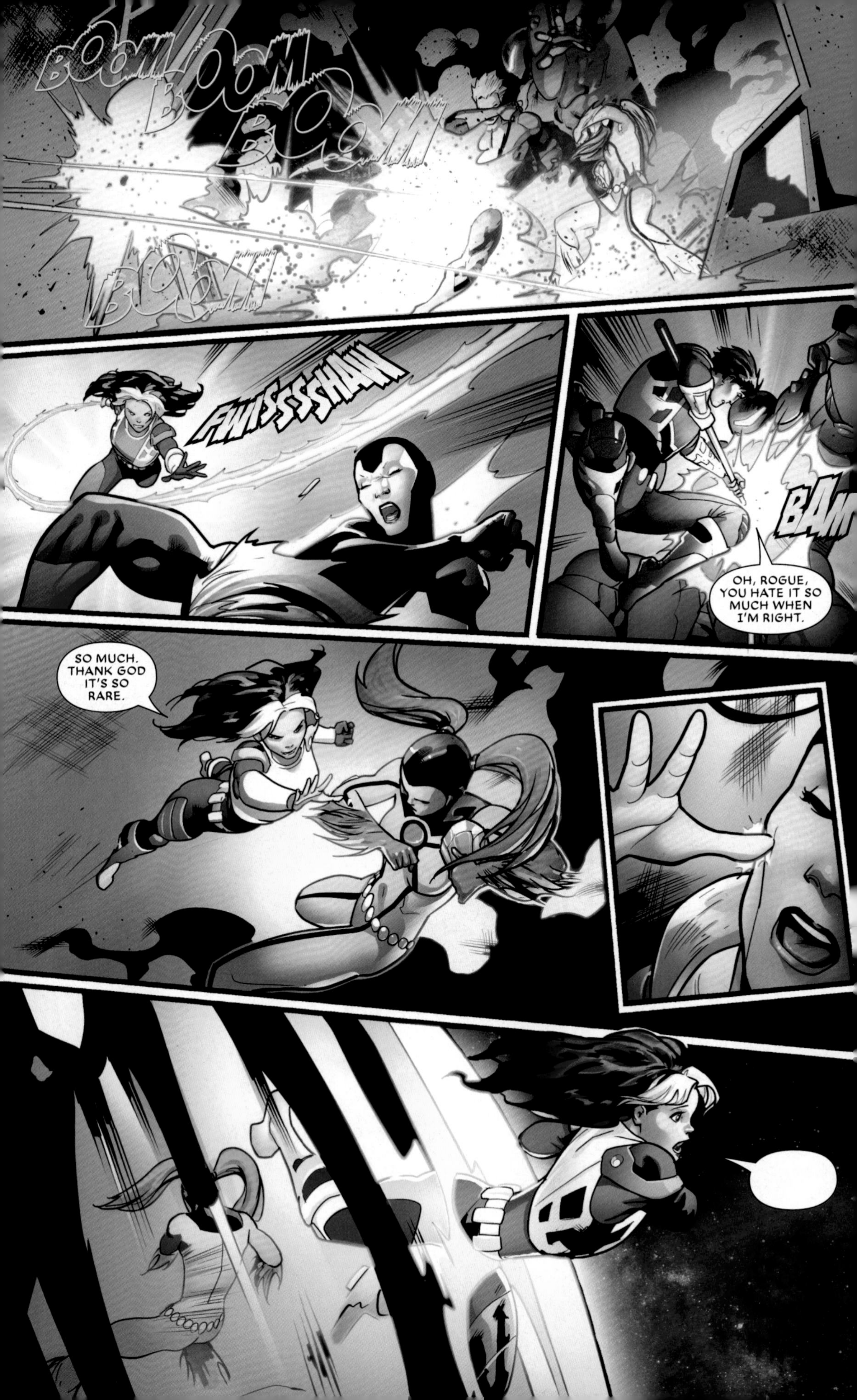
BOOM
BOOM
BOOM
BOOM
FWISSSSHAW
BAM
OH, ROGUE, YOU HATE IT SO MUCH WHEN I'M RIGHT.
SO MUCH. THANK GOD IT'S SO RARE.

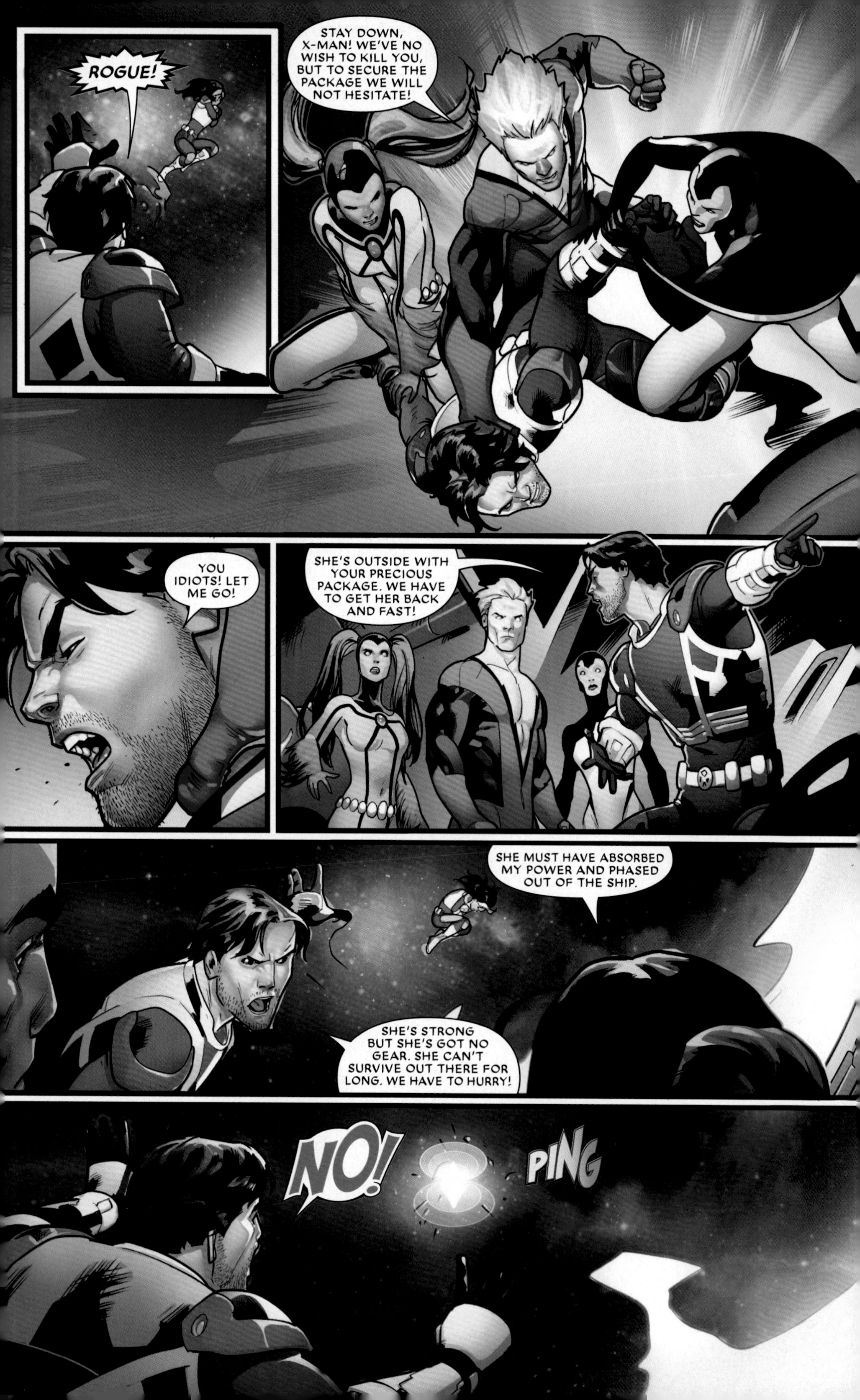
ROGUE!
STAY DOWN, X-MAN! WE'VE NO WISH TO KILL YOU, BUT TO SECURE THE PACKAGE WE WILL NOT HESITATE!
YOU IDIOTS! LET ME GO!
SHE'S OUTSIDE WITH YOUR PRECIOUS PACKAGE. WE HAVE TO GET HER BACK AND FAST!
SHE MUST HAVE ABSORBED MY POWER AND PHASED OUT OF THE SHIP.
SHE'S STRONG BUT SHE'S GOT NO GEAR. SHE CAN'T SURVIVE OUT THERE FOR LONG. WE HAVE TO HURRY!
NO!
PING

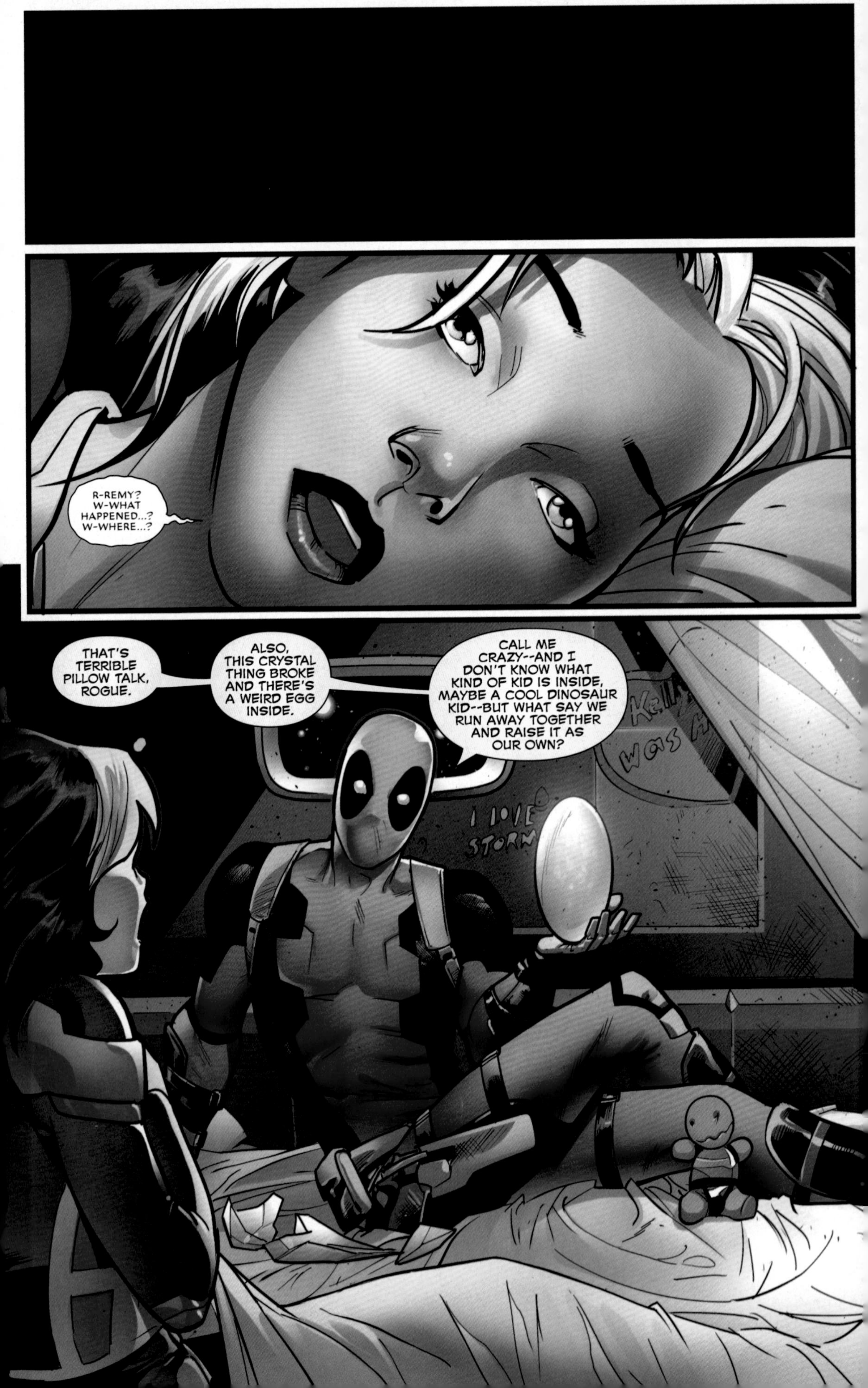
R-REMY? W-WHAT HAPPENED...? W-WHERE...?
THAT'S TERRIBLE PILLOW TALK, ROGUE.
ALSO, THIS CRYSTAL THING BROKE AND THERE'S A WEIRD EGG INSIDE.
CALL ME CRAZY--AND I DON'T KNOW WHAT KIND OF KID IS INSIDE, MAYBE A COOL DINOSAUR KID--BUT WHAT SAY WE RUN AWAY TOGETHER AND RAISE IT AS OUR OWN?
I LOVE STORM

2

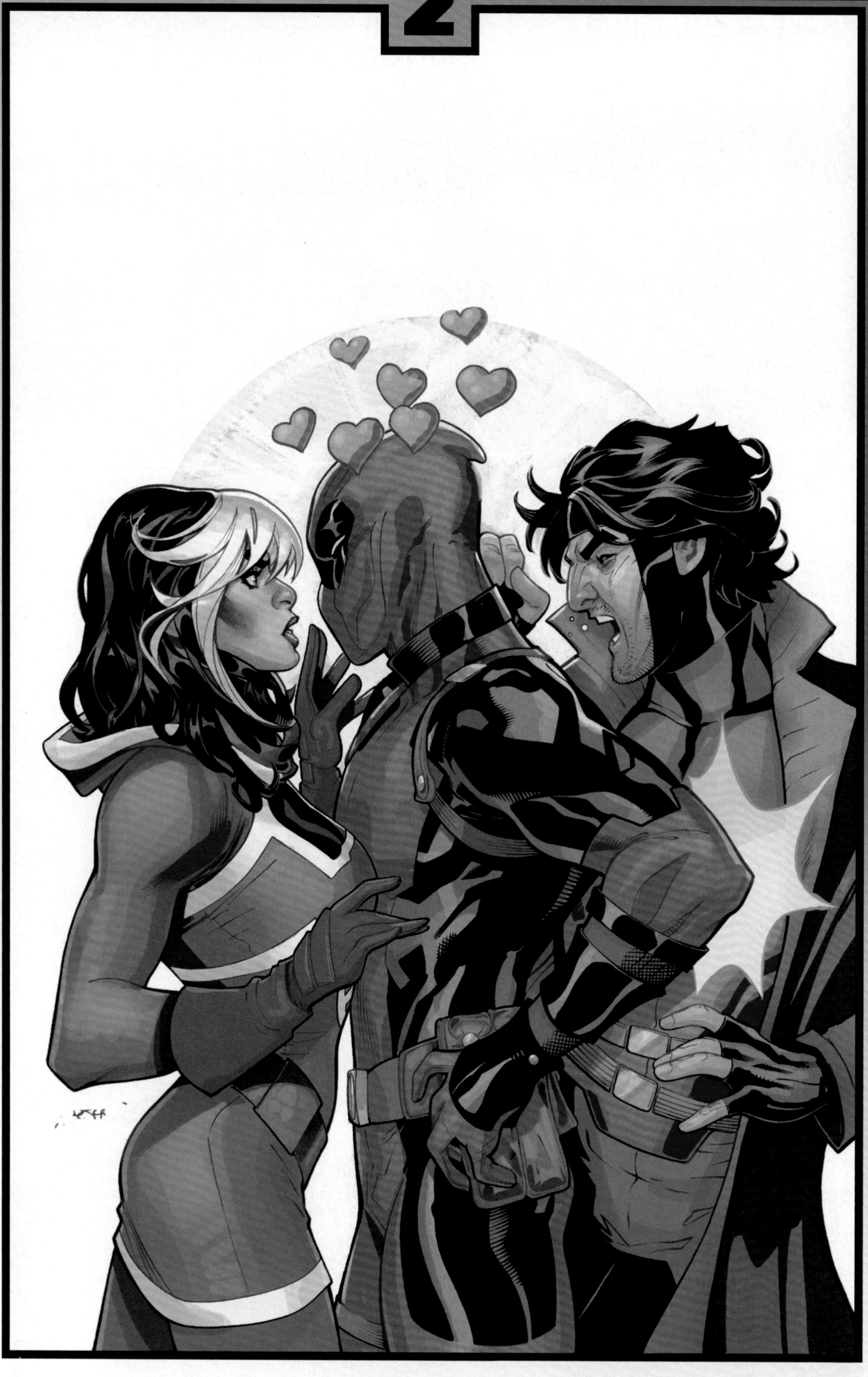

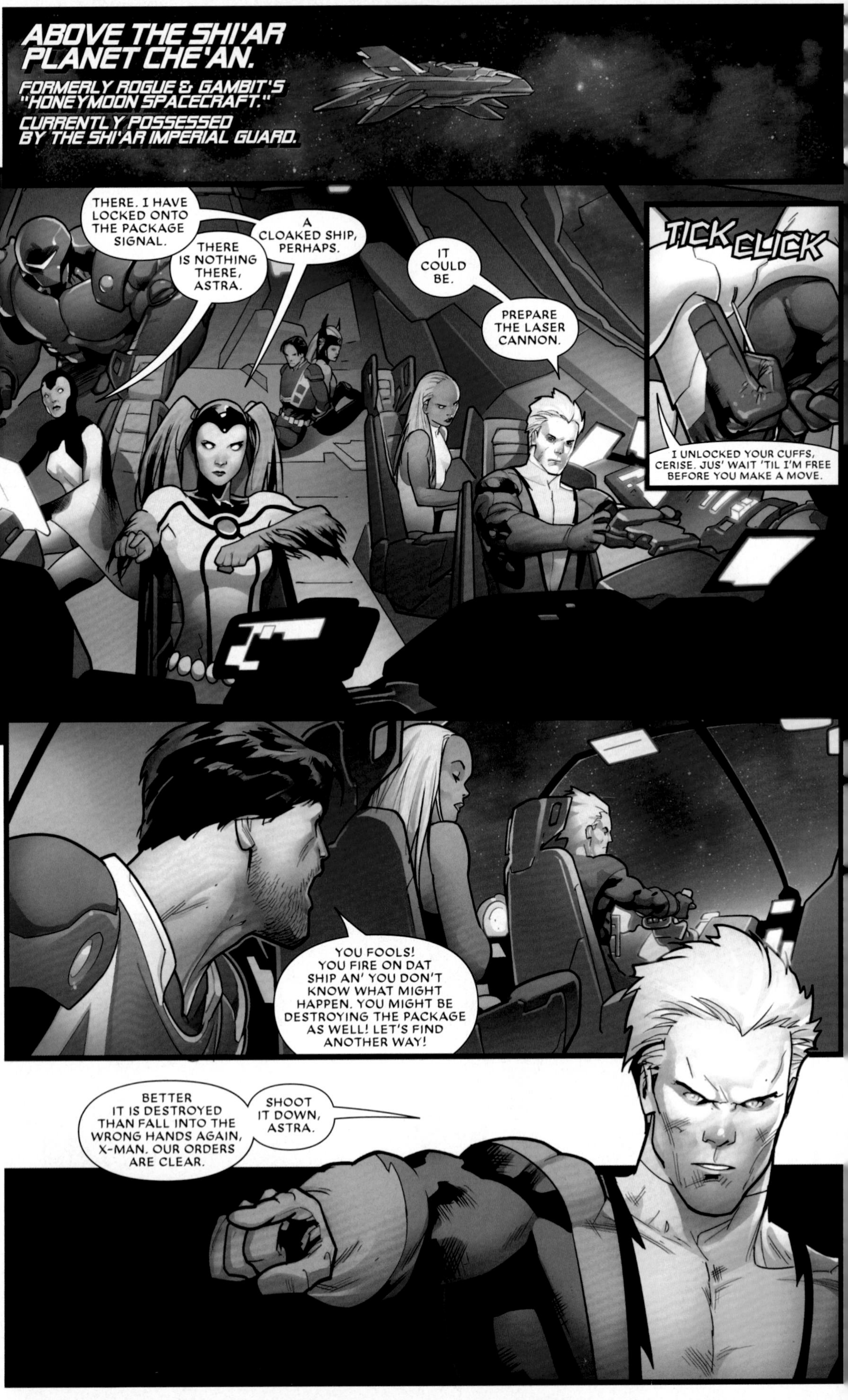
ABOVE THE SHI'AR PLANET CHE'AN.
FORMERLY ROGUE & GAMBIT'S "HONEYMOON SPACECRAFT."
CURRENTLY POSSESSED BY THE SHI'AR IMPERIAL GUARD.
THERE. I HAVE LOCKED ONTO THE PACKAGE SIGNAL.
THERE IS NOTHING THERE, ASTRA.
A CLOAKED SHIP, PERHAPS.
IT COULD BE.
PREPARE THE LASER CANNON.
TICK CLICK
I UNLOCKED YOUR CUFFS, CERISE. JUS' WAIT 'TIL I'M FREE BEFORE YOU MAKE A MOVE.
YOU FOOLS! YOU FIRE ON DAT SHIP AN' YOU DON'T KNOW WHAT MIGHT HAPPEN. YOU MIGHT BE DESTROYING THE PACKAGE AS WELL! LET'S FIND ANOTHER WAY!
BETTER IT IS DESTROYED THAN FALL INTO THE WRONG HANDS AGAIN, X-MAN. OUR ORDERS ARE CLEAR.
SHOOT IT DOWN, ASTRA.

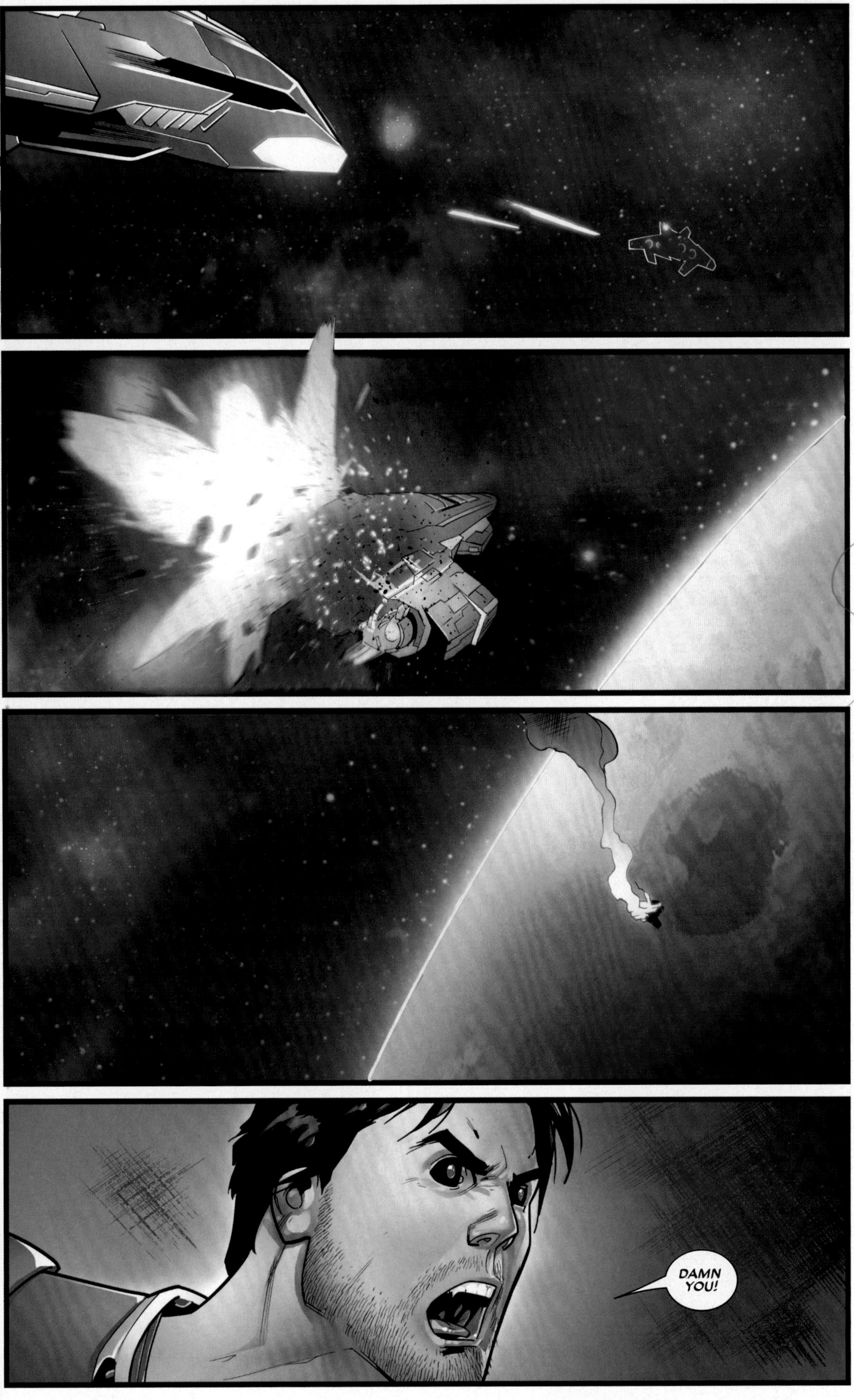
DAMN YOU!

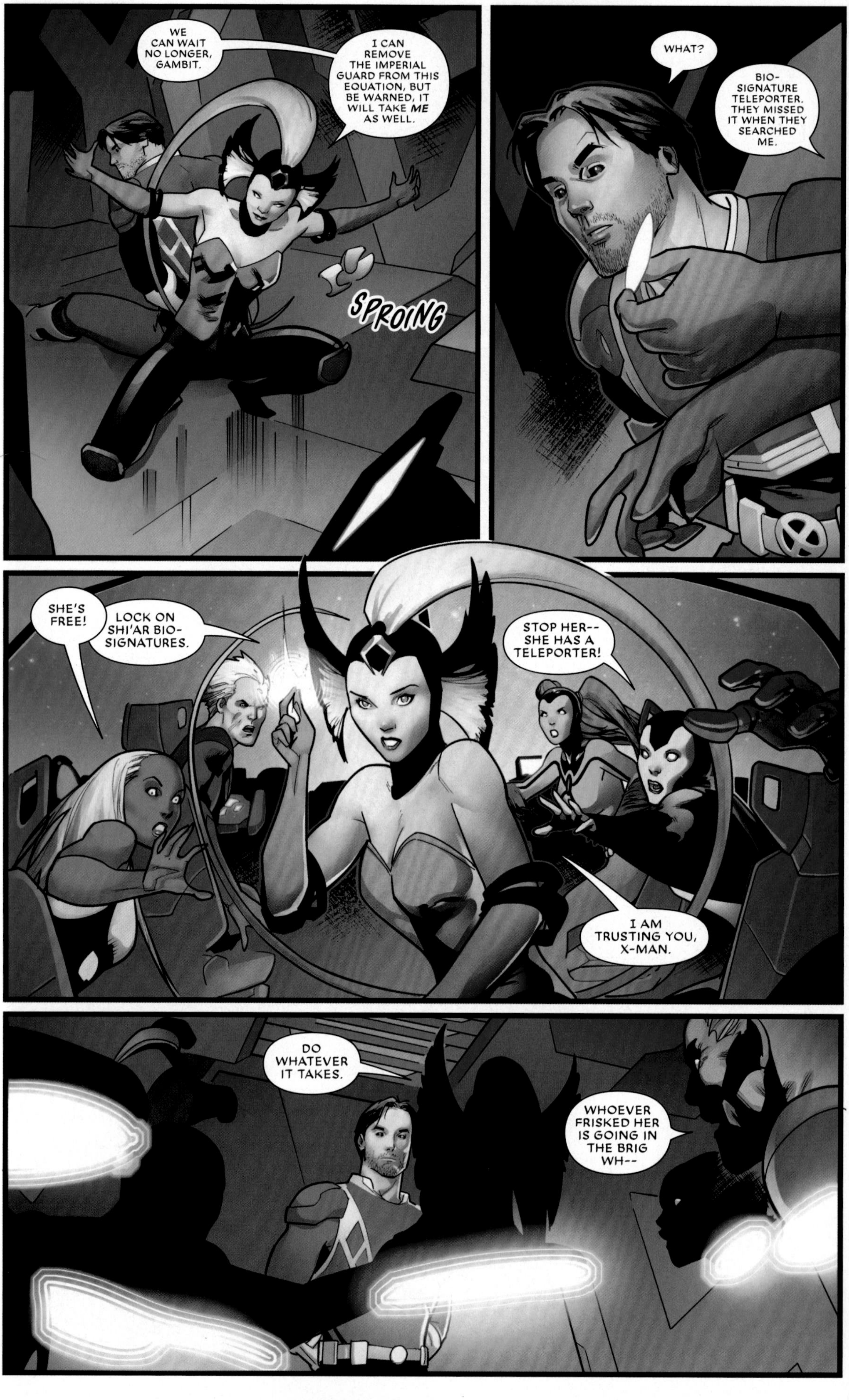

WE CAN WAIT NO LONGER, GAMBIT.
I CAN REMOVE THE IMPERIAL GUARD FROM THIS EQUATION, BUT BE WARNED, IT WILL TAKE *ME* AS WELL.
SPROING
WHAT?
BIO-SIGNATURE TELEPORTER. THEY MISSED IT WHEN THEY SEARCHED ME.
SHE'S FREE!
LOCK ON SHI'AR BIO-SIGNATURES.
STOP HER--SHE HAS A TELEPORTER!
I AM TRUSTING YOU, X-MAN.
DO WHATEVER IT TAKES.
WHOEVER FRISKED HER IS GOING IN THE BRIG WH--

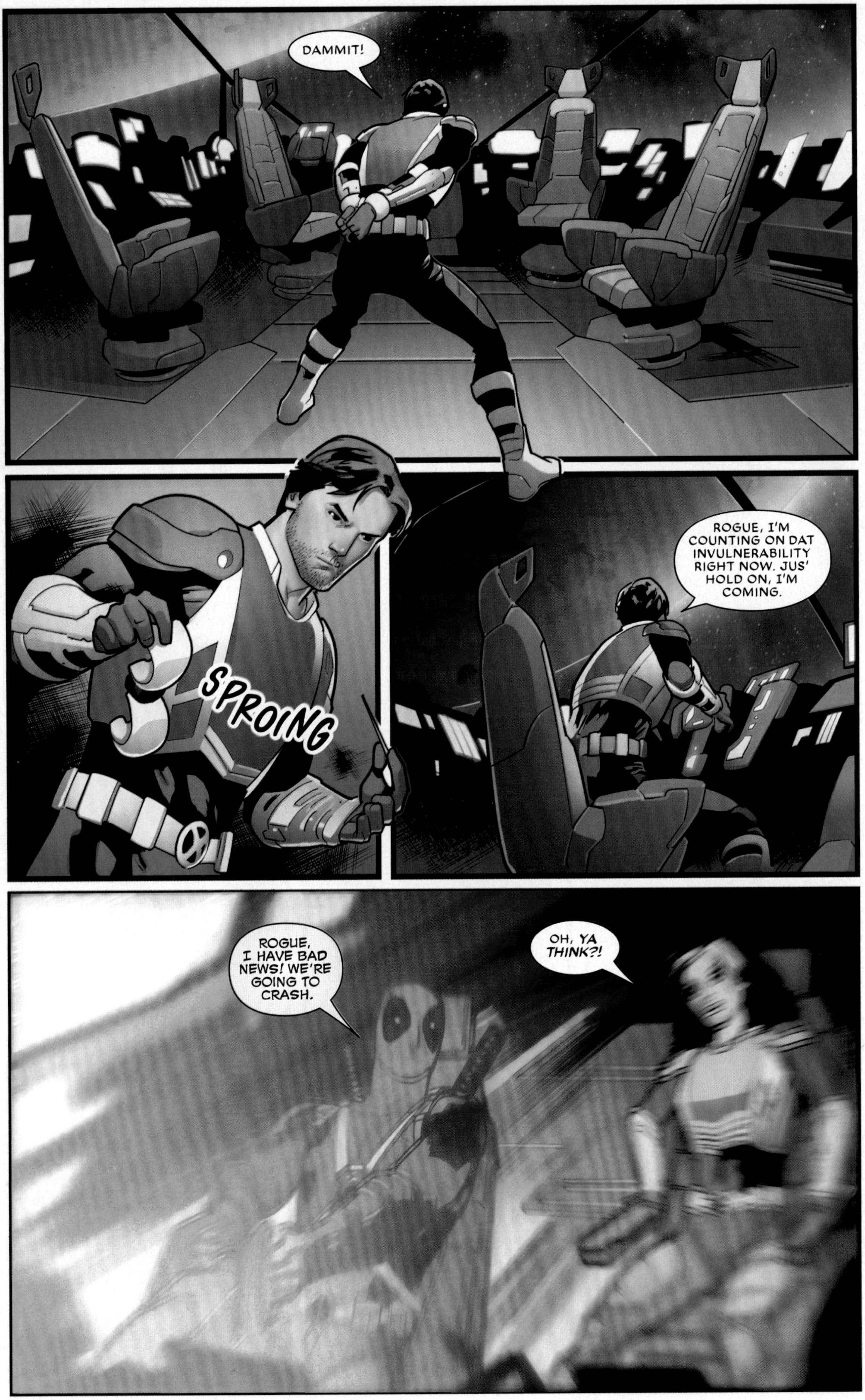
DAMMIT!
SPROING
ROGUE, I'M COUNTING ON DAT INVULNERABILITY RIGHT NOW. JUS' HOLD ON, I'M COMING.
ROGUE, I HAVE BAD NEWS! WE'RE GOING TO CRASH.
OH, YA THINK?!

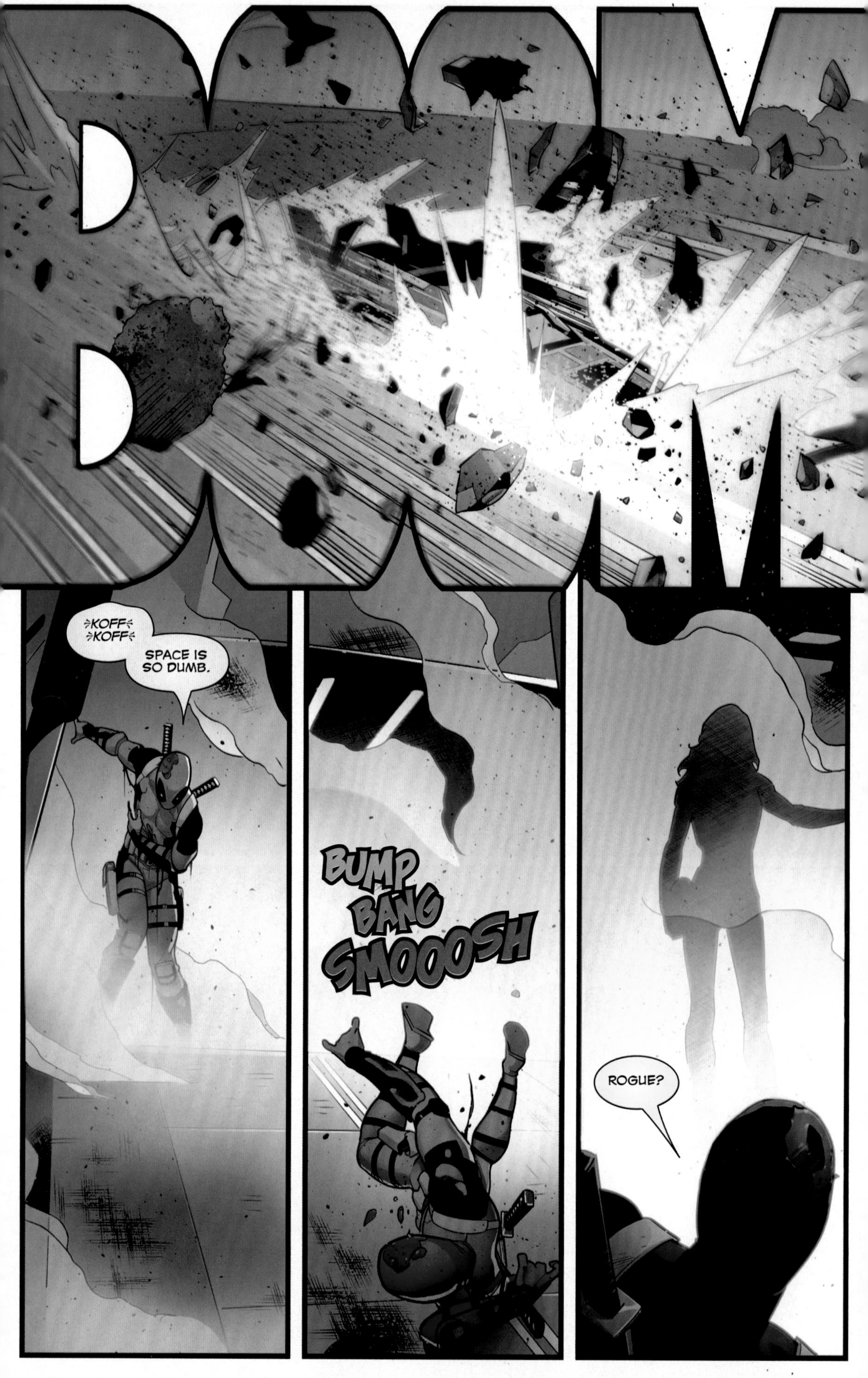
DOOM
DOOM
KOFF KOFF
SPACE IS SO DUMB.
BUMP BANG SMOOOSH
ROGUE?

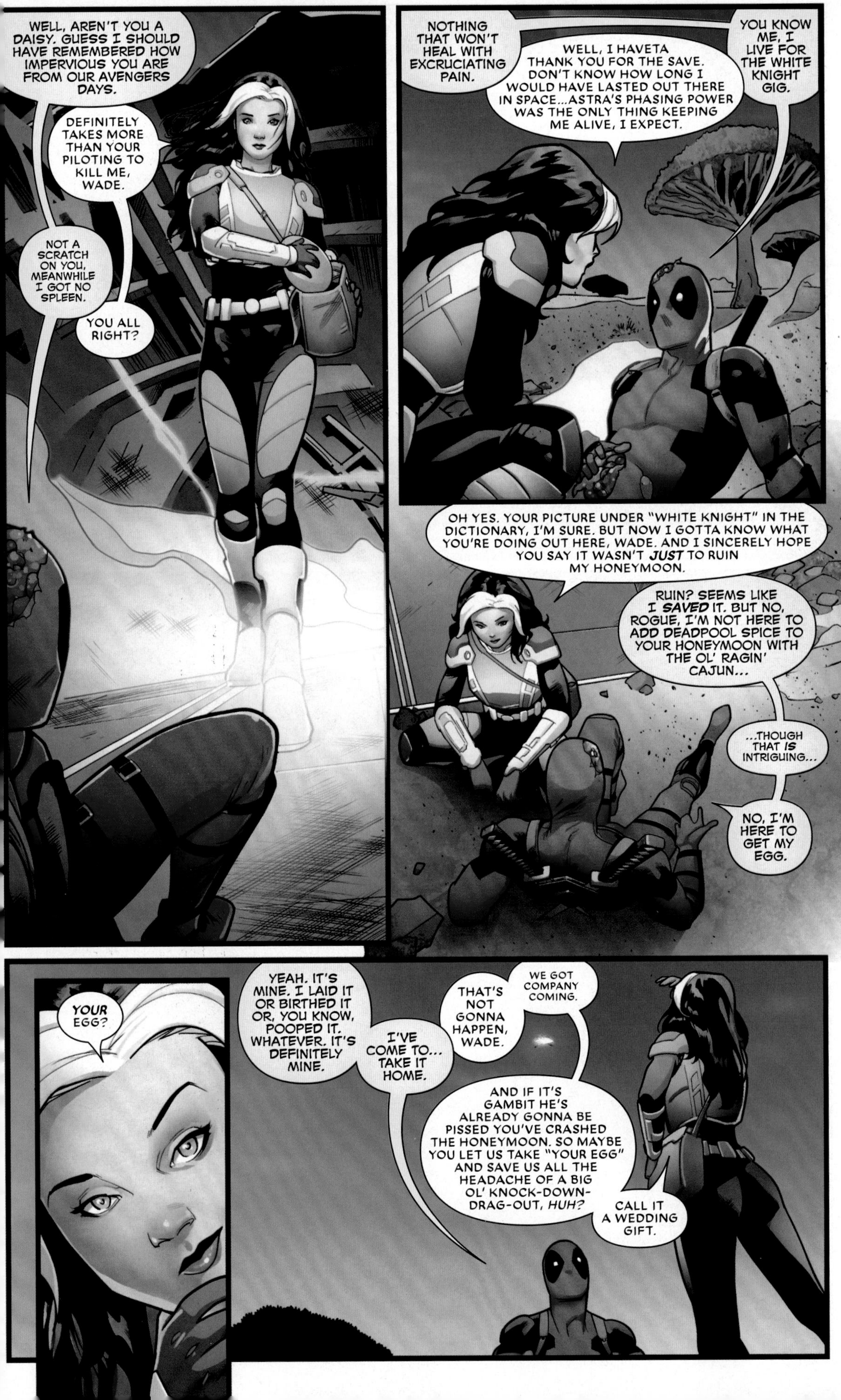

WELL, AREN'T YOU A DAISY. GUESS I SHOULD HAVE REMEMBERED HOW IMPERVIOUS YOU ARE FROM OUR AVENGERS DAYS.
DEFINITELY TAKES MORE THAN YOUR PILOTING TO KILL ME, WADE.
NOT A SCRATCH ON YOU, MEANWHILE I GOT NO SPLEEN.
YOU ALL RIGHT?
NOTHING THAT WON'T HEAL WITH EXCRUCIATING PAIN.
WELL, I HAVETA THANK YOU FOR THE SAVE. DON'T KNOW HOW LONG I WOULD HAVE LASTED OUT THERE IN SPACE...ASTRA'S PHASING POWER WAS THE ONLY THING KEEPING ME ALIVE, I EXPECT.
YOU KNOW ME, I LIVE FOR THE WHITE KNIGHT GIG.
OH YES. YOUR PICTURE UNDER "WHITE KNIGHT" IN THE DICTIONARY, I'M SURE. BUT NOW I GOTTA KNOW WHAT YOU'RE DOING OUT HERE, WADE. AND I SINCERELY HOPE YOU SAY IT WASN'T *JUST* TO RUIN MY HONEYMOON.
RUIN? SEEMS LIKE I *SAVED* IT. BUT NO, ROGUE, I'M NOT HERE TO ADD DEADPOOL SPICE TO YOUR HONEYMOON WITH THE OL' RAGIN' CAJUN...
...THOUGH THAT *IS* INTRIGUING...
NO, I'M HERE TO GET MY EGG.
YOUR EGG?
YEAH. IT'S MINE. I LAID IT OR BIRTHED IT OR, YOU KNOW, POOPED IT. WHATEVER. IT'S DEFINITELY MINE.
I'VE COME TO... TAKE IT HOME.
THAT'S NOT GONNA HAPPEN, WADE.
WE GOT COMPANY COMING.
AND IF IT'S GAMBIT HE'S ALREADY GONNA BE PISSED YOU'VE CRASHED THE HONEYMOON. SO MAYBE YOU LET US TAKE "YOUR EGG" AND SAVE US ALL THE HEADACHE OF A BIG OL' KNOCK-DOWN-DRAG-OUT, *HUH?*
CALL IT A WEDDING GIFT.

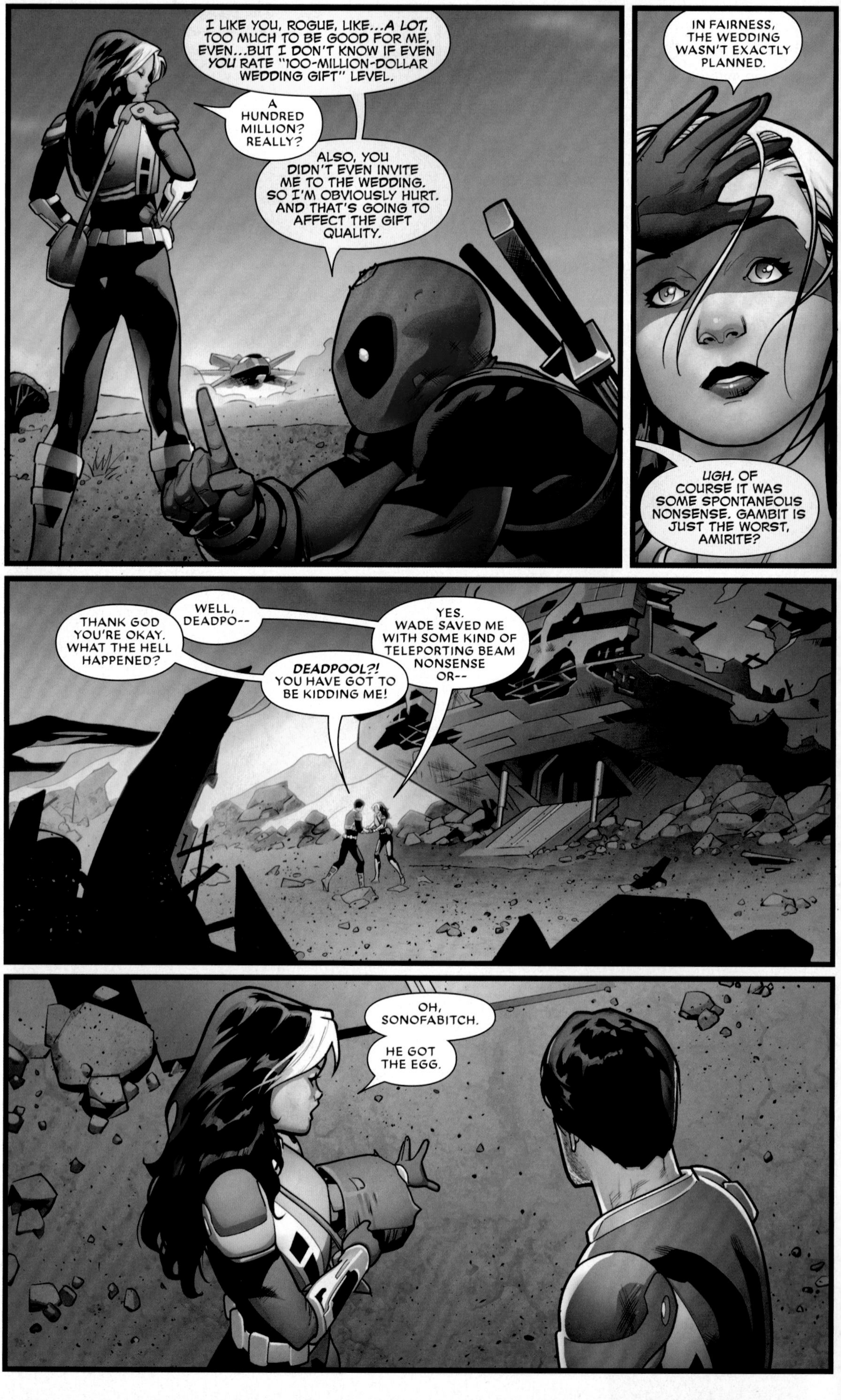

I LIKE YOU, ROGUE, LIKE...A LOT, TOO MUCH TO BE GOOD FOR ME, EVEN...BUT I DON'T KNOW IF EVEN YOU RATE "100-MILLION-DOLLAR WEDDING GIFT" LEVEL.
A HUNDRED MILLION? REALLY?
ALSO, YOU DIDN'T EVEN INVITE ME TO THE WEDDING. SO I'M OBVIOUSLY HURT. AND THAT'S GOING TO AFFECT THE GIFT QUALITY.
IN FAIRNESS, THE WEDDING WASN'T EXACTLY PLANNED.
UGH. OF COURSE IT WAS SOME SPONTANEOUS NONSENSE. GAMBIT IS JUST THE WORST, AMIRITE?
THANK GOD YOU'RE OKAY. WHAT THE HELL HAPPENED?
WELL, DEADPO--
YES. WADE SAVED ME WITH SOME KIND OF TELEPORTING BEAM NONSENSE OR--
DEADPOOL?! YOU HAVE GOT TO BE KIDDING ME!
OH, SONOFABITCH.
HE GOT THE EGG.

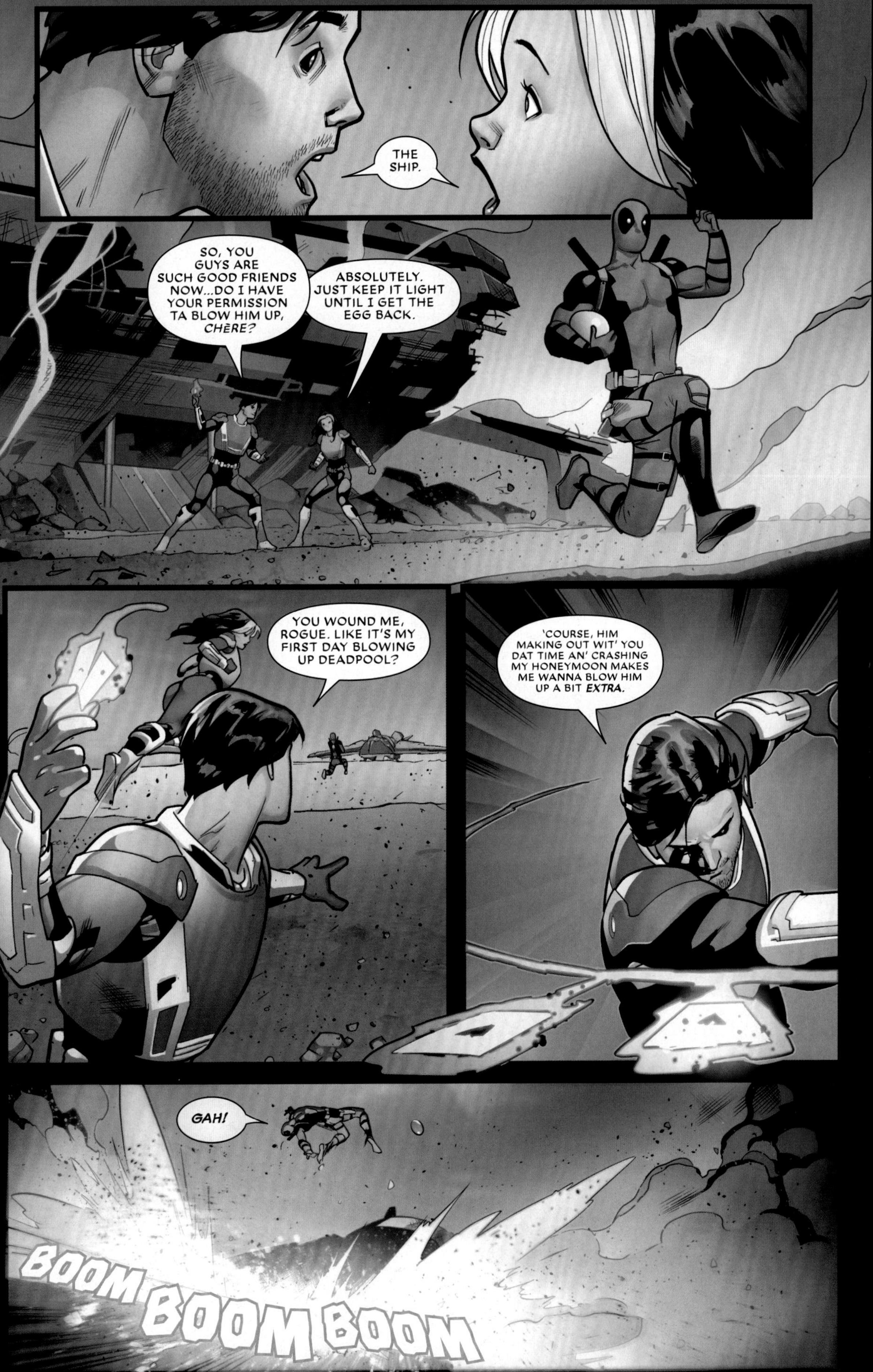
THE SHIP.
SO, YOU GUYS ARE SUCH GOOD FRIENDS NOW...DO I HAVE YOUR PERMISSION TA BLOW HIM UP, *CHÈRE?*
ABSOLUTELY. JUST KEEP IT LIGHT UNTIL I GET THE EGG BACK.
YOU WOUND ME, ROGUE. LIKE IT'S MY FIRST DAY BLOWING UP DEADPOOL?
'COURSE, HIM MAKING OUT WIT' YOU DAT TIME AN' CRASHING MY HONEYMOON MAKES ME WANNA BLOW HIM UP A BIT *EXTRA.*
GAH!
BOOM BOOM BOOM

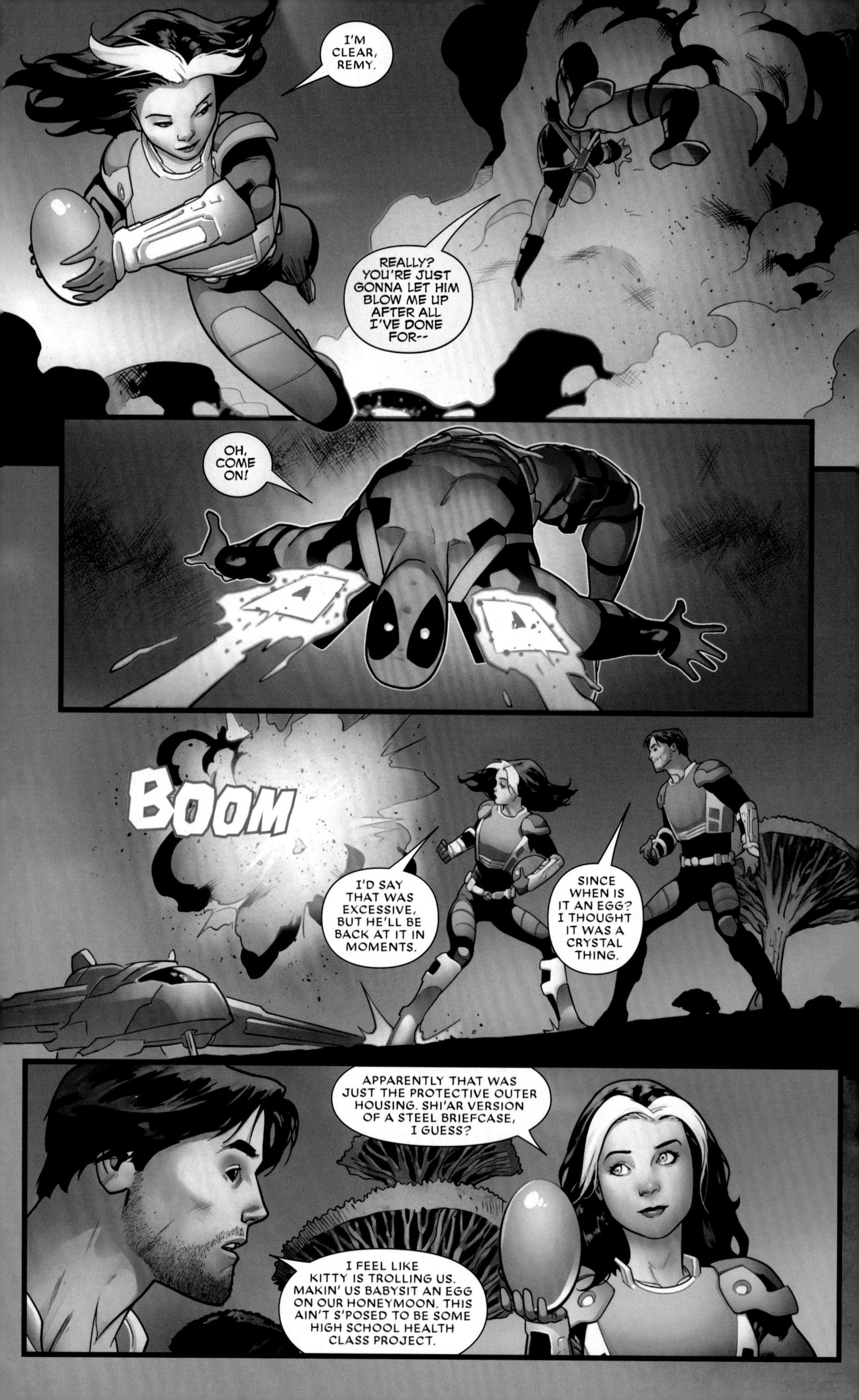
I'M CLEAR, REMY.
REALLY? YOU'RE JUST GONNA LET HIM BLOW ME UP AFTER ALL I'VE DONE FOR--
OH, COME ON!
BOOM
I'D SAY THAT WAS EXCESSIVE, BUT HE'LL BE BACK AT IT IN MOMENTS.
SINCE WHEN IS IT AN EGG? I THOUGHT IT WAS A CRYSTAL THING.
APPARENTLY THAT WAS JUST THE PROTECTIVE OUTER HOUSING. SHI'AR VERSION OF A STEEL BRIEFCASE, I GUESS?
I FEEL LIKE KITTY IS TROLLING US. MAKIN' US BABYSIT AN EGG ON OUR HONEYMOON. THIS AIN'T S'POSED TO BE SOME HIGH SCHOOL HEALTH CLASS PROJECT.

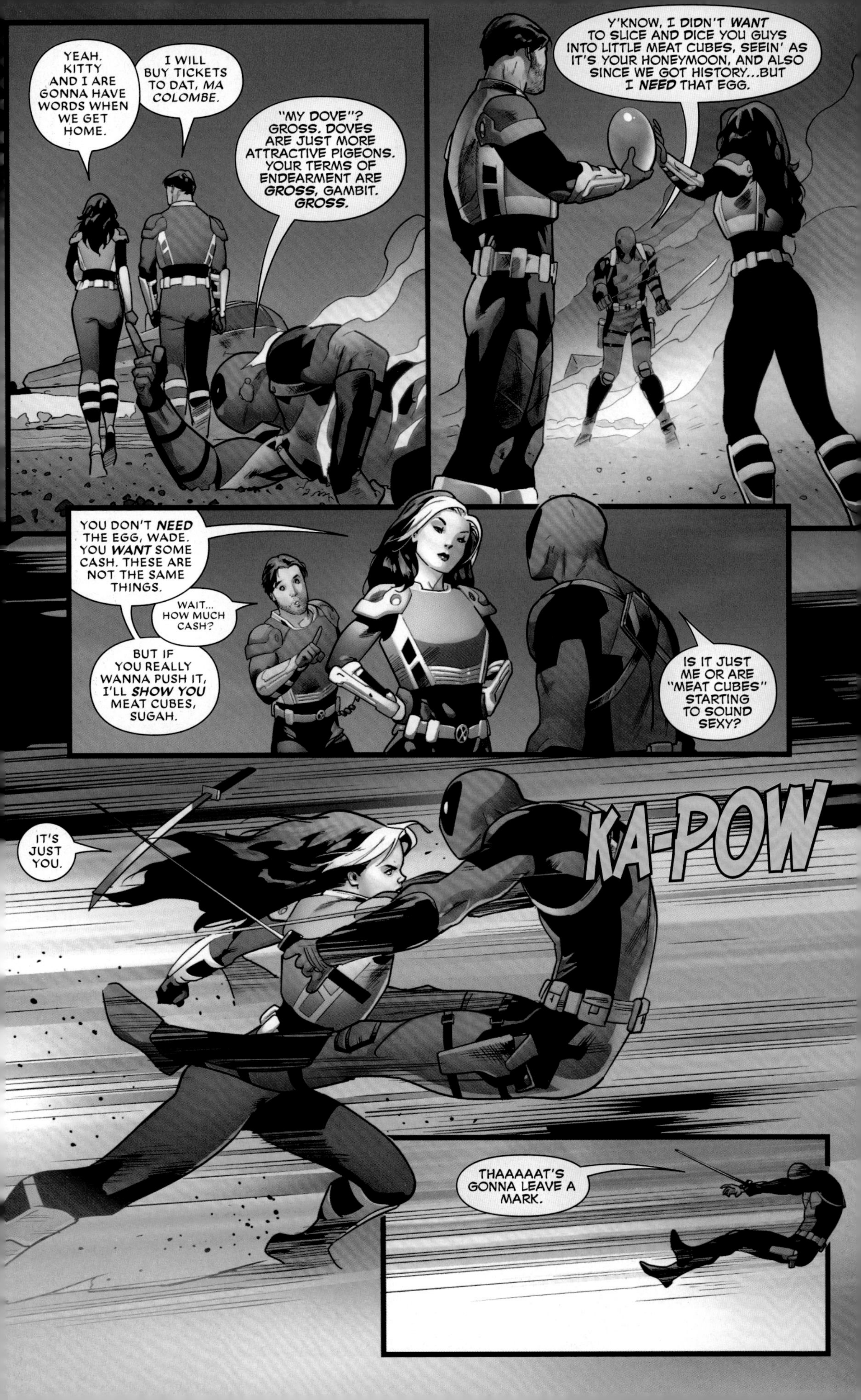
YEAH. KITTY AND I ARE GONNA HAVE WORDS WHEN WE GET HOME.
I WILL BUY TICKETS TO DAT, MA COLOMBE.
"MY DOVE"? GROSS. DOVES ARE JUST MORE ATTRACTIVE PIGEONS. YOUR TERMS OF ENDEARMENT ARE GROSS, GAMBIT. GROSS.
Y'KNOW, I DIDN'T WANT TO SLICE AND DICE YOU GUYS INTO LITTLE MEAT CUBES, SEEIN' AS IT'S YOUR HONEYMOON, AND ALSO SINCE WE GOT HISTORY...BUT I NEED THAT EGG.
YOU DON'T NEED THE EGG, WADE. YOU WANT SOME CASH. THESE ARE NOT THE SAME THINGS.
WAIT... HOW MUCH CASH?
BUT IF YOU REALLY WANNA PUSH IT, I'LL SHOW YOU MEAT CUBES, SUGAH.
IS IT JUST ME OR ARE "MEAT CUBES" STARTING TO SOUND SEXY?
IT'S JUST YOU.
KA-POW
THAAAAAT'S GONNA LEAVE A MARK.

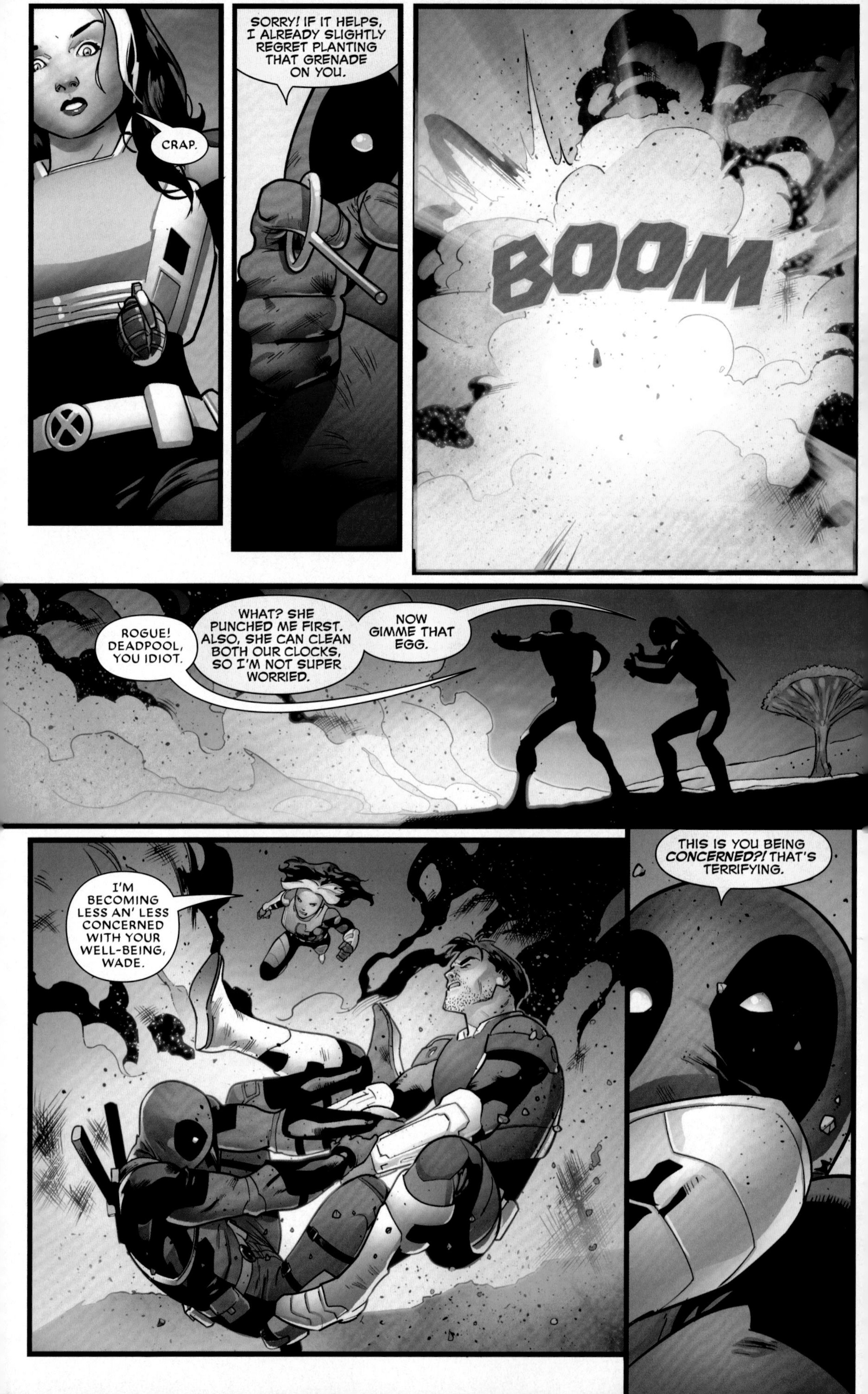
CRAP.
SORRY! IF IT HELPS, I ALREADY SLIGHTLY REGRET PLANTING THAT GRENADE ON YOU.
BOOM
ROGUE! DEADPOOL, YOU IDIOT.
WHAT? SHE PUNCHED ME FIRST. ALSO, SHE CAN CLEAN BOTH OUR CLOCKS, SO I'M NOT SUPER WORRIED.
NOW GIMME THAT EGG.
I'M BECOMING LESS AN' LESS CONCERNED WITH YOUR WELL-BEING, WADE.
THIS IS YOU BEING CONCERNED?! THAT'S TERRIFYING.

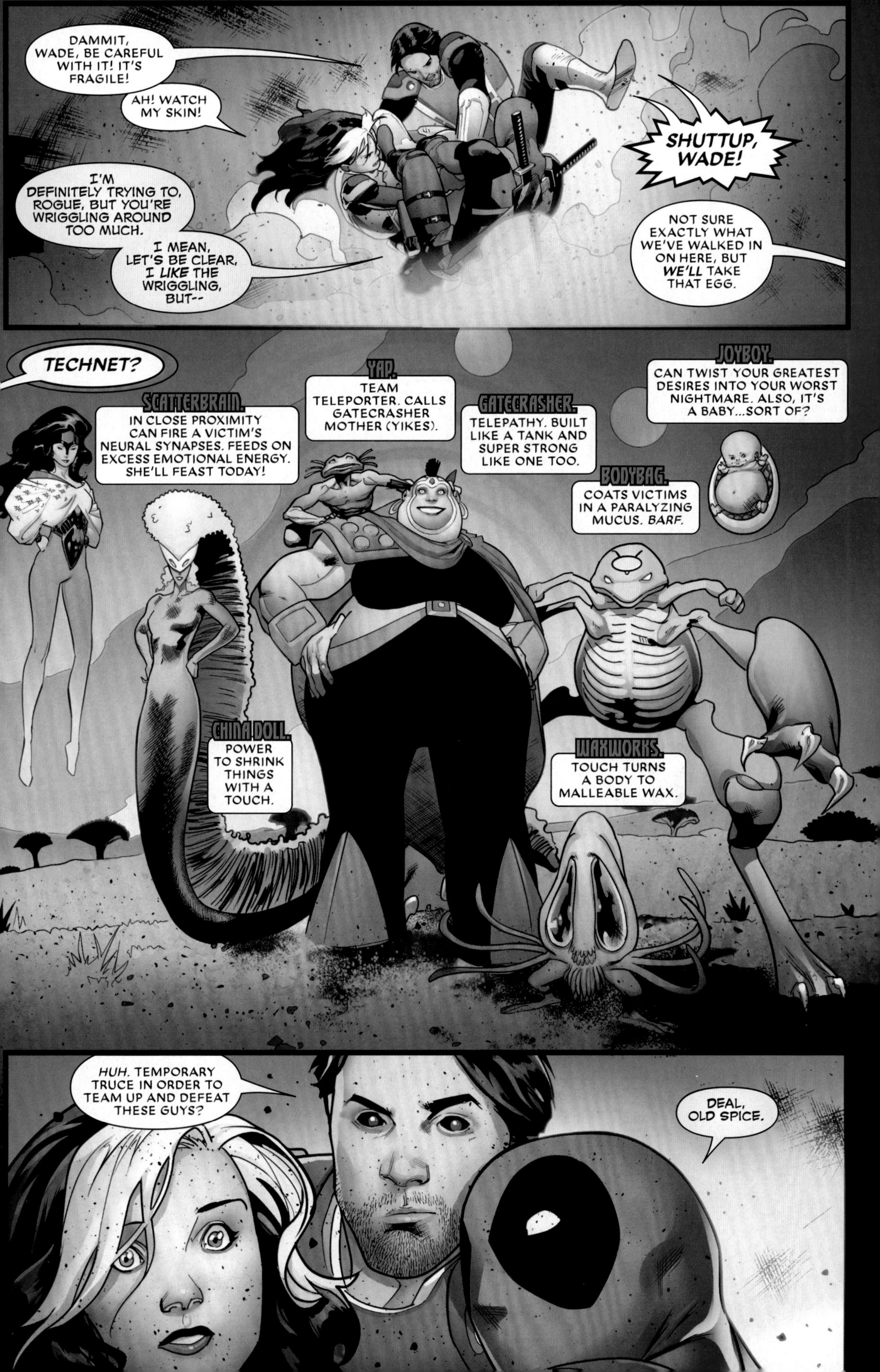
DAMMIT, WADE, BE CAREFUL WITH IT! IT'S FRAGILE!
AH! WATCH MY SKIN!
I'M DEFINITELY TRYING TO, ROGUE, BUT YOU'RE WRIGGLING AROUND TOO MUCH.
I MEAN, LET'S BE CLEAR, I LIKE THE WRIGGLING, BUT--
SHUTTUP, WADE!
NOT SURE EXACTLY WHAT WE'VE WALKED IN ON HERE, BUT WE'LL TAKE THAT EGG.
TECHNET?
SCATTERBRAIN. IN CLOSE PROXIMITY CAN FIRE A VICTIM'S NEURAL SYNAPSES. FEEDS ON EXCESS EMOTIONAL ENERGY. SHE'LL FEAST TODAY!
YAP. TEAM TELEPORTER. CALLS GATECRASHER MOTHER (YIKES).
GATECRASHER. TELEPATHY. BUILT LIKE A TANK AND SUPER STRONG LIKE ONE TOO.
JOYBOY. CAN TWIST YOUR GREATEST DESIRES INTO YOUR WORST NIGHTMARE. ALSO, IT'S A BABY...SORT OF?
BODYBAG. COATS VICTIMS IN A PARALYZING MUCUS. BARF.
CHINA DOLL. POWER TO SHRINK THINGS WITH A TOUCH.
WAXWORKS. TOUCH TURNS A BODY TO MALLEABLE WAX.
HUH. TEMPORARY TRUCE IN ORDER TO TEAM UP AND DEFEAT THESE GUYS?
DEAL, OLD SPICE.

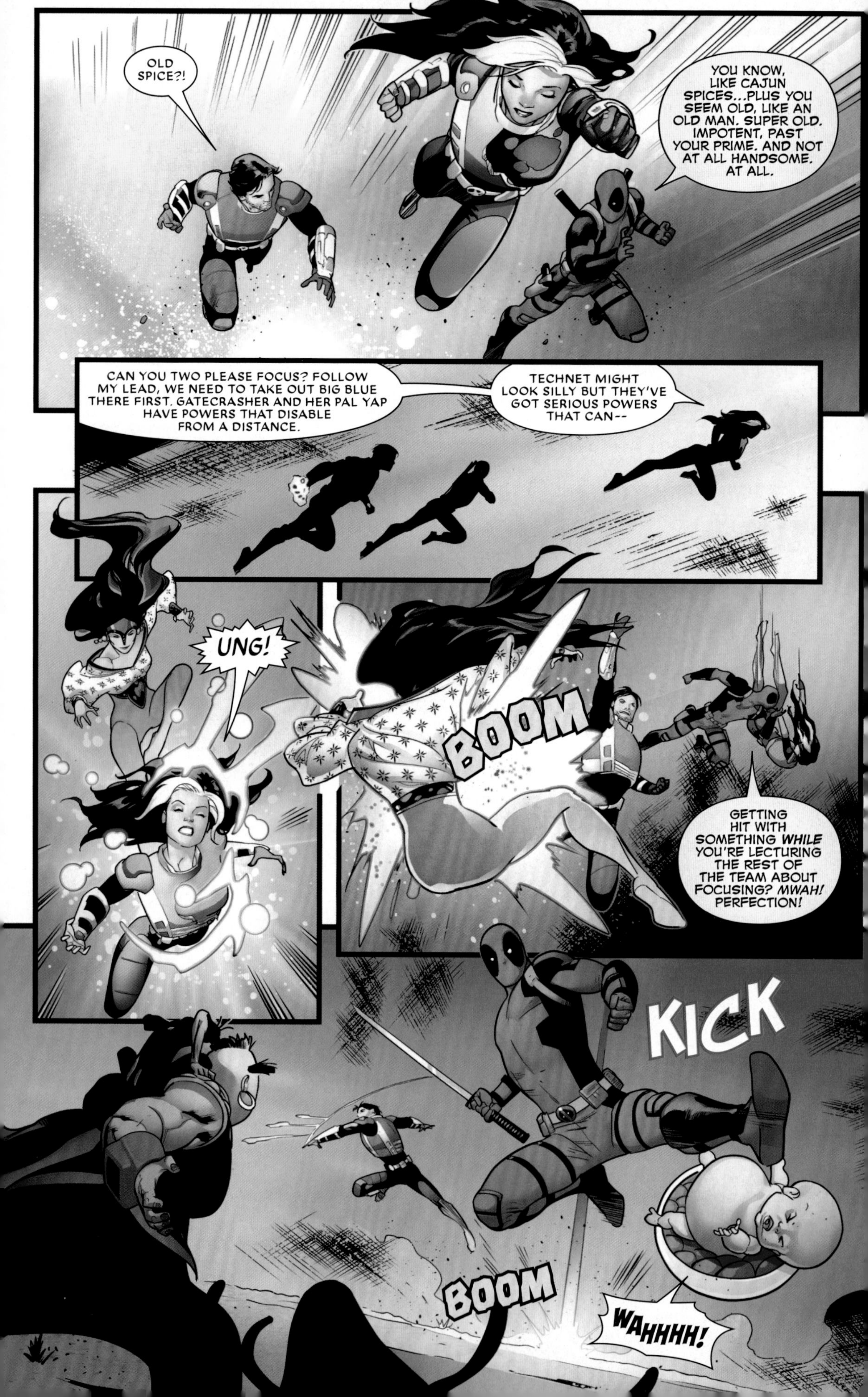
OLD SPICE?!
YOU KNOW, LIKE CAJUN SPICES...PLUS YOU SEEM OLD, LIKE AN OLD MAN. SUPER OLD. IMPOTENT, PAST YOUR PRIME. AND NOT AT ALL HANDSOME. AT ALL.
CAN YOU TWO PLEASE FOCUS? FOLLOW MY LEAD, WE NEED TO TAKE OUT BIG BLUE THERE FIRST. GATECRASHER AND HER PAL YAP HAVE POWERS THAT DISABLE FROM A DISTANCE.
TECHNET MIGHT LOOK SILLY BUT THEY'VE GOT SERIOUS POWERS THAT CAN--
UNG!
BOOM
GETTING HIT WITH SOMETHING *WHILE* YOU'RE LECTURING THE REST OF THE TEAM ABOUT FOCUSING? *MWAH!* PERFECTION!
KICK
BOOM
WAHHHH!

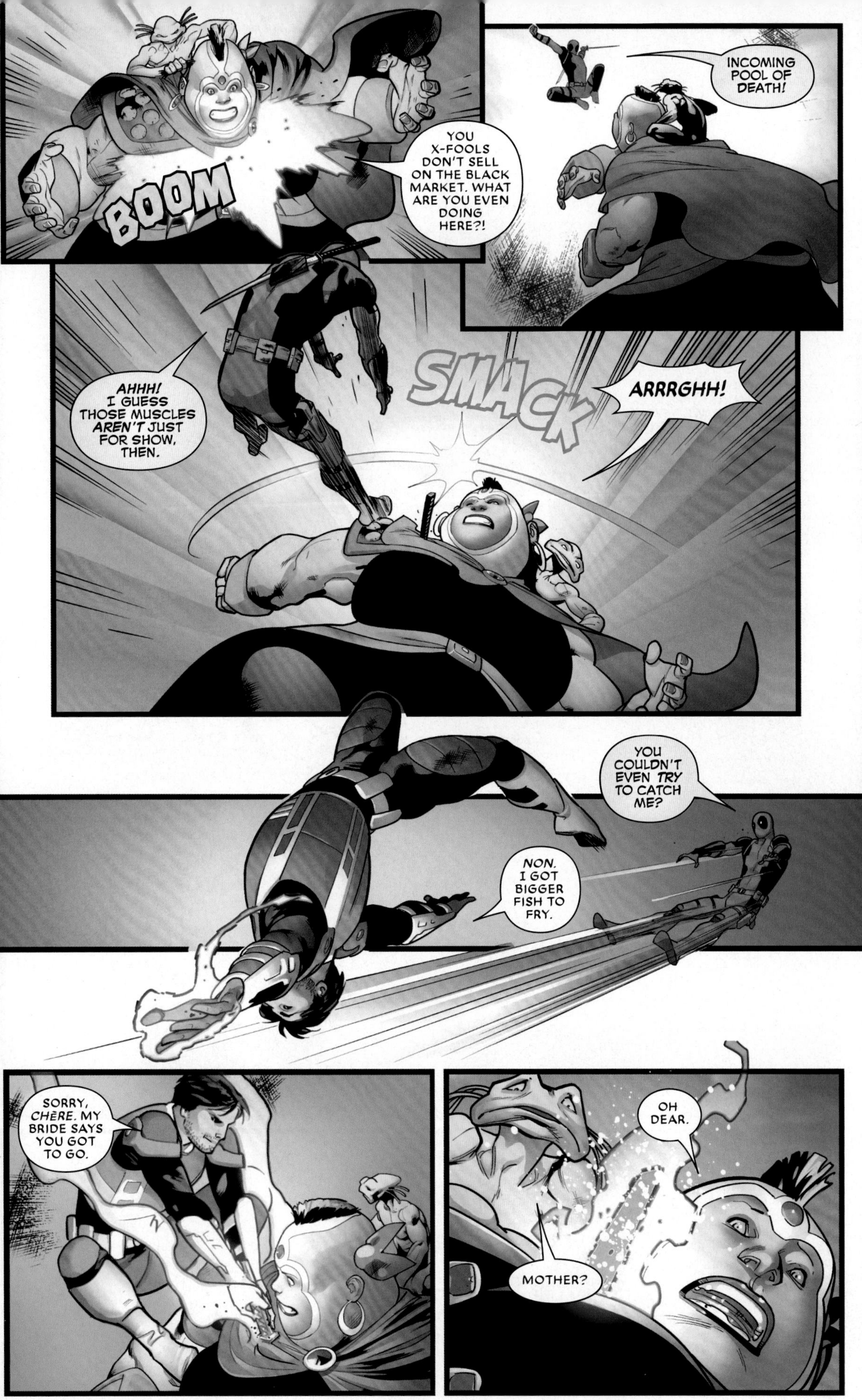
BOOM
YOU X-FOOLS DON'T SELL ON THE BLACK MARKET. WHAT ARE YOU EVEN DOING HERE?!
INCOMING POOL OF DEATH!
AHHH! I GUESS THOSE MUSCLES AREN'T JUST FOR SHOW, THEN.
SMACK
ARRRGHH!
YOU COULDN'T EVEN TRY TO CATCH ME?
NON. I GOT BIGGER FISH TO FRY.
SORRY, CHÈRE. MY BRIDE SAYS YOU GOT TO GO.
OH DEAR.
MOTHER?

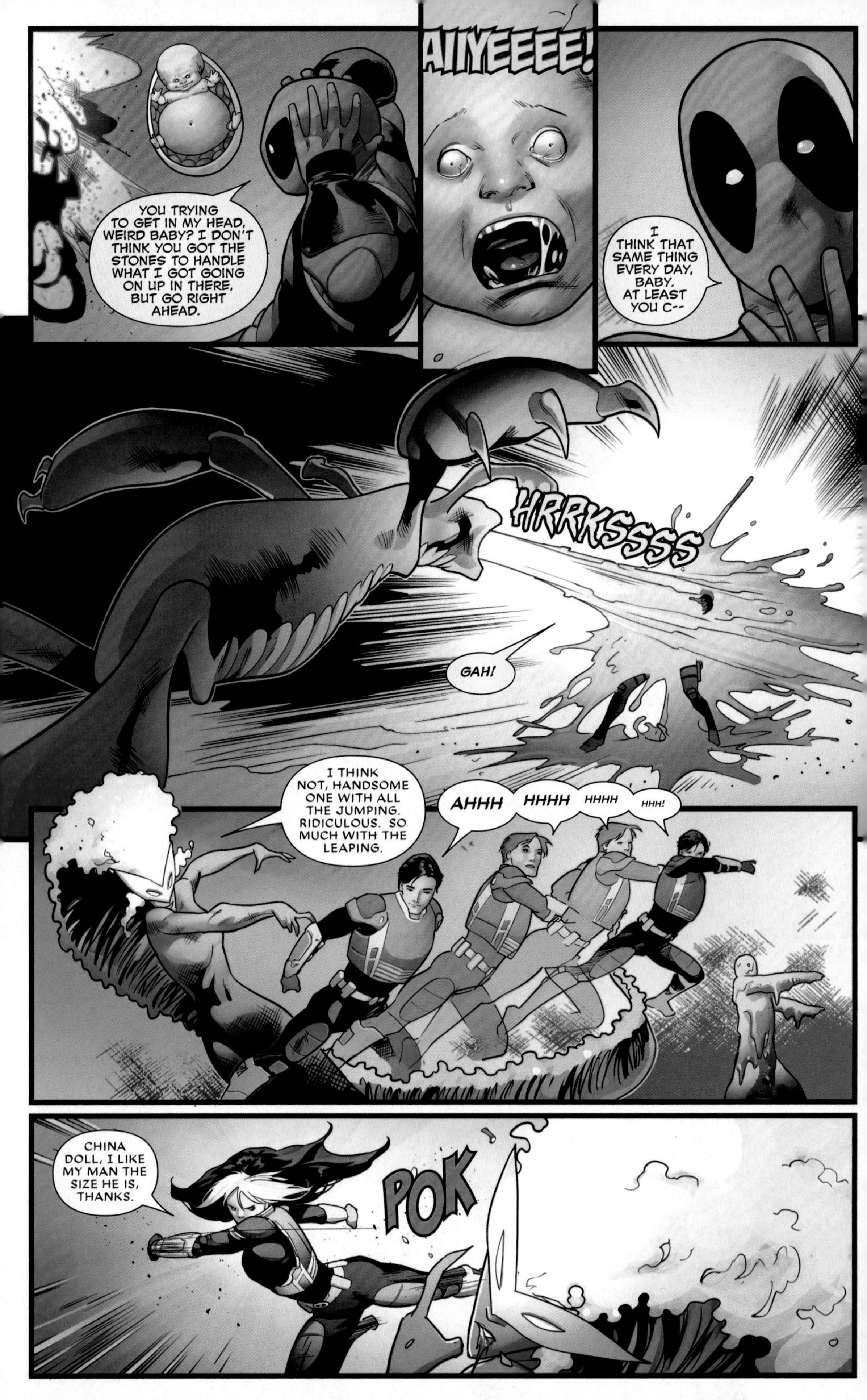
YOU TRYING TO GET IN MY HEAD, WEIRD BABY? I DON'T THINK YOU GOT THE STONES TO HANDLE WHAT I GOT GOING ON UP IN THERE, BUT GO RIGHT AHEAD.
AIIYEEEE!
I THINK THAT SAME THING EVERY DAY, BABY. AT LEAST YOU C--
HRRKSSSS
GAH!
I THINK NOT, HANDSOME ONE WITH ALL THE JUMPING. RIDICULOUS. SO MUCH WITH THE LEAPING.
AHHH
HHHH
HHHH
HHH!
CHINA DOLL, I LIKE MY MAN THE SIZE HE IS, THANKS.
POK

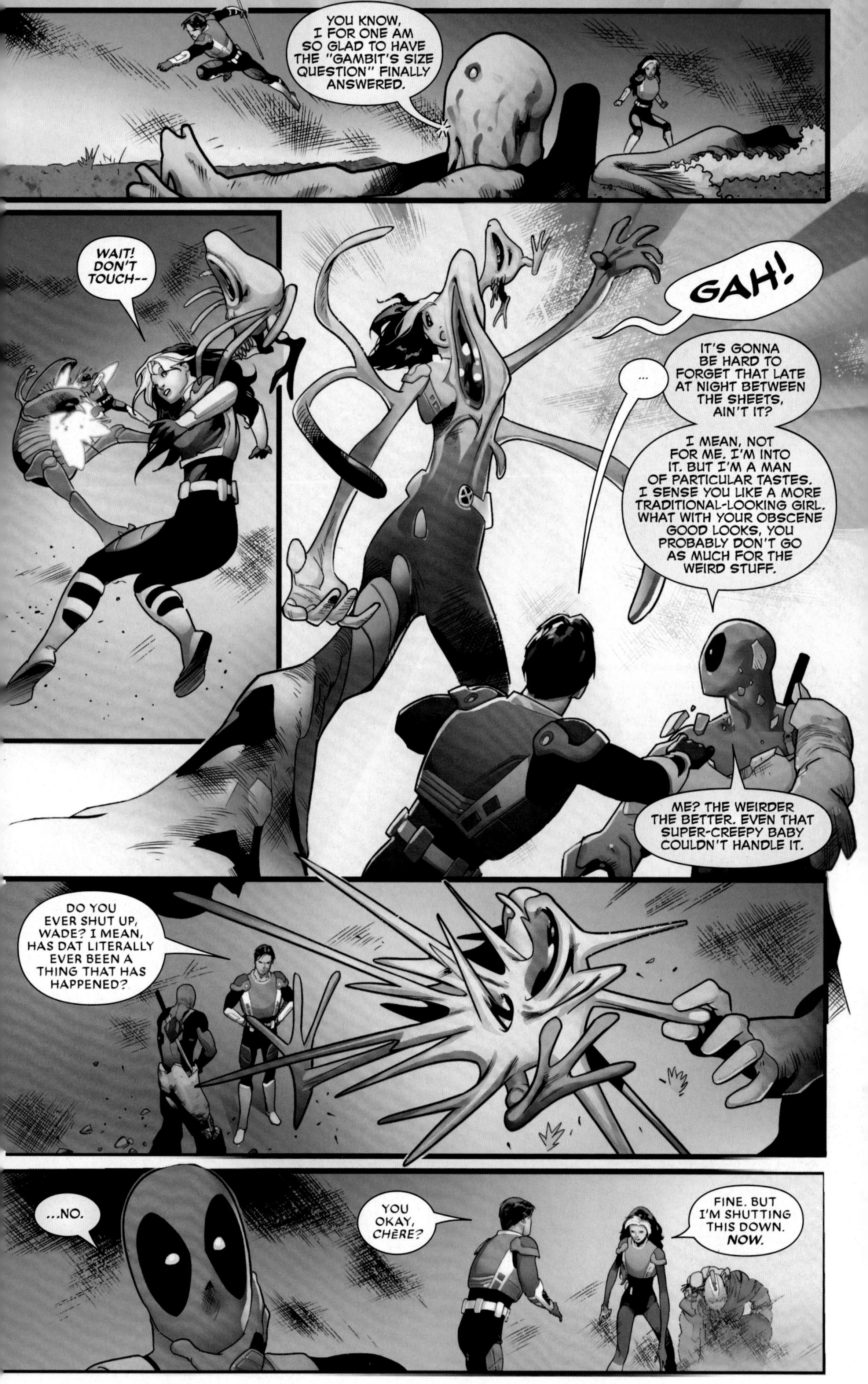
YOU KNOW, I FOR ONE AM SO GLAD TO HAVE THE "GAMBIT'S SIZE QUESTION" FINALLY ANSWERED.
WAIT! DON'T TOUCH--
GAH!
...
IT'S GONNA BE HARD TO FORGET THAT LATE AT NIGHT BETWEEN THE SHEETS, AIN'T IT?
I MEAN, NOT FOR ME. I'M INTO IT. BUT I'M A MAN OF PARTICULAR TASTES. I SENSE YOU LIKE A MORE TRADITIONAL-LOOKING GIRL. WHAT WITH YOUR OBSCENE GOOD LOOKS, YOU PROBABLY DON'T GO AS MUCH FOR THE WEIRD STUFF.
ME? THE WEIRDER THE BETTER. EVEN THAT SUPER-CREEPY BABY COULDN'T HANDLE IT.
DO YOU EVER SHUT UP, WADE? I MEAN, HAS DAT LITERALLY EVER BEEN A THING THAT HAS HAPPENED?
...NO.
YOU OKAY, CHÈRE?
FINE. BUT I'M SHUTTING THIS DOWN. NOW.

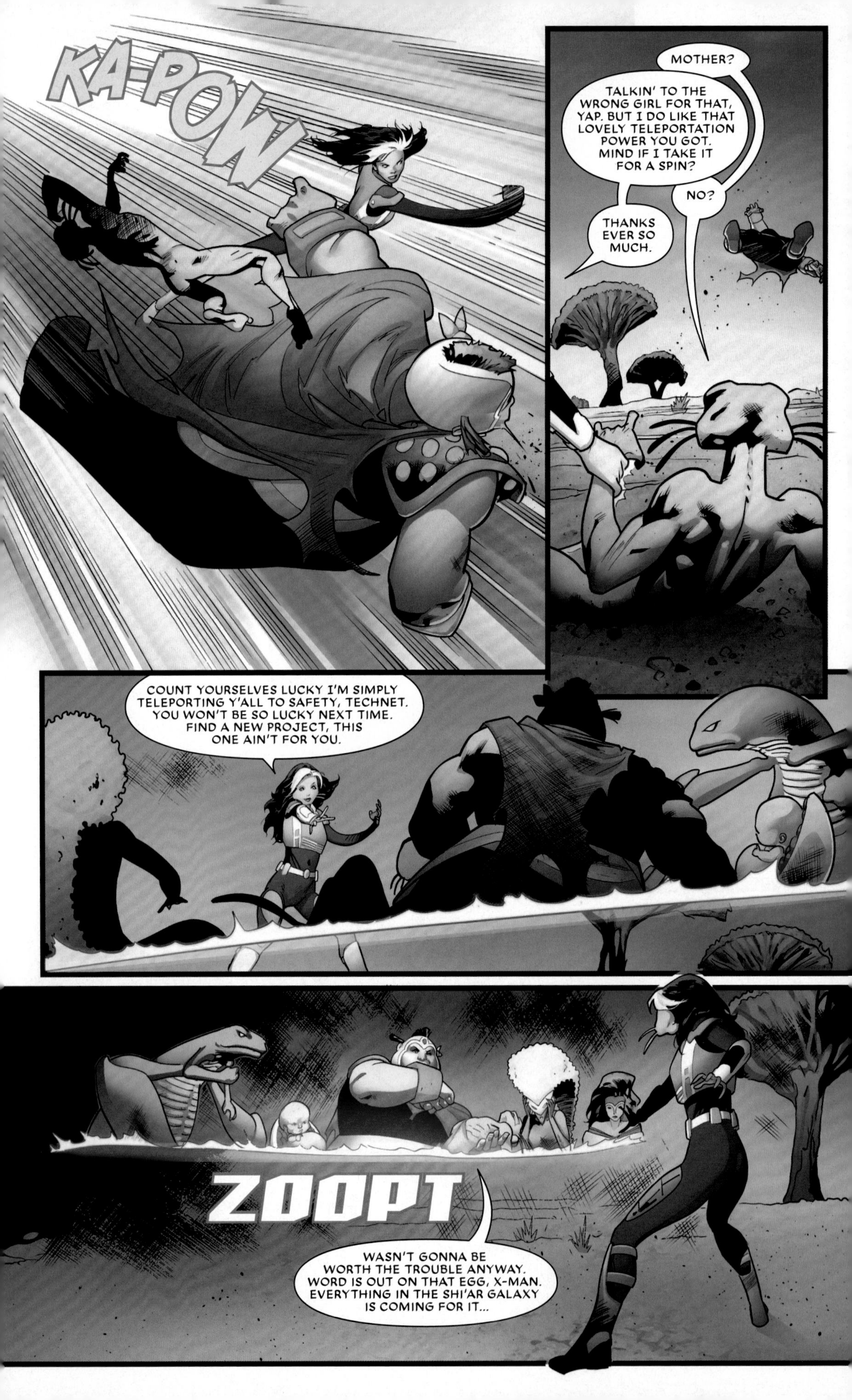
KA-POW
MOTHER?
TALKIN' TO THE WRONG GIRL FOR THAT, YAP. BUT I DO LIKE THAT LOVELY TELEPORTATION POWER YOU GOT. MIND IF I TAKE IT FOR A SPIN?
NO?
THANKS EVER SO MUCH.
COUNT YOURSELVES LUCKY I'M SIMPLY TELEPORTING Y'ALL TO SAFETY, TECHNET. YOU WON'T BE SO LUCKY NEXT TIME. FIND A NEW PROJECT, THIS ONE AIN'T FOR YOU.
ZOOPT
WASN'T GONNA BE WORTH THE TROUBLE ANYWAY. WORD IS OUT ON THAT EGG, X-MAN. EVERYTHING IN THE SHI'AR GALAXY IS COMING FOR IT...

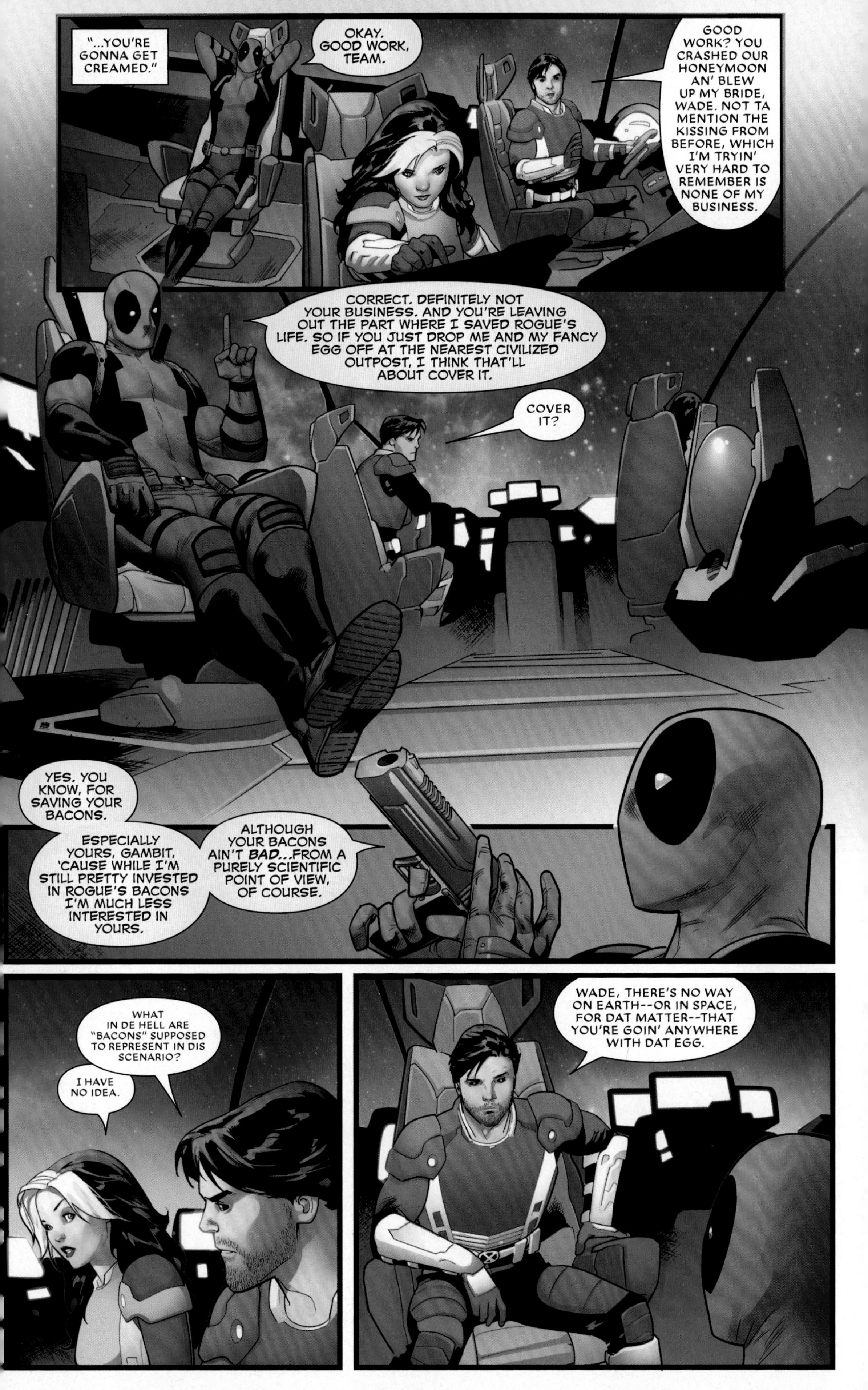
"...YOU'RE GONNA GET CREAMED."
OKAY. GOOD WORK, TEAM.
GOOD WORK? YOU CRASHED OUR HONEYMOON AN' BLEW UP MY BRIDE, WADE. NOT TA MENTION THE KISSING FROM BEFORE, WHICH I'M TRYIN' VERY HARD TO REMEMBER IS NONE OF MY BUSINESS.
CORRECT. DEFINITELY NOT YOUR BUSINESS. AND YOU'RE LEAVING OUT THE PART WHERE I SAVED ROGUE'S LIFE. SO IF YOU JUST DROP ME AND MY FANCY EGG OFF AT THE NEAREST CIVILIZED OUTPOST, I THINK THAT'LL ABOUT COVER IT.
COVER IT?
YES. YOU KNOW, FOR SAVING YOUR BACONS.
ESPECIALLY YOURS, GAMBIT, 'CAUSE WHILE I'M STILL PRETTY INVESTED IN ROGUE'S BACONS I'M MUCH LESS INTERESTED IN YOURS.
ALTHOUGH YOUR BACONS AIN'T BAD...FROM A PURELY SCIENTIFIC POINT OF VIEW, OF COURSE.
WHAT IN DE HELL ARE "BACONS" SUPPOSED TO REPRESENT IN DIS SCENARIO?
I HAVE NO IDEA.
WADE, THERE'S NO WAY ON EARTH--OR IN SPACE, FOR DAT MATTER--THAT YOU'RE GOIN' ANYWHERE WITH DAT EGG.

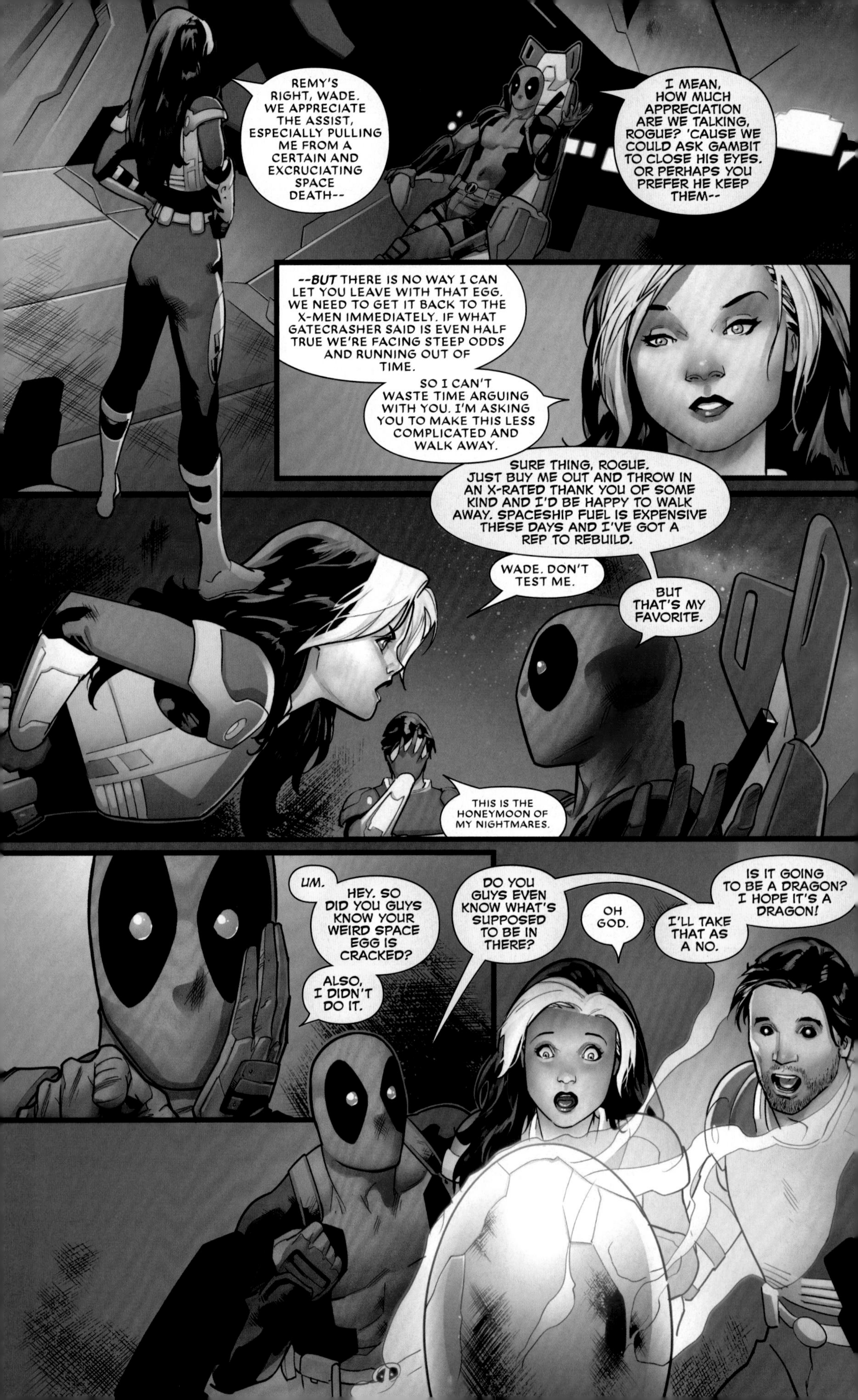
REMY'S RIGHT, WADE. WE APPRECIATE THE ASSIST, ESPECIALLY PULLING ME FROM A CERTAIN AND EXCRUCIATING SPACE DEATH--
I MEAN, HOW MUCH APPRECIATION ARE WE TALKING, ROGUE? 'CAUSE WE COULD ASK GAMBIT TO CLOSE HIS EYES. OR PERHAPS YOU PREFER HE KEEP THEM--
--BUT THERE IS NO WAY I CAN LET YOU LEAVE WITH THAT EGG. WE NEED TO GET IT BACK TO THE X-MEN IMMEDIATELY. IF WHAT GATECRASHER SAID IS EVEN HALF TRUE WE'RE FACING STEEP ODDS AND RUNNING OUT OF TIME.
SO I CAN'T WASTE TIME ARGUING WITH YOU. I'M ASKING YOU TO MAKE THIS LESS COMPLICATED AND WALK AWAY.
SURE THING, ROGUE. JUST BUY ME OUT AND THROW IN AN X-RATED THANK YOU OF SOME KIND AND I'D BE HAPPY TO WALK AWAY. SPACESHIP FUEL IS EXPENSIVE THESE DAYS AND I'VE GOT A REP TO REBUILD.
WADE. DON'T TEST ME.
BUT THAT'S MY FAVORITE.
THIS IS THE HONEYMOON OF MY NIGHTMARES.
UM.
HEY. SO DID YOU GUYS KNOW YOUR WEIRD SPACE EGG IS CRACKED?
ALSO, I DIDN'T DO IT.
DO YOU GUYS EVEN KNOW WHAT'S SUPPOSED TO BE IN THERE?
OH GOD.
I'LL TAKE THAT AS A NO.
IS IT GOING TO BE A DRAGON? I HOPE IT'S A DRAGON!

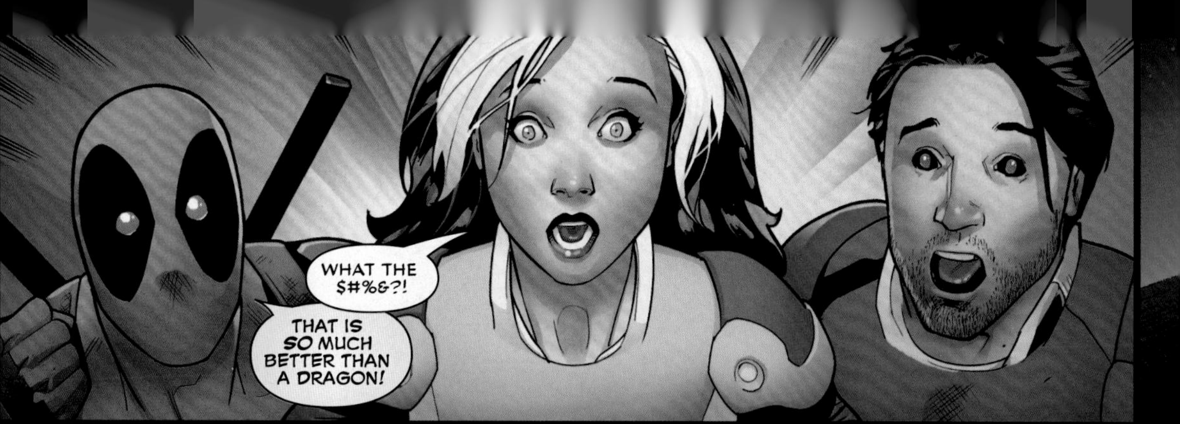
WHAT THE $#%&?!
THAT IS SO MUCH BETTER THAN A DRAGON!

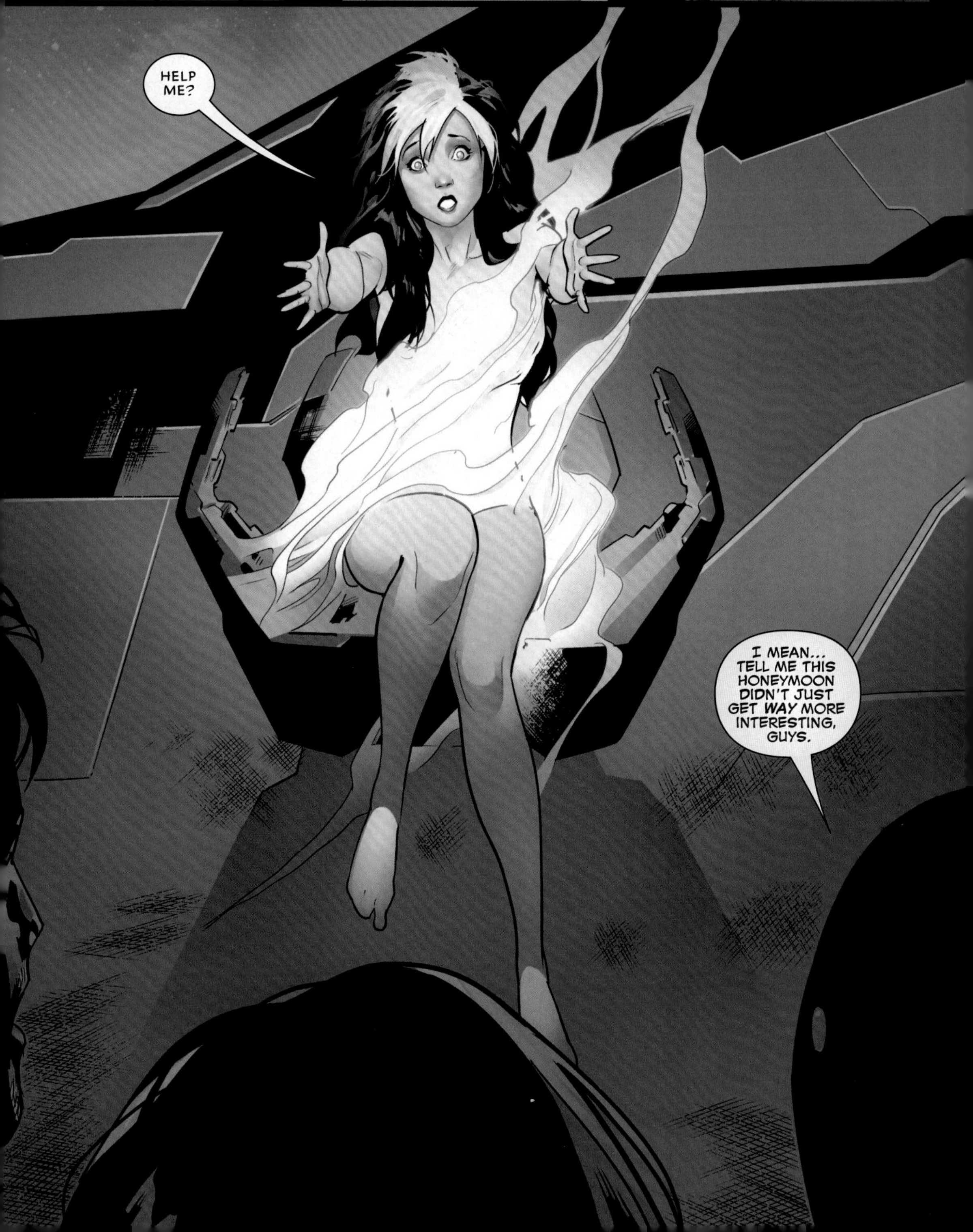
HELP ME?
I MEAN... TELL ME THIS HONEYMOON DIDN'T JUST GET WAY MORE INTERESTING, GUYS.

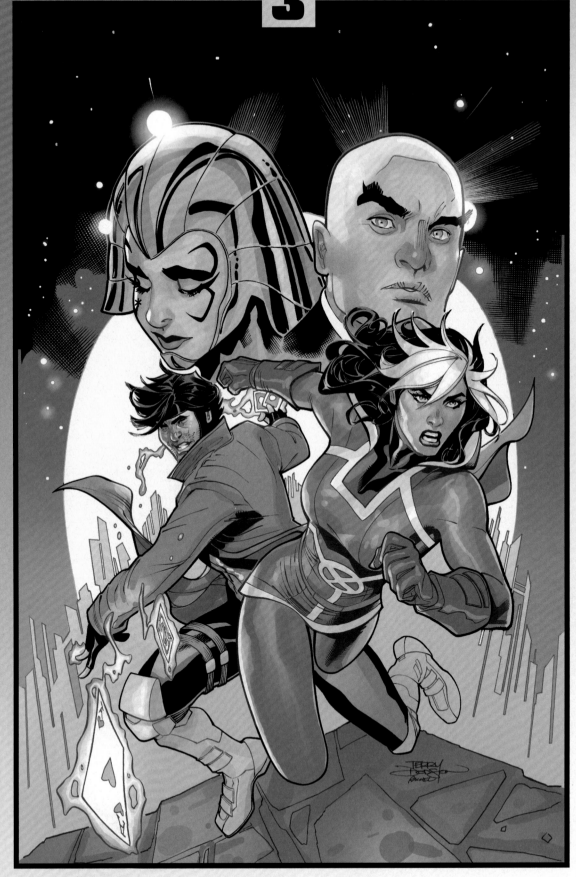

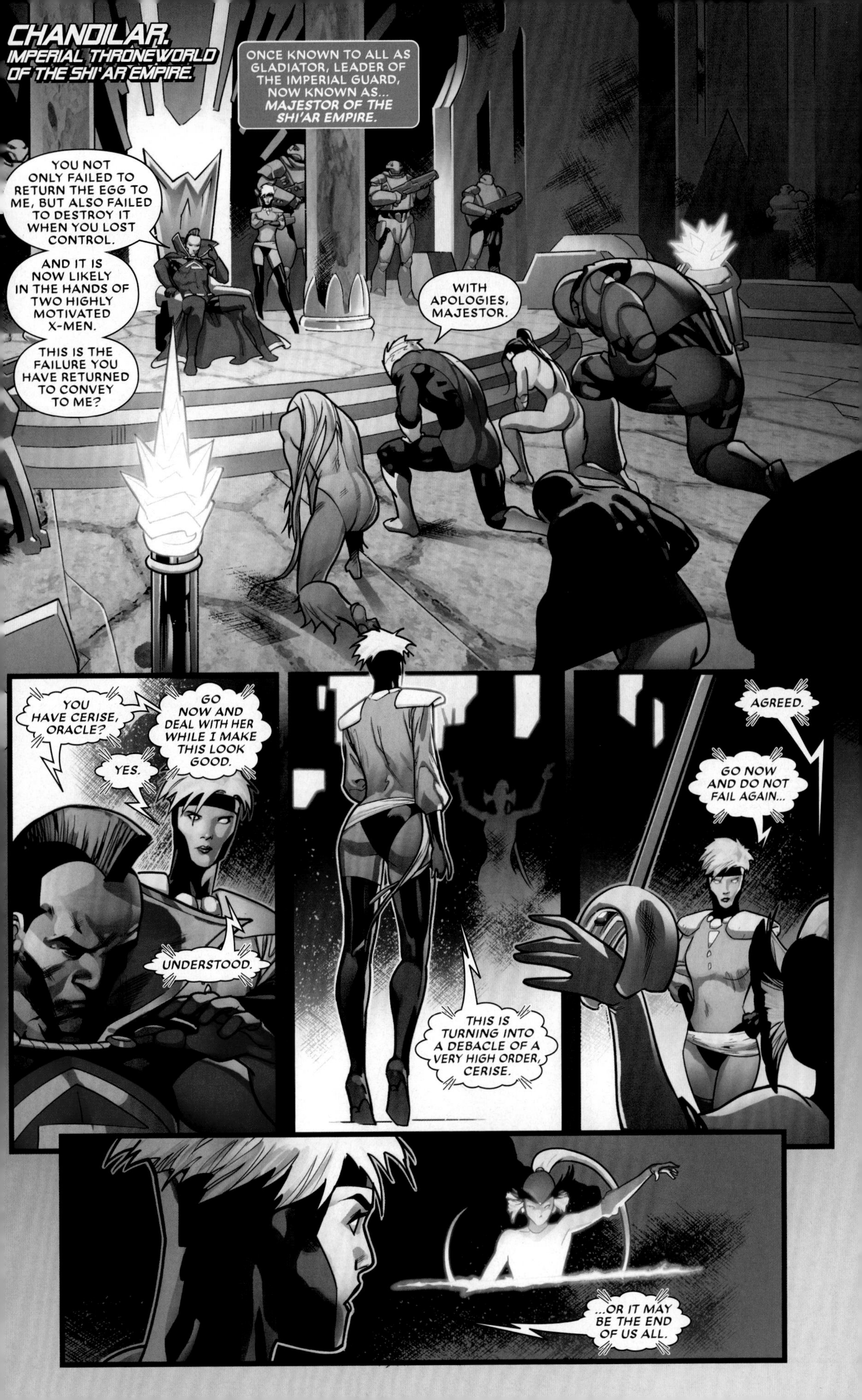
CHANDILAR.
IMPERIAL THRONEWORLD OF THE SHI'AR EMPIRE.
ONCE KNOWN TO ALL AS GLADIATOR, LEADER OF THE IMPERIAL GUARD, NOW KNOWN AS... *MAJESTOR OF THE SHI'AR EMPIRE.*
YOU NOT ONLY FAILED TO RETURN THE EGG TO ME, BUT ALSO FAILED TO DESTROY IT WHEN YOU LOST CONTROL.
AND IT IS NOW LIKELY IN THE HANDS OF TWO HIGHLY MOTIVATED X-MEN.
THIS IS THE FAILURE YOU HAVE RETURNED TO CONVEY TO ME?
WITH APOLOGIES, MAJESTOR.
YOU HAVE CERISE, ORACLE?
YES.
GO NOW AND DEAL WITH HER WHILE I MAKE THIS LOOK GOOD.
UNDERSTOOD.
THIS IS TURNING INTO A DEBACLE OF A VERY HIGH ORDER, CERISE.
AGREED.
GO NOW AND DO NOT FAIL AGAIN...
...OR IT MAY BE THE END OF US ALL.

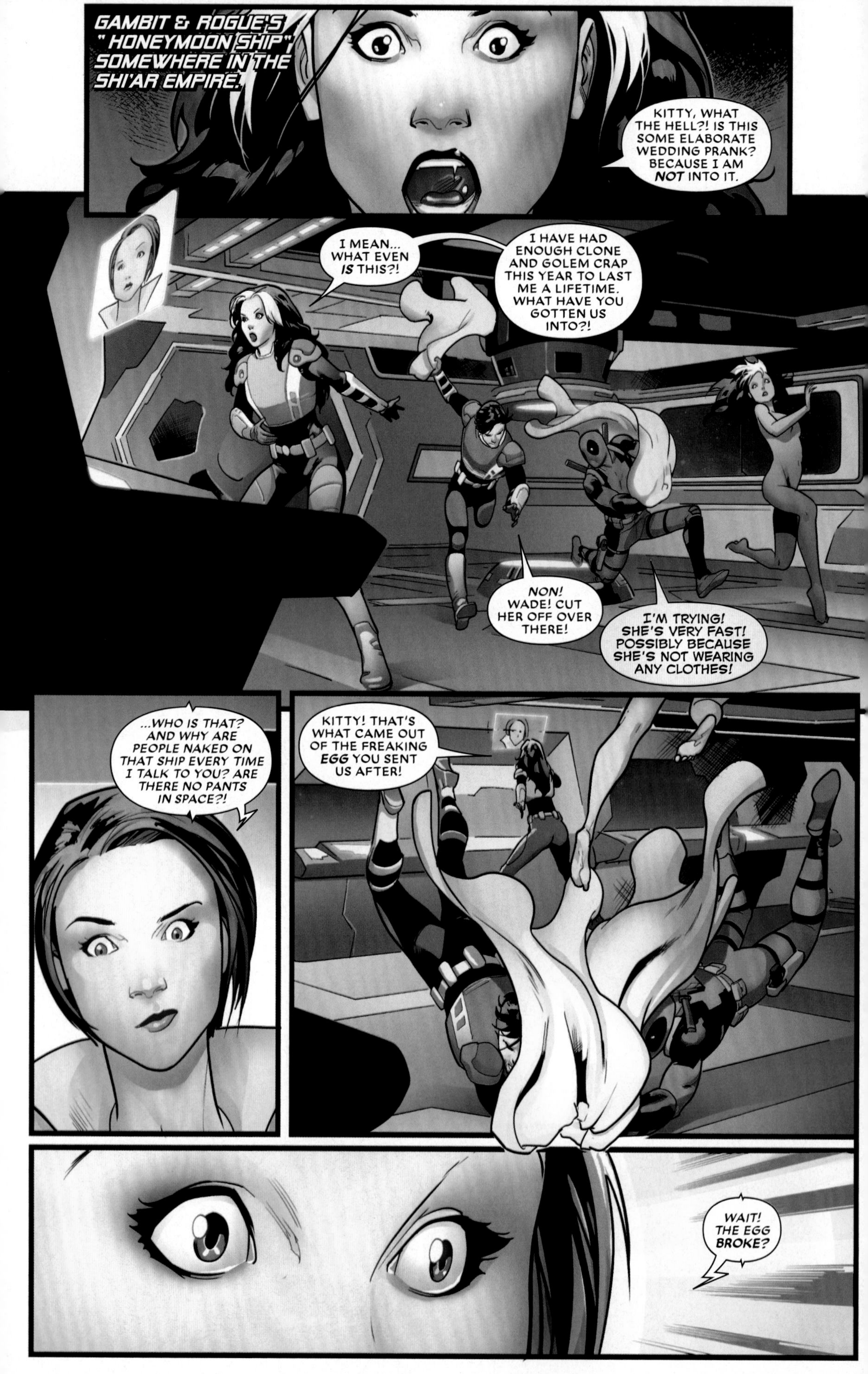
GAMBIT & ROGUE'S "HONEYMOON SHIP" SOMEWHERE IN THE SHI'AR EMPIRE.
KITTY, WHAT THE HELL?! IS THIS SOME ELABORATE WEDDING PRANK? BECAUSE I AM NOT INTO IT.
I MEAN... WHAT EVEN IS THIS?!
I HAVE HAD ENOUGH CLONE AND GOLEM CRAP THIS YEAR TO LAST ME A LIFETIME. WHAT HAVE YOU GOTTEN US INTO?!
NON! WADE! CUT HER OFF OVER THERE!
I'M TRYING! SHE'S VERY FAST! POSSIBLY BECAUSE SHE'S NOT WEARING ANY CLOTHES!
...WHO IS THAT? AND WHY ARE PEOPLE NAKED ON THAT SHIP EVERY TIME I TALK TO YOU? ARE THERE NO PANTS IN SPACE?!
KITTY! THAT'S WHAT CAME OUT OF THE FREAKING EGG YOU SENT US AFTER!
WAIT! THE EGG BROKE?

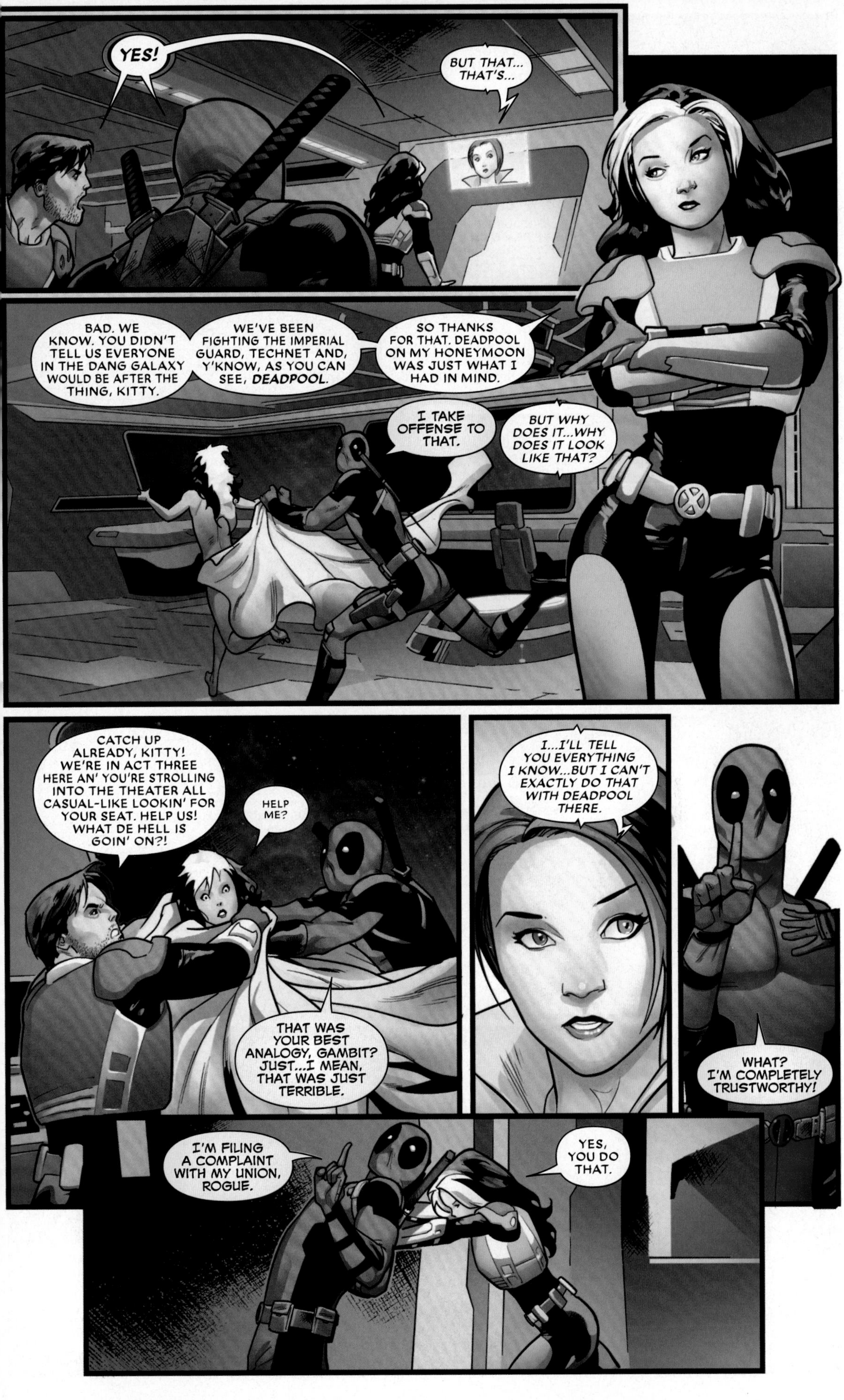
YES!
BUT THAT... THAT'S...
BAD. WE KNOW. YOU DIDN'T TELL US EVERYONE IN THE DANG GALAXY WOULD BE AFTER THE THING, KITTY.
WE'VE BEEN FIGHTING THE IMPERIAL GUARD, TECHNET AND, Y'KNOW, AS YOU CAN SEE, DEADPOOL.
SO THANKS FOR THAT. DEADPOOL ON MY HONEYMOON WAS JUST WHAT I HAD IN MIND.
I TAKE OFFENSE TO THAT.
BUT WHY DOES IT...WHY DOES IT LOOK LIKE THAT?
CATCH UP ALREADY, KITTY! WE'RE IN ACT THREE HERE AN' YOU'RE STROLLING INTO THE THEATER ALL CASUAL-LIKE LOOKIN' FOR YOUR SEAT. HELP US! WHAT DE HELL IS GOIN' ON?!
HELP ME?
THAT WAS YOUR BEST ANALOGY, GAMBIT? JUST...I MEAN, THAT WAS JUST TERRIBLE.
I...I'LL TELL YOU EVERYTHING I KNOW...BUT I CAN'T EXACTLY DO THAT WITH DEADPOOL THERE.
WHAT? I'M COMPLETELY TRUSTWORTHY!
I'M FILING A COMPLAINT WITH MY UNION, ROGUE.
YES, YOU DO THAT.

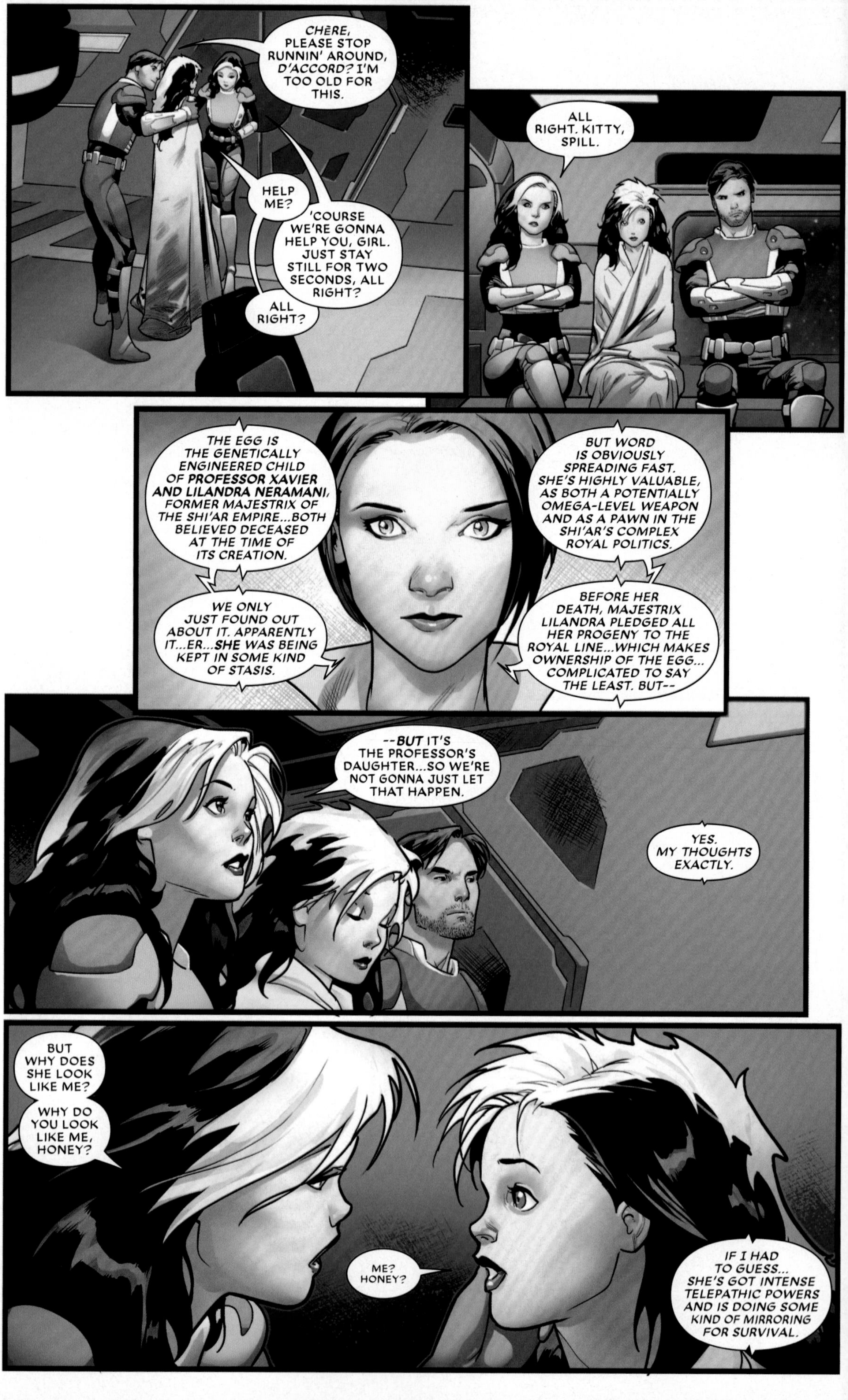
CHÈRE, PLEASE STOP RUNNIN' AROUND, D'ACCORD? I'M TOO OLD FOR THIS.
HELP ME?
'COURSE WE'RE GONNA HELP YOU, GIRL. JUST STAY STILL FOR TWO SECONDS, ALL RIGHT?
ALL RIGHT?
ALL RIGHT. KITTY, SPILL.
THE EGG IS THE GENETICALLY ENGINEERED CHILD OF PROFESSOR XAVIER AND LILANDRA NERAMANI, FORMER MAJESTRIX OF THE SHI'AR EMPIRE...BOTH BELIEVED DECEASED AT THE TIME OF ITS CREATION.
WE ONLY JUST FOUND OUT ABOUT IT. APPARENTLY IT...ER...SHE WAS BEING KEPT IN SOME KIND OF STASIS.
BUT WORD IS OBVIOUSLY SPREADING FAST. SHE'S HIGHLY VALUABLE, AS BOTH A POTENTIALLY OMEGA-LEVEL WEAPON AND AS A PAWN IN THE SHI'AR'S COMPLEX ROYAL POLITICS.
BEFORE HER DEATH, MAJESTRIX LILANDRA PLEDGED ALL HER PROGENY TO THE ROYAL LINE...WHICH MAKES OWNERSHIP OF THE EGG... COMPLICATED TO SAY THE LEAST. BUT--
--BUT IT'S THE PROFESSOR'S DAUGHTER...SO WE'RE NOT GONNA JUST LET THAT HAPPEN.
YES. MY THOUGHTS EXACTLY.
BUT WHY DOES SHE LOOK LIKE ME?
WHY DO YOU LOOK LIKE ME, HONEY?
ME? HONEY?
IF I HAD TO GUESS... SHE'S GOT INTENSE TELEPATHIC POWERS AND IS DOING SOME KIND OF MIRRORING FOR SURVIVAL.

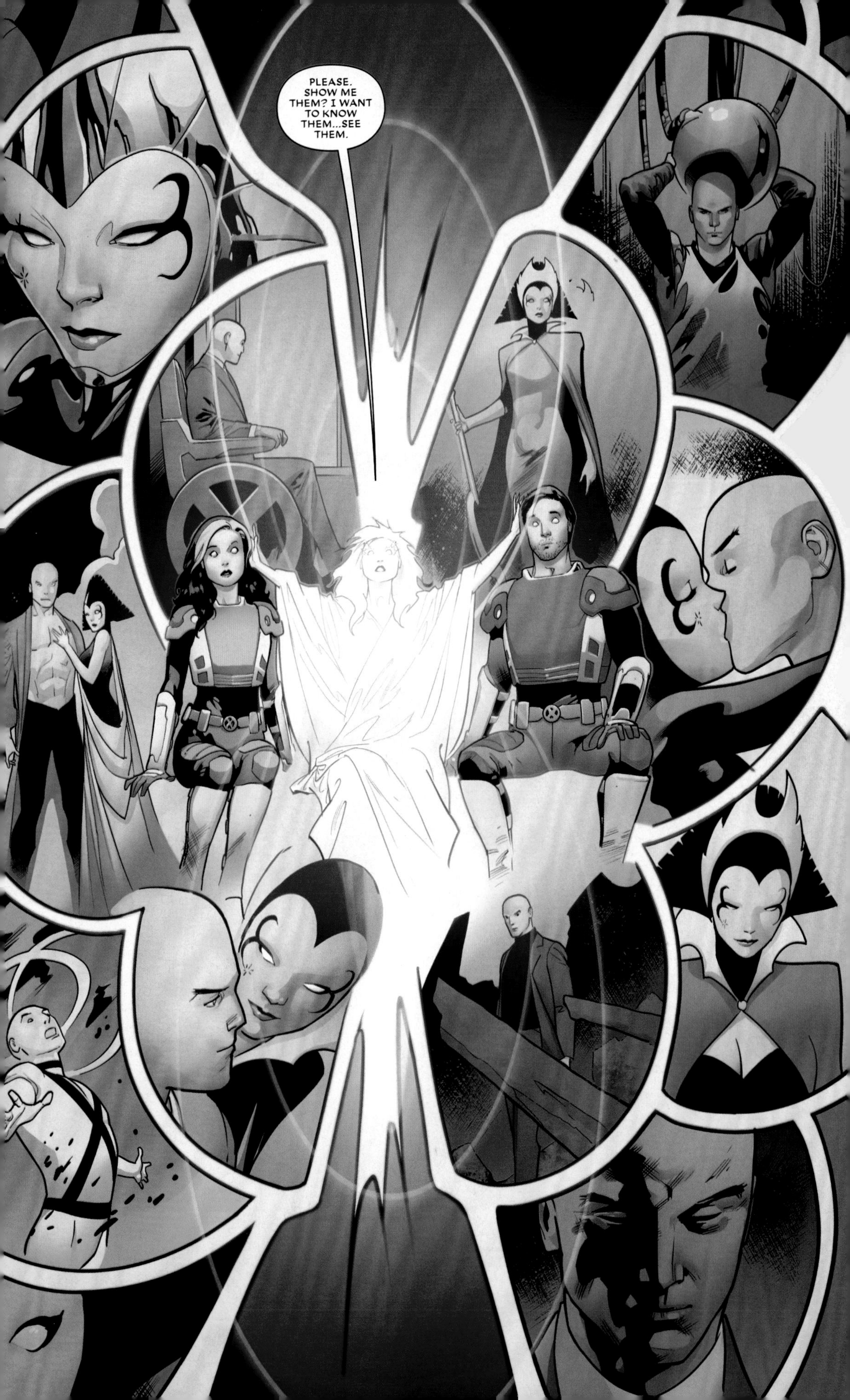
PLEASE. SHOW ME THEM? I WANT TO KNOW THEM...SEE THEM.

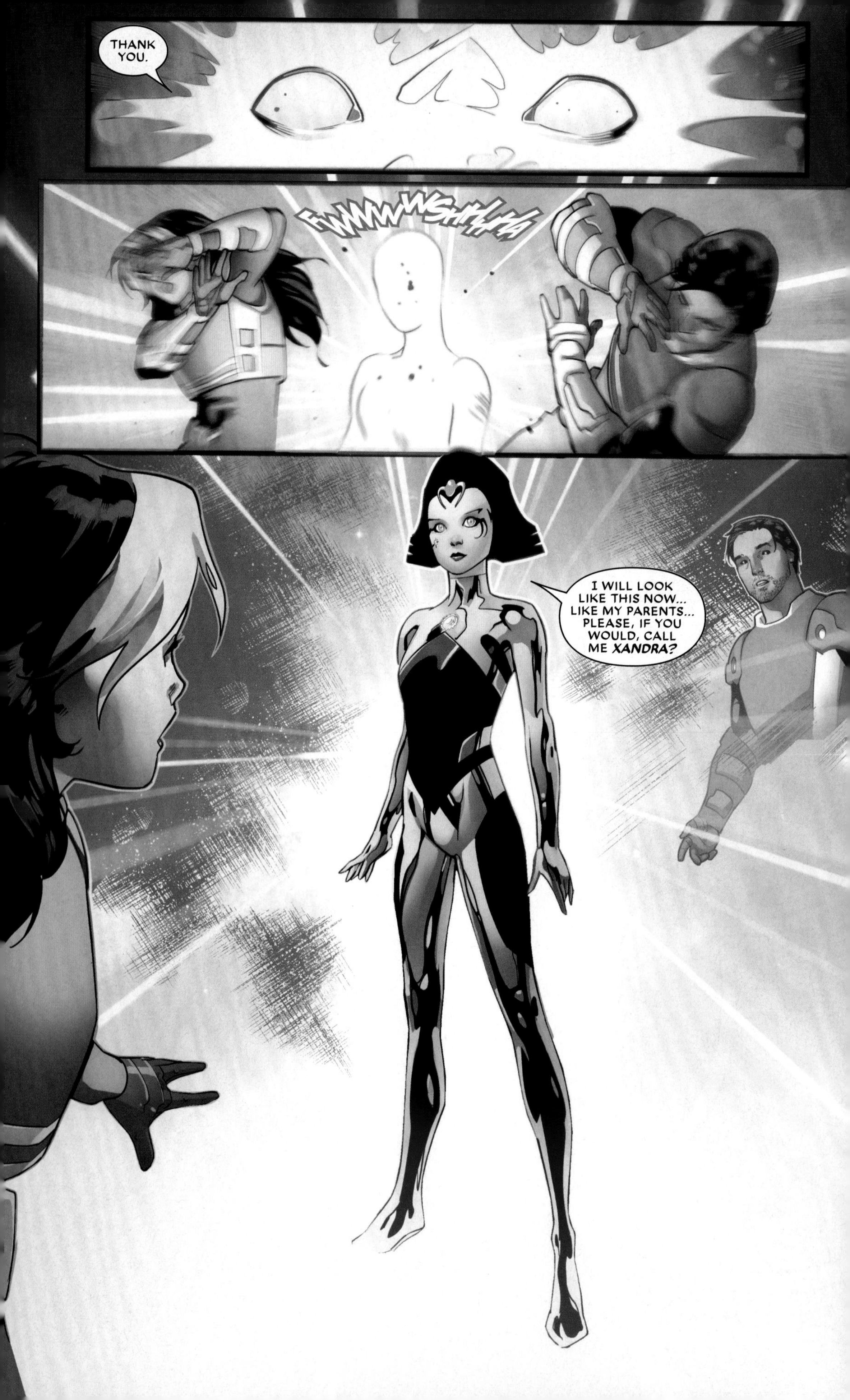
THANK YOU.
FWWWWSHHHHA
I WILL LOOK LIKE THIS NOW... LIKE MY PARENTS... PLEASE, IF YOU WOULD, CALL ME XANDRA?

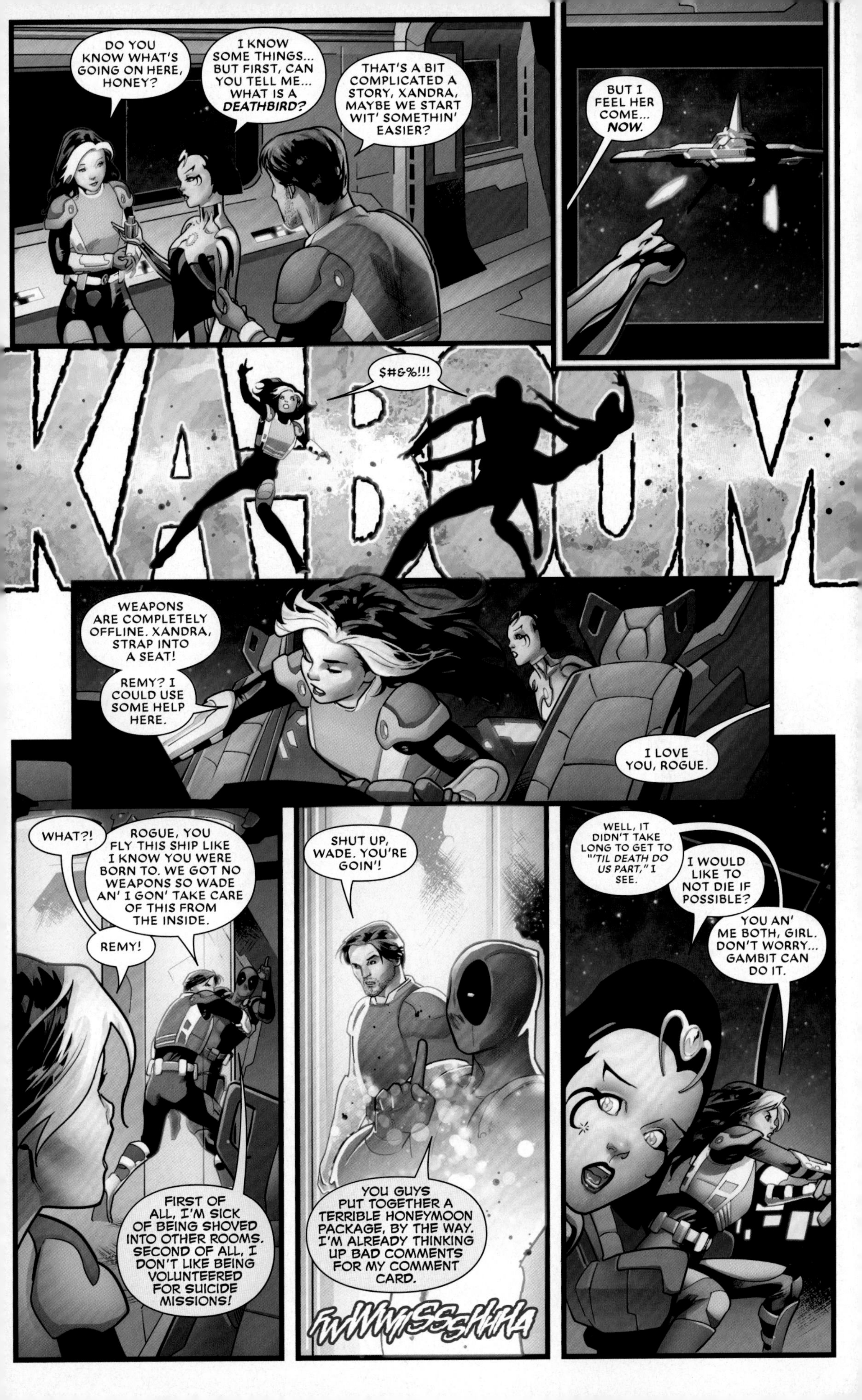
DO YOU KNOW WHAT'S GOING ON HERE, HONEY?
I KNOW SOME THINGS... BUT FIRST, CAN YOU TELL ME... WHAT IS A *DEATHBIRD?*
THAT'S A BIT COMPLICATED A STORY, XANDRA, MAYBE WE START WIT' SOMETHIN' EASIER?
BUT I FEEL HER COME... *NOW.*
KABOOM
$#&%!!!
WEAPONS ARE COMPLETELY OFFLINE. XANDRA, STRAP INTO A SEAT!
REMY? I COULD USE SOME HELP HERE.
I LOVE YOU, ROGUE.
WHAT?!
ROGUE, YOU FLY THIS SHIP LIKE I KNOW YOU WERE BORN TO. WE GOT NO WEAPONS SO WADE AN' I GON' TAKE CARE OF THIS FROM THE INSIDE.
REMY!
FIRST OF ALL, I'M SICK OF BEING SHOVED INTO OTHER ROOMS. SECOND OF ALL, I DON'T LIKE BEING VOLUNTEERED FOR SUICIDE MISSIONS!
SHUT UP, WADE. YOU'RE GOIN'!
YOU GUYS PUT TOGETHER A TERRIBLE HONEYMOON PACKAGE, BY THE WAY. I'M ALREADY THINKING UP BAD COMMENTS FOR MY COMMENT CARD.
WELL, IT DIDN'T TAKE LONG TO GET TO "*'TIL DEATH DO US PART,*" I SEE.
I WOULD LIKE TO NOT DIE IF POSSIBLE?
YOU AN' ME BOTH, GIRL. DON'T WORRY... GAMBIT CAN DO IT.

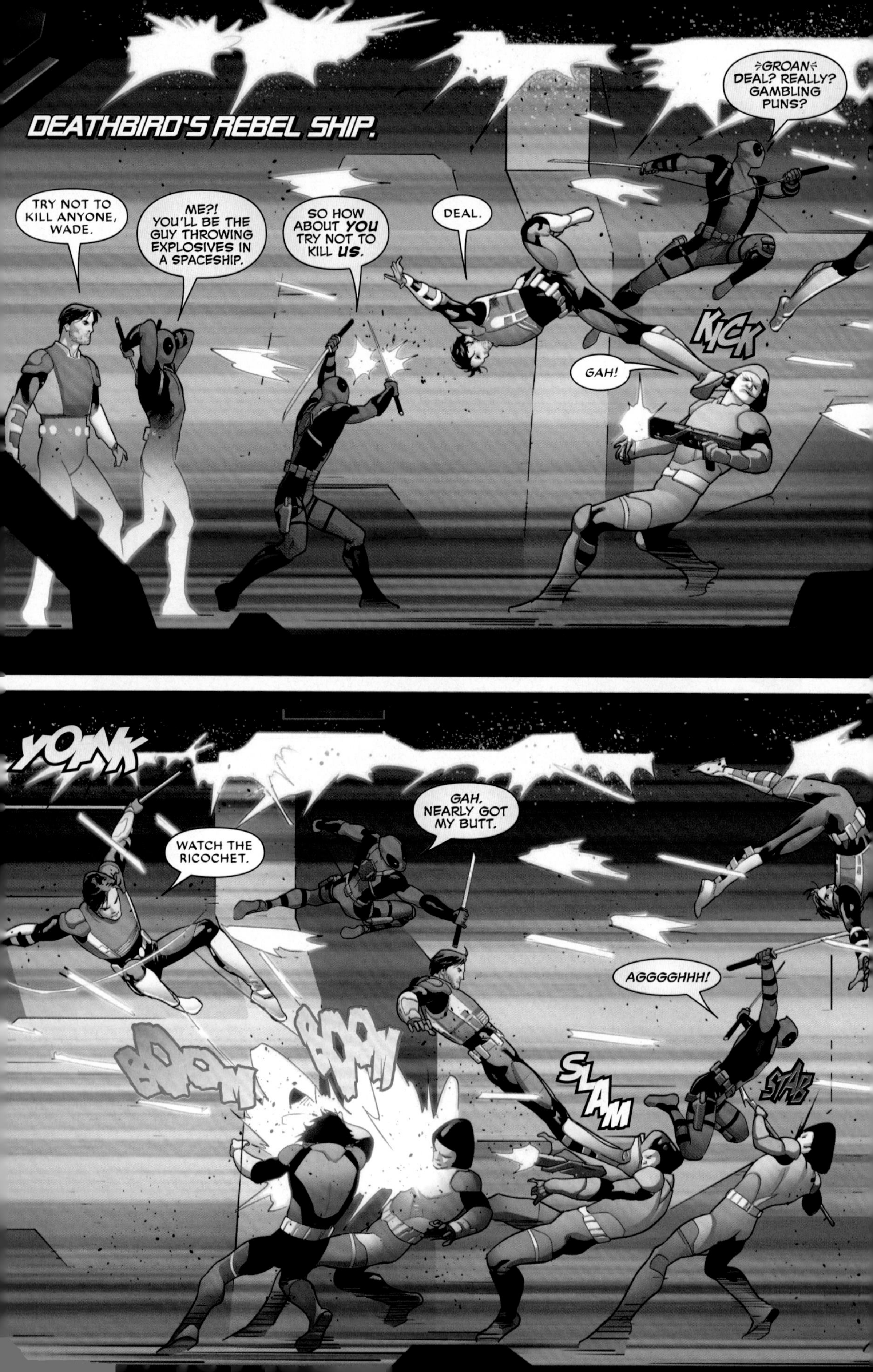
DEATHBIRD'S REBEL SHIP.
TRY NOT TO KILL ANYONE, WADE.
ME?! YOU'LL BE THE GUY THROWING EXPLOSIVES IN A SPACESHIP.
SO HOW ABOUT YOU TRY NOT TO KILL US.
DEAL.
GROAN DEAL? REALLY? GAMBLING PUNS?
KICK
GAH!
YOINK
WATCH THE RICOCHET.
GAH. NEARLY GOT MY BUTT.
AGGGGHHH!
BOOM
BOOM
SLAM
STAB

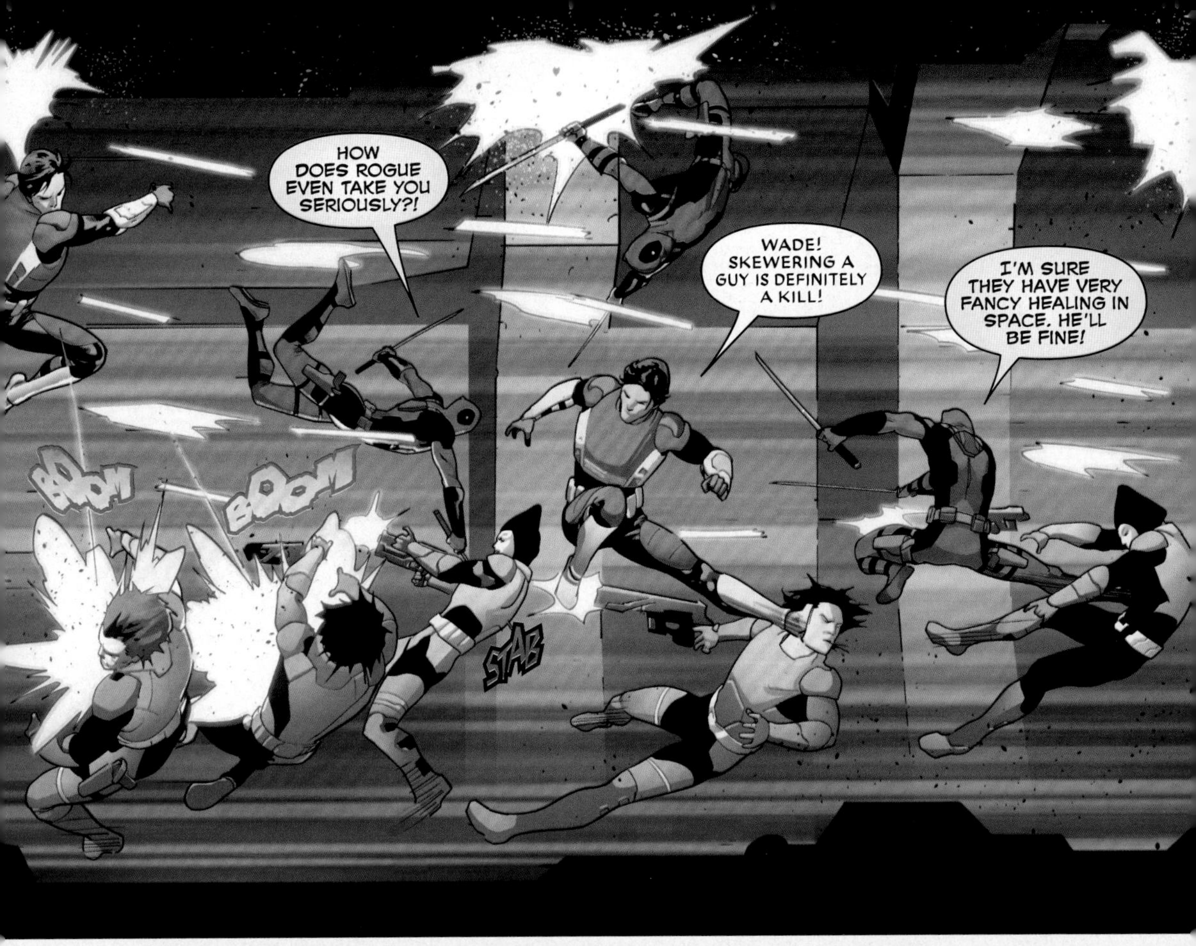
HOW DOES ROGUE EVEN TAKE YOU SERIOUSLY?!
BOOM
BOOM
STAB
WADE! SKEWERING A GUY IS DEFINITELY A KILL!
I'M SURE THEY HAVE VERY FANCY HEALING IN SPACE. HE'LL BE FINE!

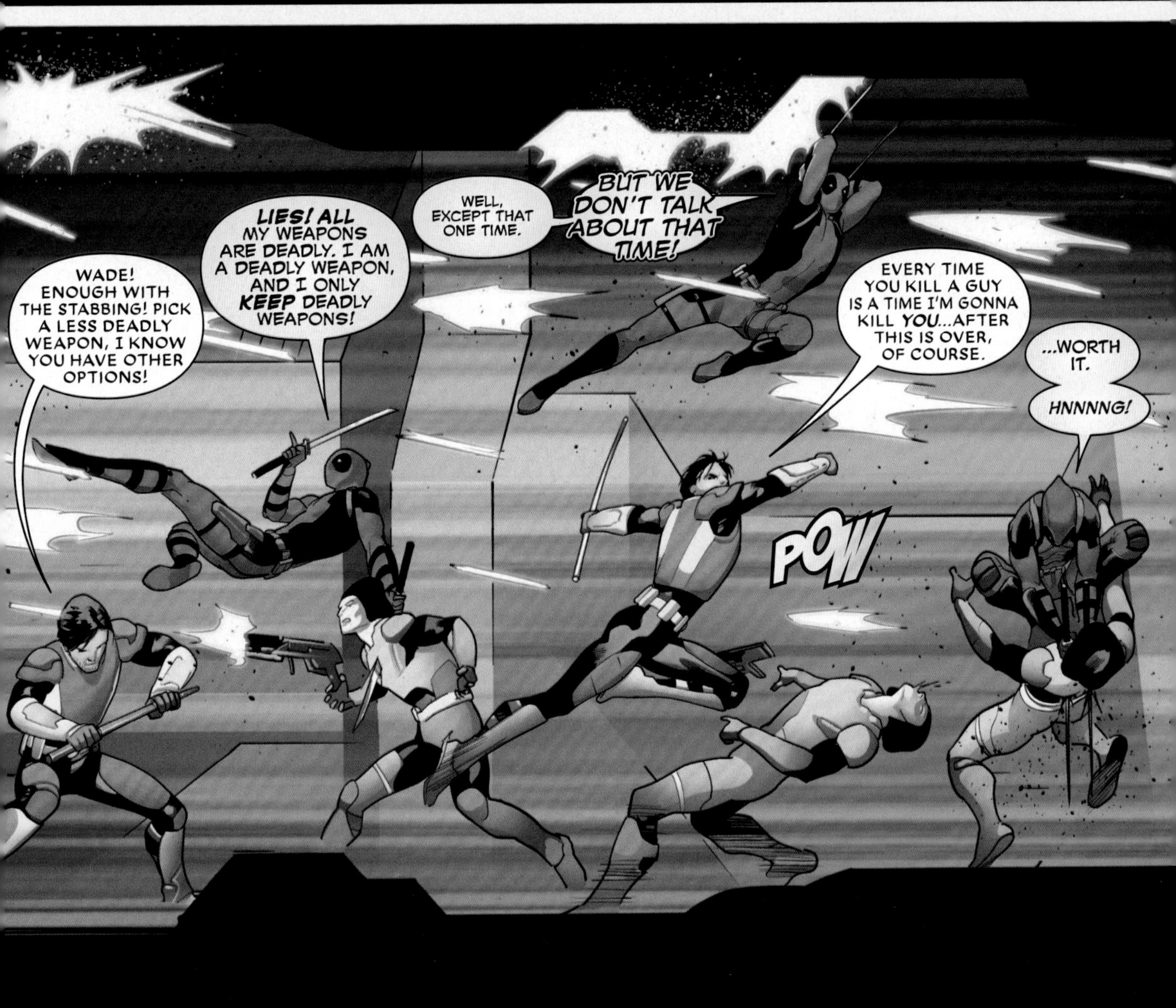
WADE! ENOUGH WITH THE STABBING! PICK A LESS DEADLY WEAPON, I KNOW YOU HAVE OTHER OPTIONS!
LIES! ALL MY WEAPONS ARE DEADLY. I AM A DEADLY WEAPON, AND I ONLY KEEP DEADLY WEAPONS!
WELL, EXCEPT THAT ONE TIME.
BUT WE DON'T TALK ABOUT THAT TIME!
EVERY TIME YOU KILL A GUY IS A TIME I'M GONNA KILL YOU...AFTER THIS IS OVER, OF COURSE.
POW
...WORTH IT.
HNNNNG!

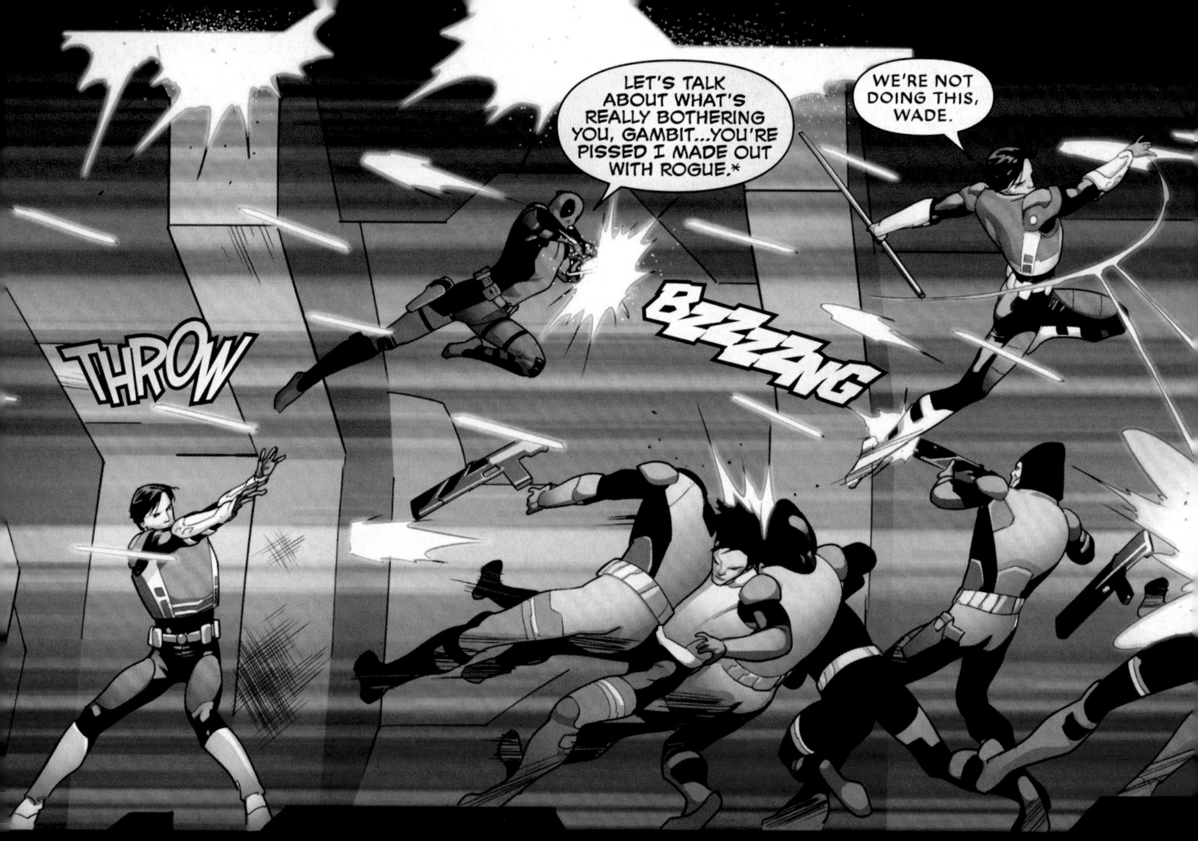
LET'S TALK ABOUT WHAT'S REALLY BOTHERING YOU, GAMBIT...YOU'RE PISSED I MADE OUT WITH ROGUE.*
WE'RE NOT DOING THIS, WADE.
THROW
BZZZZNG

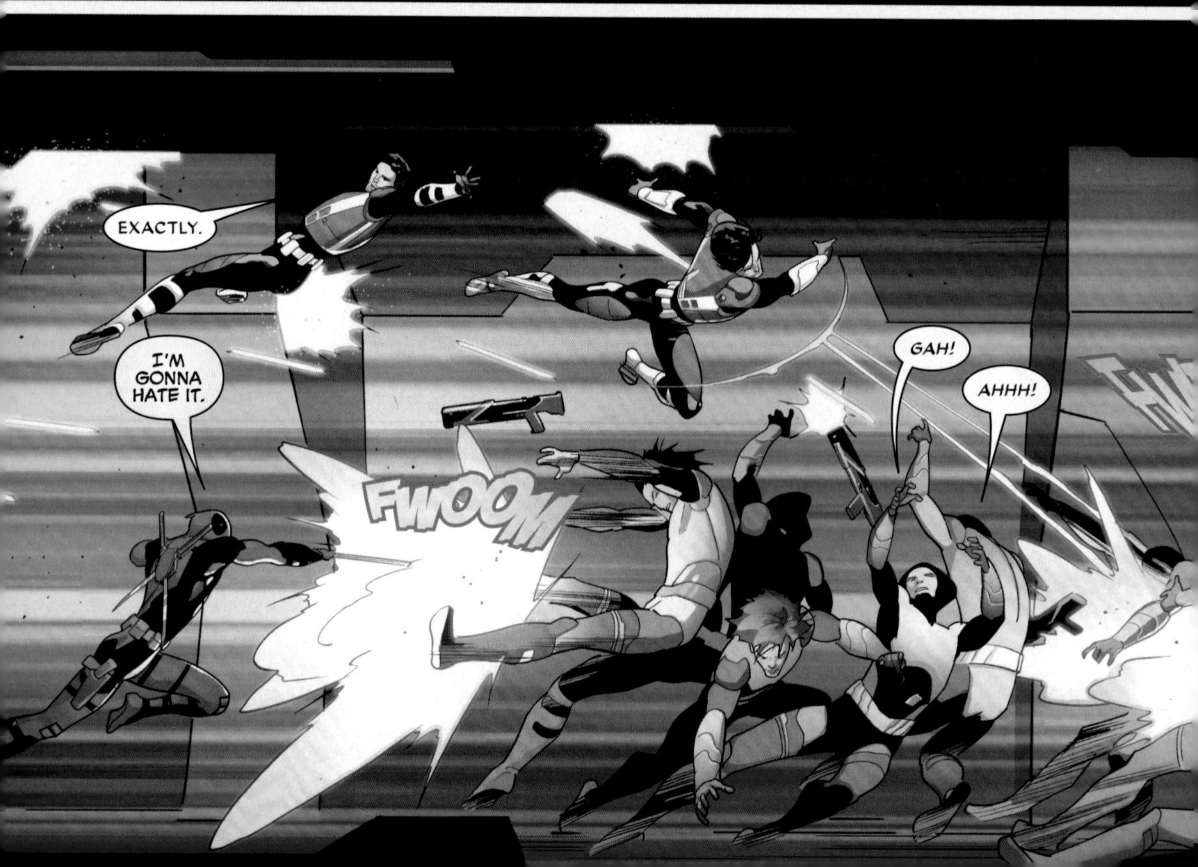
EXACTLY.
I'M GONNA HATE IT.
GAH!
AHHH!
FWOOM

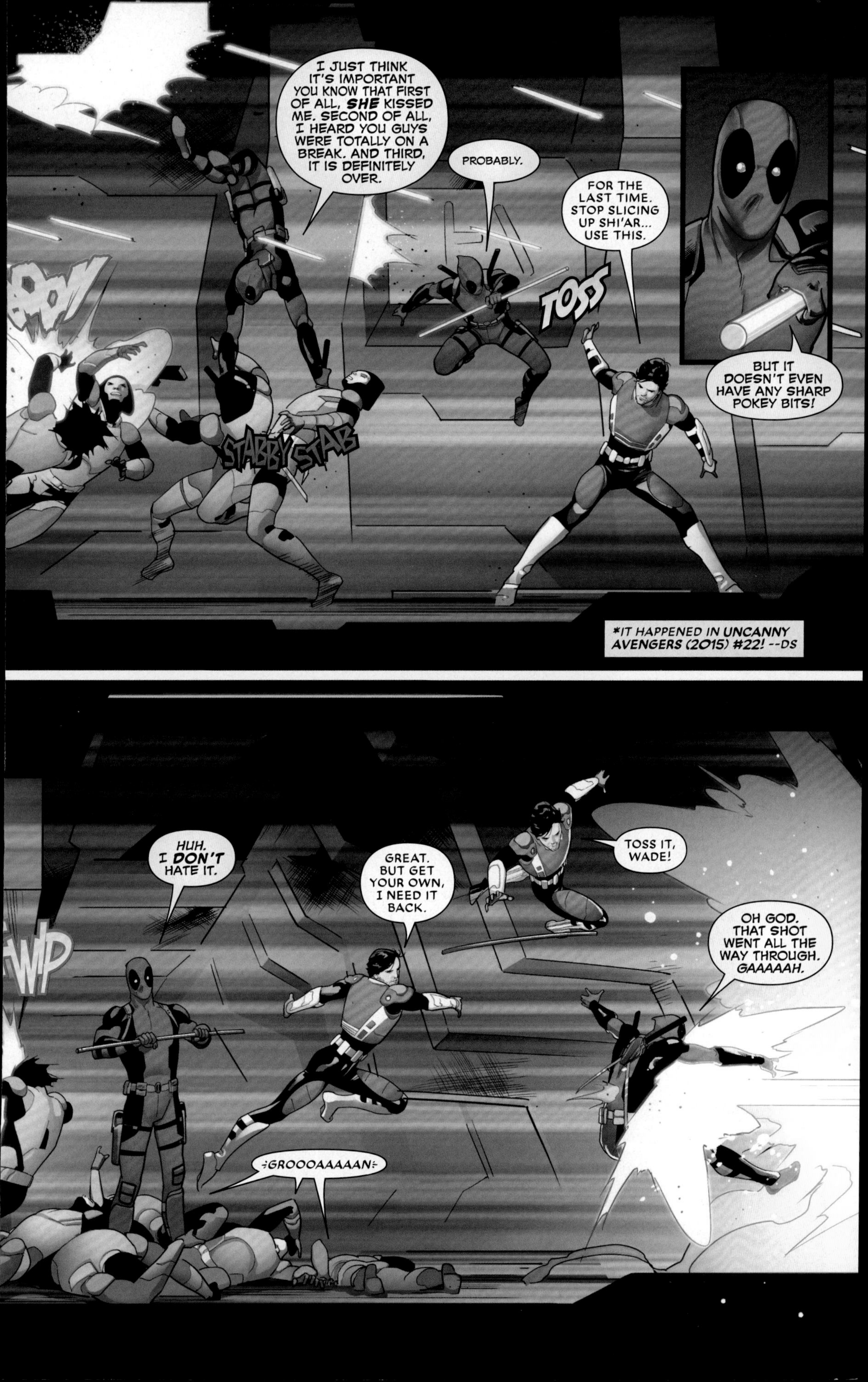
I JUST THINK IT'S IMPORTANT YOU KNOW THAT FIRST OF ALL, **SHE** KISSED ME. SECOND OF ALL, I HEARD YOU GUYS WERE TOTALLY ON A BREAK. AND THIRD, IT IS DEFINITELY OVER.
PROBABLY.
FOR THE LAST TIME. STOP SLICING UP SHI'AR... USE THIS.
TOSS
STABBY STAB
BUT IT DOESN'T EVEN HAVE ANY SHARP POKEY BITS!
*IT HAPPENED IN UNCANNY AVENGERS (2015) #22! --DS
HUH. I **DON'T** HATE IT.
GREAT. BUT GET YOUR OWN, I NEED IT BACK.
TOSS IT, WADE!
OH GOD. THAT SHOT WENT ALL THE WAY THROUGH. GAAAAAH.
÷GROOOAAAAAN÷

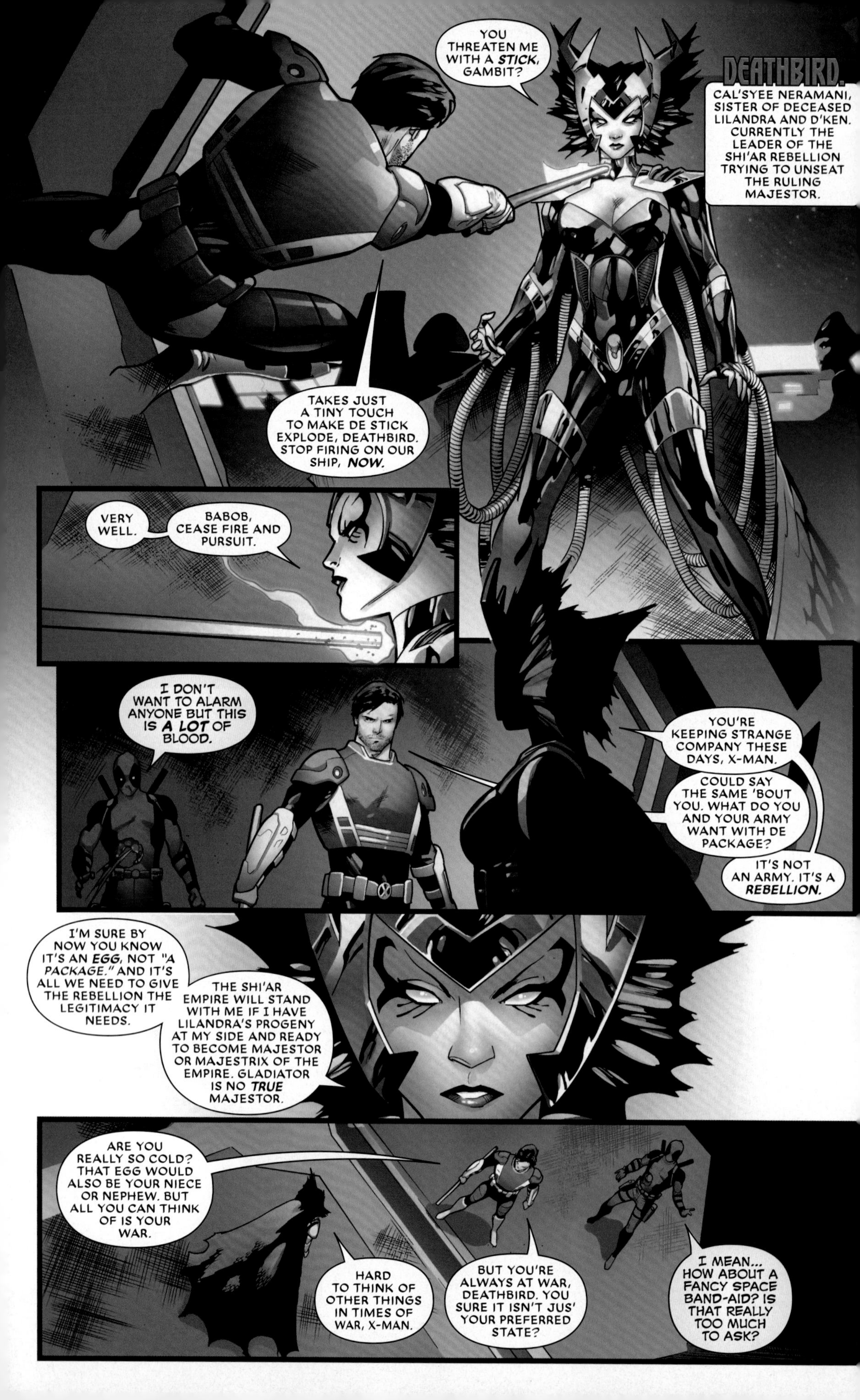
YOU THREATEN ME WITH A STICK, GAMBIT?
DEATHBIRD.
CAL'SYEE NERAMANI, SISTER OF DECEASED LILANDRA AND D'KEN. CURRENTLY THE LEADER OF THE SHI'AR REBELLION TRYING TO UNSEAT THE RULING MAJESTOR.
TAKES JUST A TINY TOUCH TO MAKE DE STICK EXPLODE, DEATHBIRD. STOP FIRING ON OUR SHIP, NOW.
VERY WELL.
BABOB, CEASE FIRE AND PURSUIT.
I DON'T WANT TO ALARM ANYONE BUT THIS IS A LOT OF BLOOD.
YOU'RE KEEPING STRANGE COMPANY THESE DAYS, X-MAN.
COULD SAY THE SAME 'BOUT YOU. WHAT DO YOU AND YOUR ARMY WANT WITH DE PACKAGE?
IT'S NOT AN ARMY. IT'S A REBELLION.
I'M SURE BY NOW YOU KNOW IT'S AN EGG, NOT "A PACKAGE." AND IT'S ALL WE NEED TO GIVE THE REBELLION THE LEGITIMACY IT NEEDS.
THE SHI'AR EMPIRE WILL STAND WITH ME IF I HAVE LILANDRA'S PROGENY AT MY SIDE AND READY TO BECOME MAJESTOR OR MAJESTRIX OF THE EMPIRE. GLADIATOR IS NO TRUE MAJESTOR.
ARE YOU REALLY SO COLD? THAT EGG WOULD ALSO BE YOUR NIECE OR NEPHEW. BUT ALL YOU CAN THINK OF IS YOUR WAR.
HARD TO THINK OF OTHER THINGS IN TIMES OF WAR, X-MAN.
BUT YOU'RE ALWAYS AT WAR, DEATHBIRD. YOU SURE IT ISN'T JUS' YOUR PREFERRED STATE?
I MEAN... HOW ABOUT A FANCY SPACE BAND-AID? IS THAT REALLY TOO MUCH TO ASK?

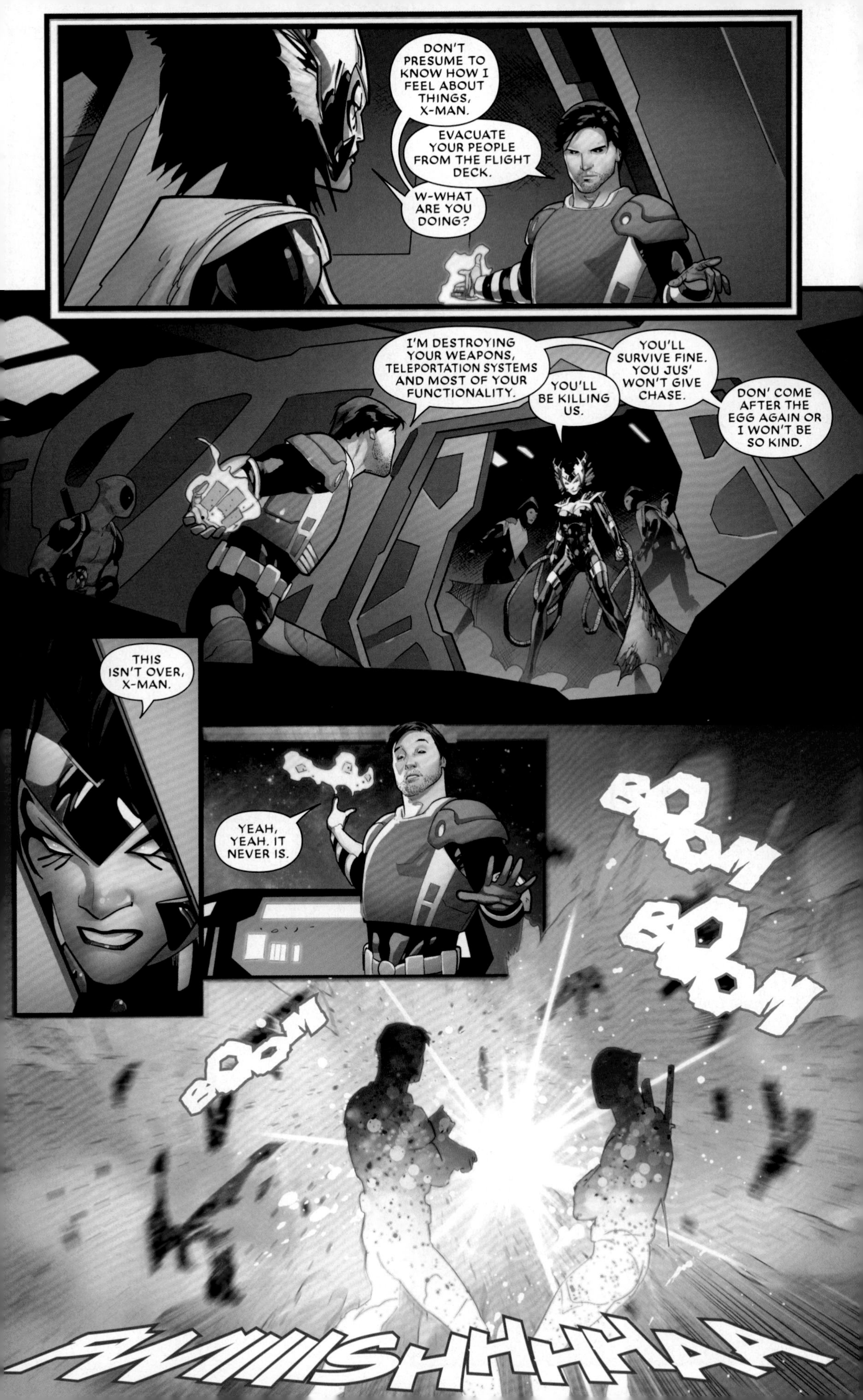
DON'T PRESUME TO KNOW HOW I FEEL ABOUT THINGS, X-MAN.
EVACUATE YOUR PEOPLE FROM THE FLIGHT DECK.
W-WHAT ARE YOU DOING?
I'M DESTROYING YOUR WEAPONS, TELEPORTATION SYSTEMS AND MOST OF YOUR FUNCTIONALITY.
YOU'LL BE KILLING US.
YOU'LL SURVIVE FINE. YOU JUS' WON'T GIVE CHASE.
DON' COME AFTER THE EGG AGAIN OR I WON'T BE SO KIND.
THIS ISN'T OVER, X-MAN.
YEAH, YEAH. IT NEVER IS.
BOOM
BOOM
BOOM
BOOM
FWIIIISHHHHAA

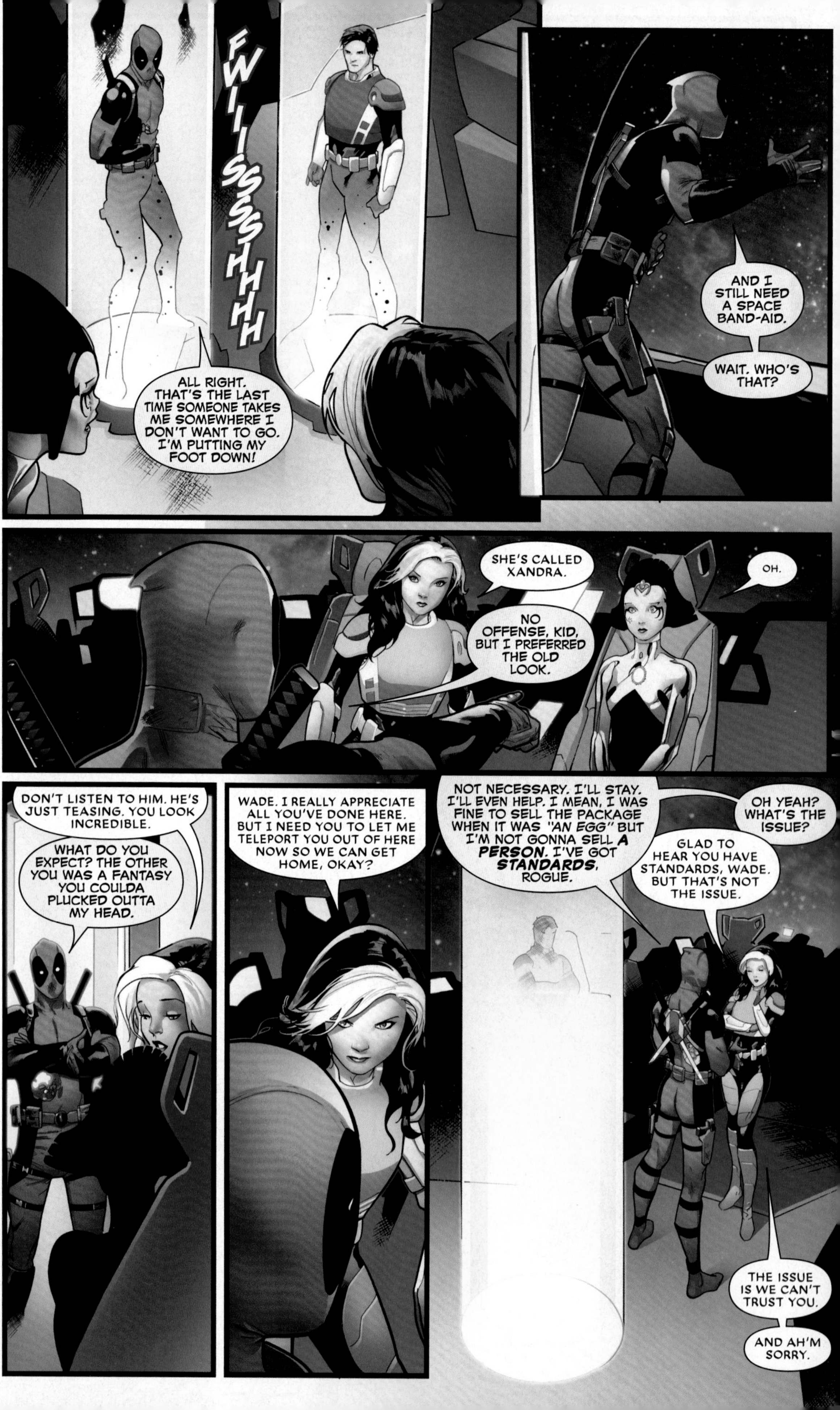
FWIIIISSSSHHHH
ALL RIGHT. THAT'S THE LAST TIME SOMEONE TAKES ME SOMEWHERE I DON'T WANT TO GO. I'M PUTTING MY FOOT DOWN!
AND I STILL NEED A SPACE BAND-AID.
WAIT. WHO'S THAT?
SHE'S CALLED XANDRA.
OH.
NO OFFENSE, KID, BUT I PREFERRED THE OLD LOOK.
DON'T LISTEN TO HIM. HE'S JUST TEASING. YOU LOOK INCREDIBLE.
WHAT DO YOU EXPECT? THE OTHER YOU WAS A FANTASY YOU COULDA PLUCKED OUTTA MY HEAD.
WADE. I REALLY APPRECIATE ALL YOU'VE DONE HERE. BUT I NEED YOU TO LET ME TELEPORT YOU OUT OF HERE NOW SO WE CAN GET HOME, OKAY?
NOT NECESSARY. I'LL STAY. I'LL EVEN HELP. I MEAN, I WAS FINE TO SELL THE PACKAGE WHEN IT WAS "AN EGG" BUT I'M NOT GONNA SELL A PERSON. I'VE GOT STANDARDS, ROGUE.
OH YEAH? WHAT'S THE ISSUE?
GLAD TO HEAR YOU HAVE STANDARDS, WADE. BUT THAT'S NOT THE ISSUE.
THE ISSUE IS WE CAN'T TRUST YOU.
AND AH'M SORRY.

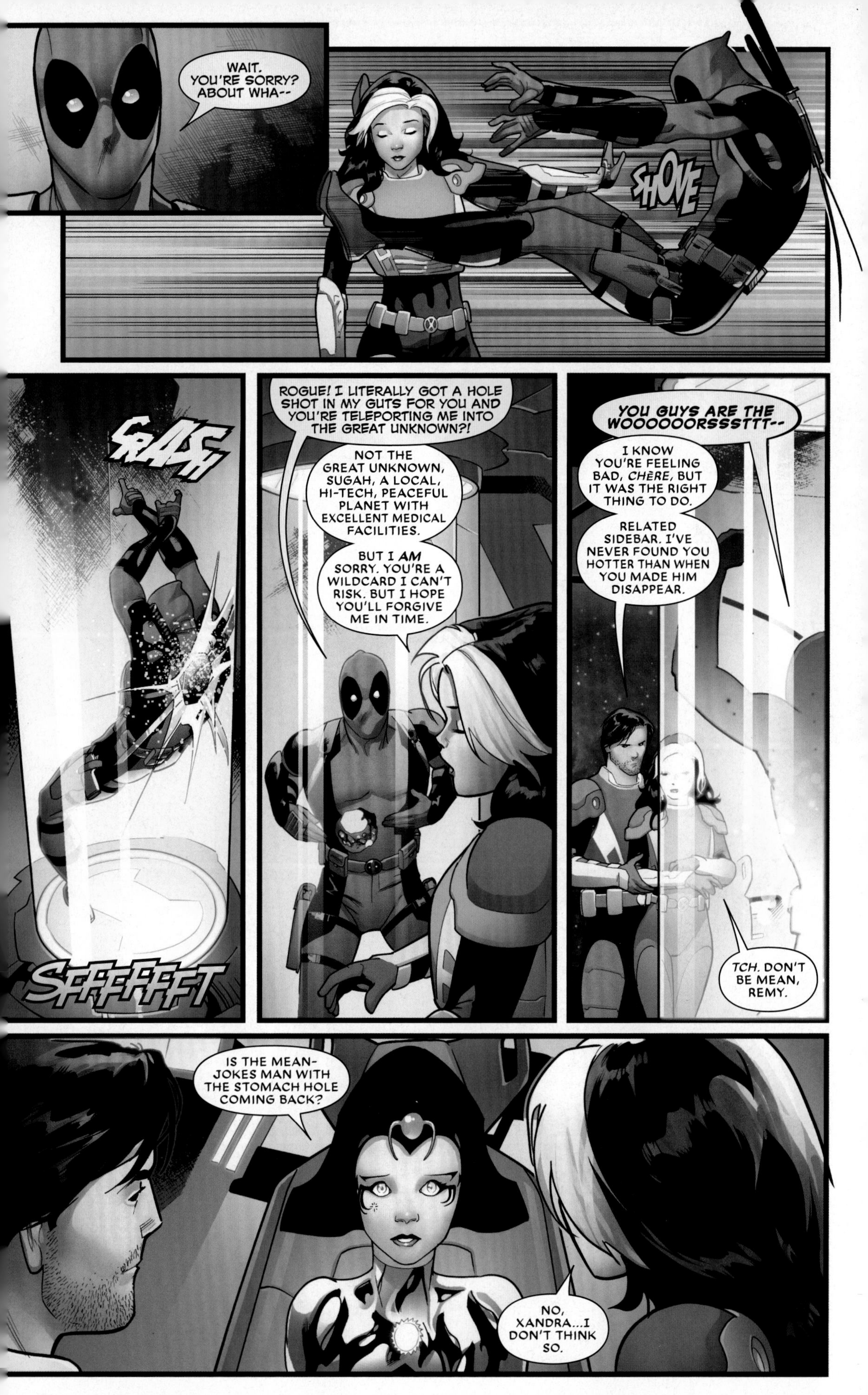
WAIT. YOU'RE SORRY? ABOUT WHA--
SHOVE
SFFFFFFT
ROGUE! I LITERALLY GOT A HOLE SHOT IN MY GUTS FOR YOU AND YOU'RE TELEPORTING ME INTO THE GREAT UNKNOWN?!
NOT THE GREAT UNKNOWN, SUGAH, A LOCAL, HI-TECH, PEACEFUL PLANET WITH EXCELLENT MEDICAL FACILITIES.
BUT I *AM* SORRY. YOU'RE A WILDCARD I CAN'T RISK. BUT I HOPE YOU'LL FORGIVE ME IN TIME.
YOU GUYS ARE THE WOOOOOORSSSTTT--
I KNOW YOU'RE FEELING BAD, *CHÈRE*, BUT IT WAS THE RIGHT THING TO DO.
RELATED SIDEBAR. I'VE NEVER FOUND YOU HOTTER THAN WHEN YOU MADE HIM DISAPPEAR.
TCH. DON'T BE MEAN, REMY.
IS THE MEAN-JOKES MAN WITH THE STOMACH HOLE COMING BACK?
NO, XANDRA...I DON'T THINK SO.

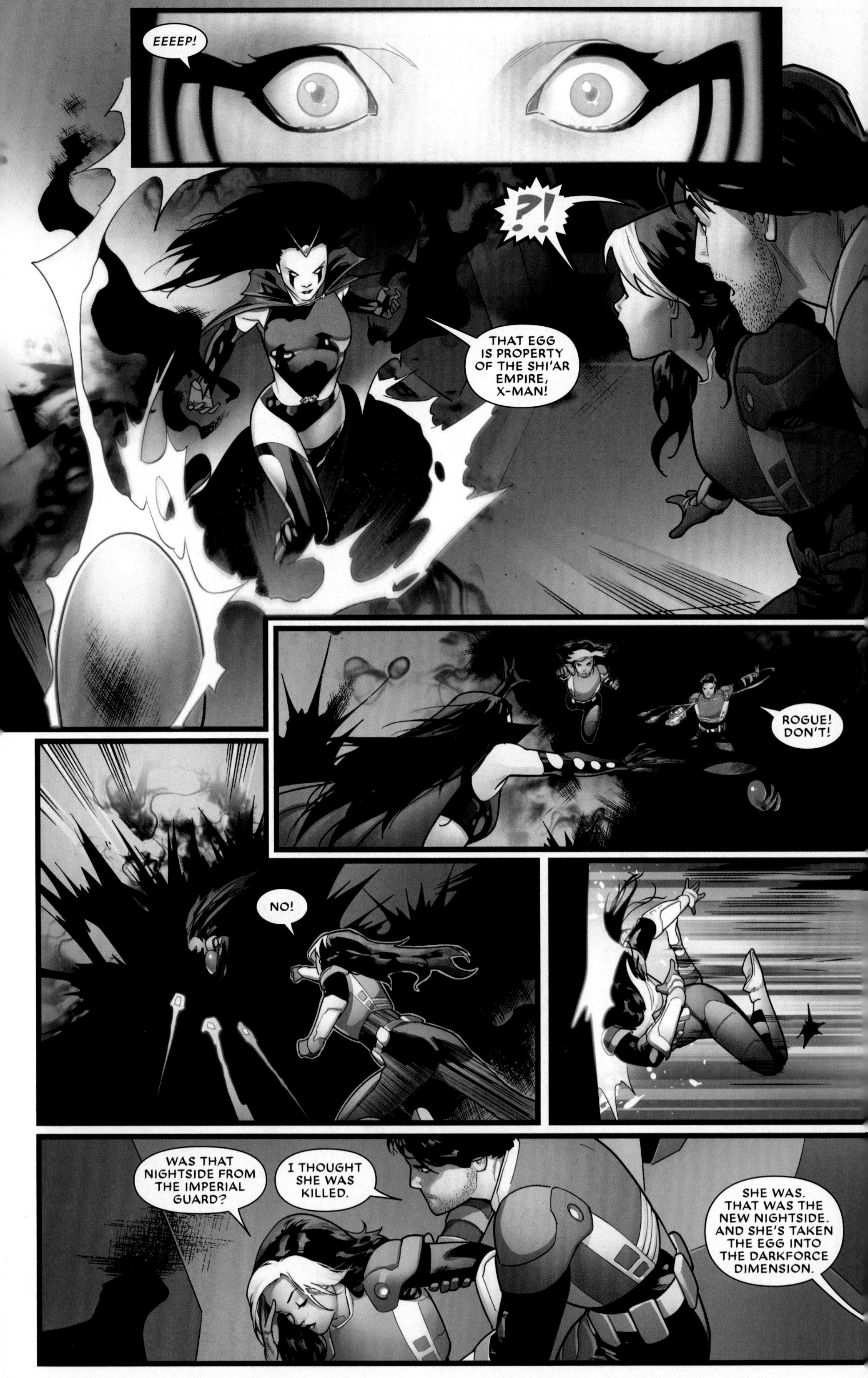
EEEEP!
?!
THAT EGG IS PROPERTY OF THE SHI'AR EMPIRE, X-MAN!
ROGUE! DON'T!
NO!
WAS THAT NIGHTSIDE FROM THE IMPERIAL GUARD?
I THOUGHT SHE WAS KILLED.
SHE WAS. THAT WAS THE NEW NIGHTSIDE. AND SHE'S TAKEN THE EGG INTO THE DARKFORCE DIMENSION.

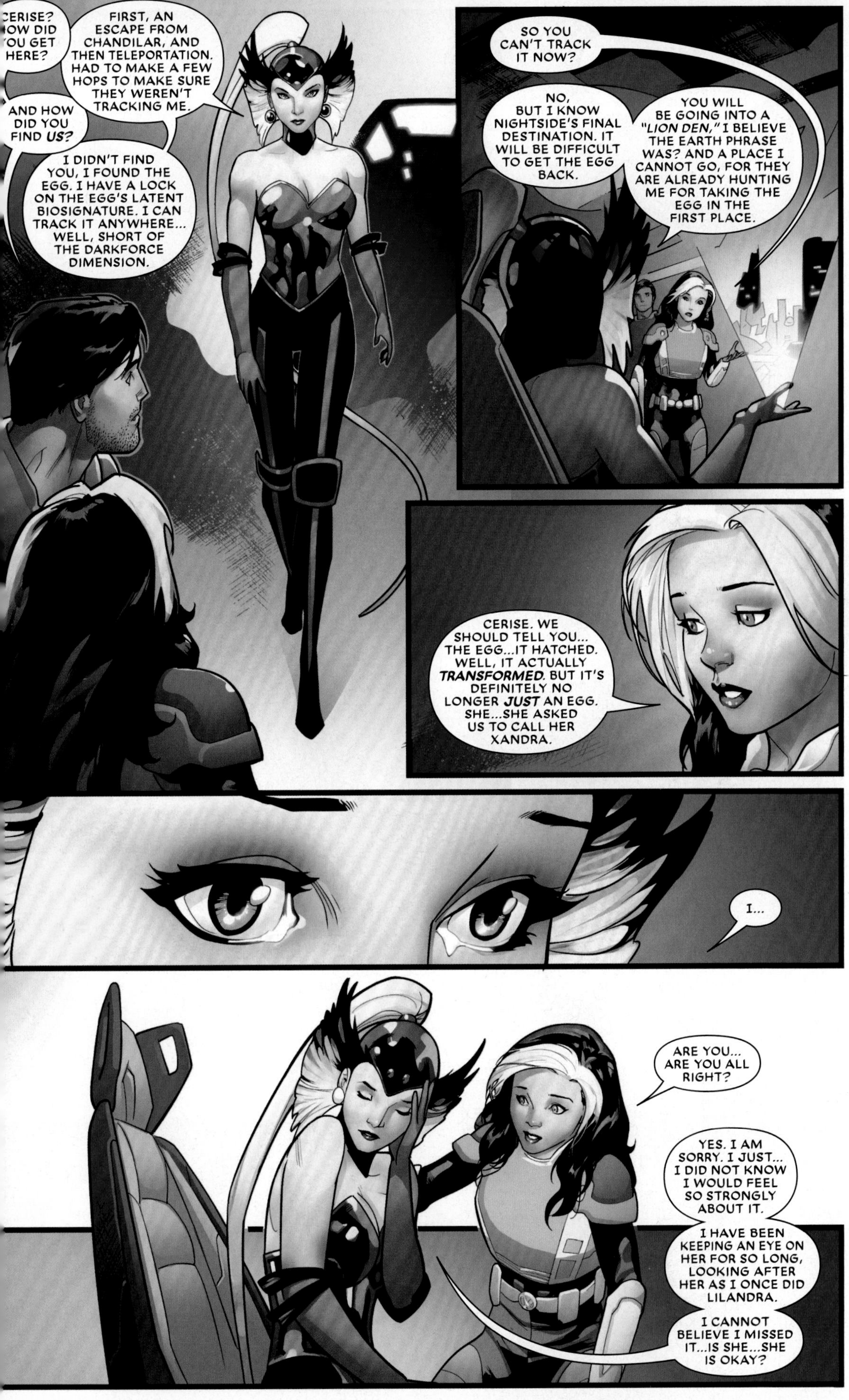
CERISE? HOW DID YOU GET HERE?
FIRST, AN ESCAPE FROM CHANDILAR, AND THEN TELEPORTATION. HAD TO MAKE A FEW HOPS TO MAKE SURE THEY WEREN'T TRACKING ME.
AND HOW DID YOU FIND US?
I DIDN'T FIND YOU, I FOUND THE EGG. I HAVE A LOCK ON THE EGG'S LATENT BIOSIGNATURE. I CAN TRACK IT ANYWHERE... WELL, SHORT OF THE DARKFORCE DIMENSION.
SO YOU CAN'T TRACK IT NOW?
NO, BUT I KNOW NIGHTSIDE'S FINAL DESTINATION. IT WILL BE DIFFICULT TO GET THE EGG BACK.
YOU WILL BE GOING INTO A "LION DEN," I BELIEVE THE EARTH PHRASE WAS? AND A PLACE I CANNOT GO, FOR THEY ARE ALREADY HUNTING ME FOR TAKING THE EGG IN THE FIRST PLACE.
CERISE. WE SHOULD TELL YOU... THE EGG...IT HATCHED. WELL, IT ACTUALLY TRANSFORMED. BUT IT'S DEFINITELY NO LONGER JUST AN EGG. SHE...SHE ASKED US TO CALL HER XANDRA.
I...
ARE YOU... ARE YOU ALL RIGHT?
YES. I AM SORRY. I JUST... I DID NOT KNOW I WOULD FEEL SO STRONGLY ABOUT IT.
I HAVE BEEN KEEPING AN EYE ON HER FOR SO LONG, LOOKING AFTER HER AS I ONCE DID LILANDRA.
I CANNOT BELIEVE I MISSED IT...IS SHE...SHE IS OKAY?

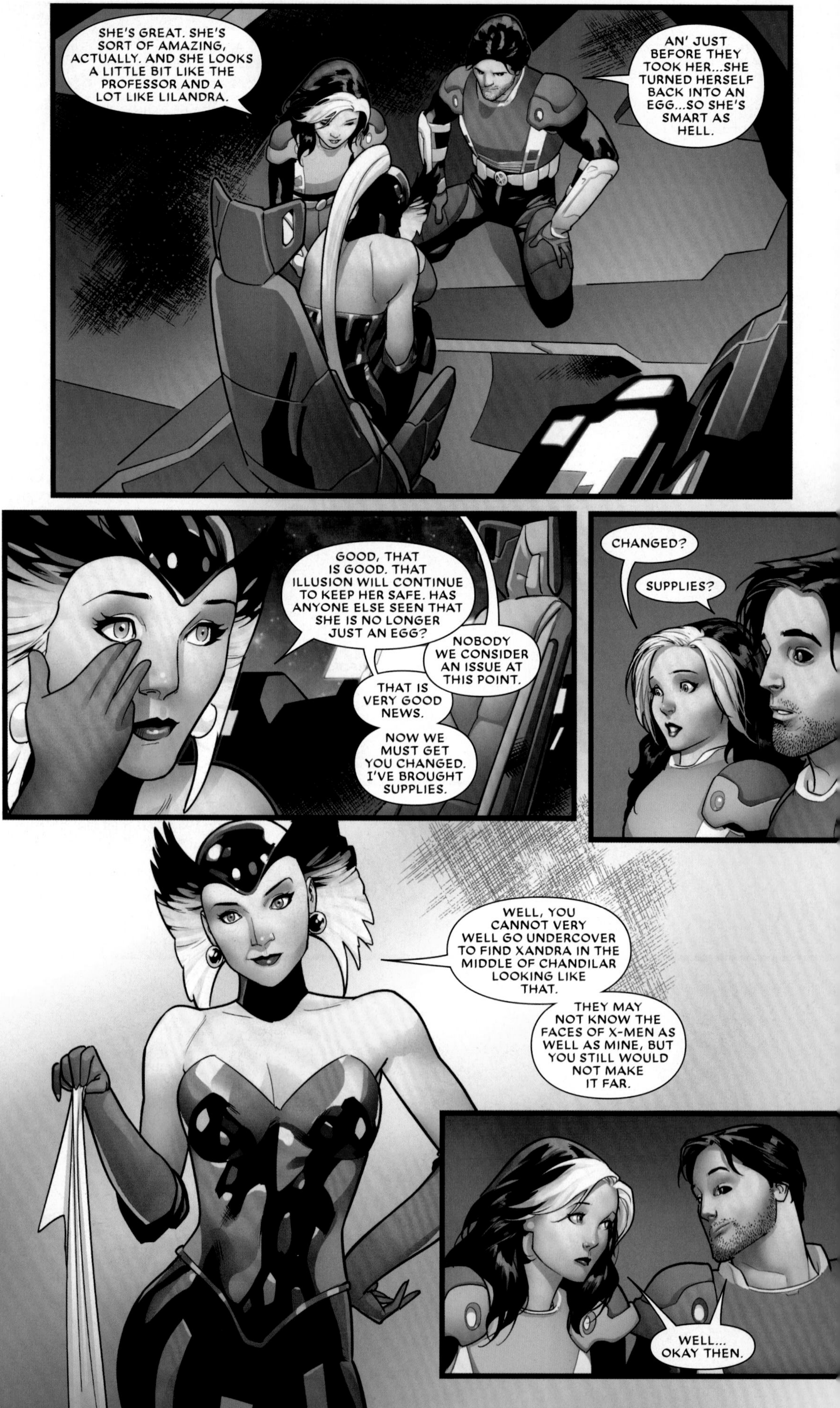
SHE'S GREAT. SHE'S SORT OF AMAZING, ACTUALLY. AND SHE LOOKS A LITTLE BIT LIKE THE PROFESSOR AND A LOT LIKE LILANDRA.
AN' JUST BEFORE THEY TOOK HER...SHE TURNED HERSELF BACK INTO AN EGG...SO SHE'S SMART AS HELL.
GOOD, THAT IS GOOD. THAT ILLUSION WILL CONTINUE TO KEEP HER SAFE. HAS ANYONE ELSE SEEN THAT SHE IS NO LONGER JUST AN EGG?
NOBODY WE CONSIDER AN ISSUE AT THIS POINT.
THAT IS VERY GOOD NEWS.
NOW WE MUST GET YOU CHANGED. I'VE BROUGHT SUPPLIES.
CHANGED?
SUPPLIES?
WELL, YOU CANNOT VERY WELL GO UNDERCOVER TO FIND XANDRA IN THE MIDDLE OF CHANDILAR LOOKING LIKE THAT.
THEY MAY NOT KNOW THE FACES OF X-MEN AS WELL AS MINE, BUT YOU STILL WOULD NOT MAKE IT FAR.
WELL... OKAY THEN.

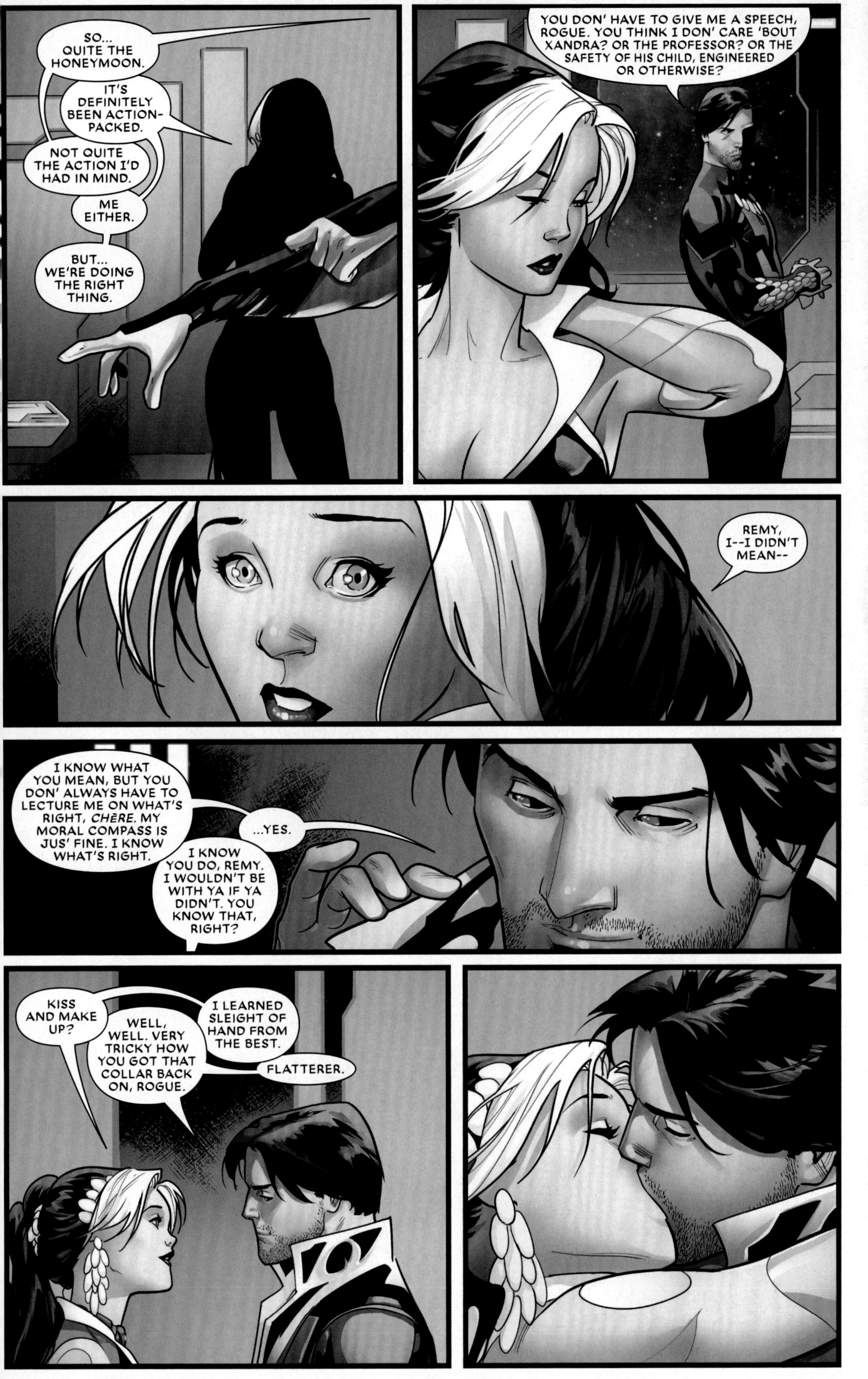
SO... QUITE THE HONEYMOON.
IT'S DEFINITELY BEEN ACTION-PACKED.
NOT QUITE THE ACTION I'D HAD IN MIND.
ME EITHER.
BUT... WE'RE DOING THE RIGHT THING.
YOU DON' HAVE TO GIVE ME A SPEECH, ROGUE. YOU THINK I DON' CARE 'BOUT XANDRA? OR THE PROFESSOR? OR THE SAFETY OF HIS CHILD, ENGINEERED OR OTHERWISE?
REMY, I--I DIDN'T MEAN--
I KNOW WHAT YOU MEAN, BUT YOU DON' ALWAYS HAVE TO LECTURE ME ON WHAT'S RIGHT, *CHÈRE*. MY MORAL COMPASS IS JUS' FINE. I KNOW WHAT'S RIGHT.
I KNOW YOU DO, REMY. I WOULDN'T BE WITH YA IF YA DIDN'T. YOU KNOW THAT, RIGHT?
...YES.
KISS AND MAKE UP?
WELL, WELL. VERY TRICKY HOW YOU GOT THAT COLLAR BACK ON, ROGUE.
I LEARNED SLEIGHT OF HAND FROM THE BEST.
FLATTERER.

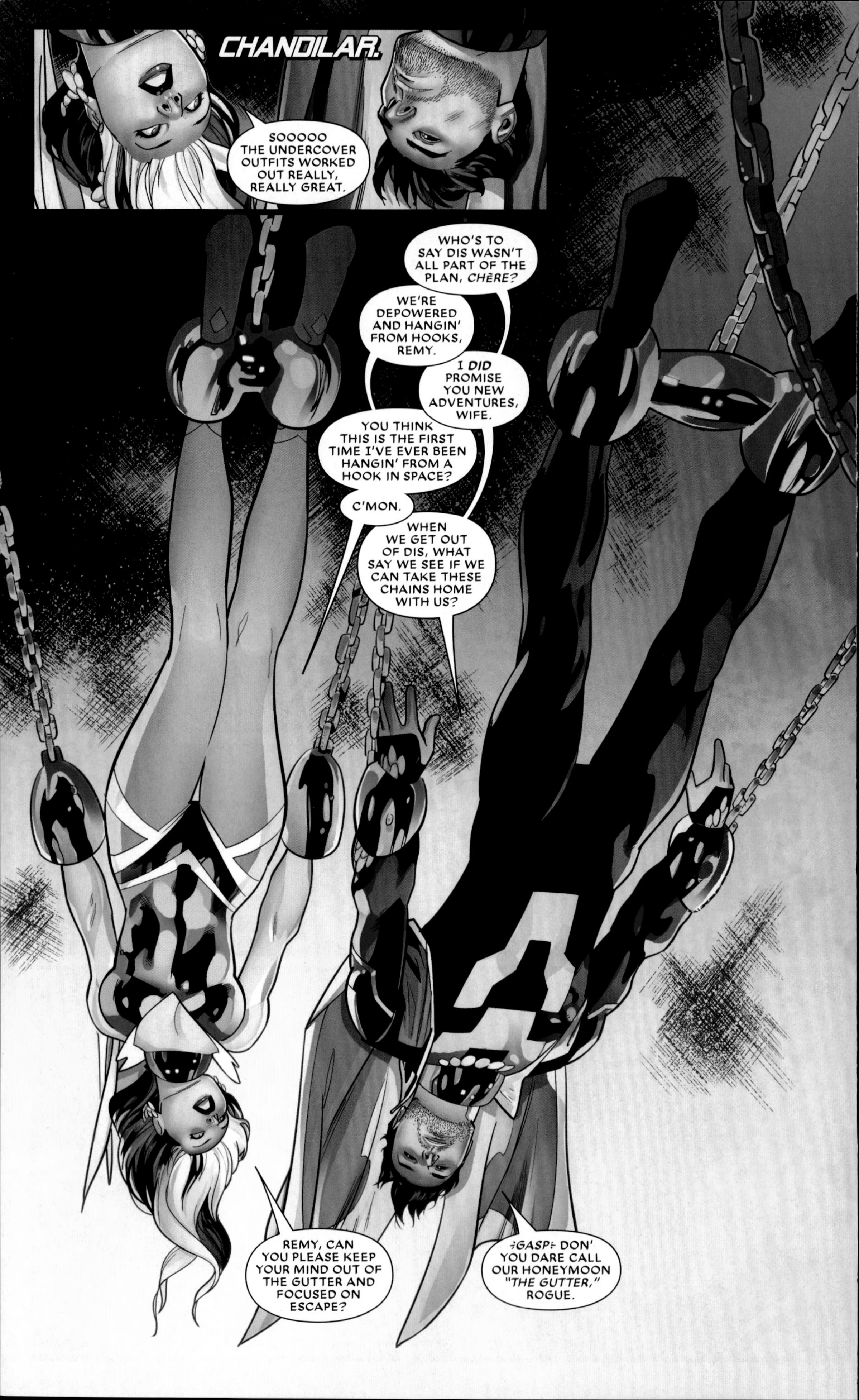
CHANDILAR.
SOOOOO THE UNDERCOVER OUTFITS WORKED OUT REALLY, REALLY GREAT.
WHO'S TO SAY DIS WASN'T ALL PART OF THE PLAN, *CHÈRE?*
WE'RE DEPOWERED AND HANGIN' FROM HOOKS, REMY.
I ***DID*** PROMISE YOU NEW ADVENTURES, WIFE.
YOU THINK THIS IS THE FIRST TIME I'VE EVER BEEN HANGIN' FROM A HOOK IN SPACE?
C'MON.
WHEN WE GET OUT OF DIS, WHAT SAY WE SEE IF WE CAN TAKE THESE CHAINS HOME WITH US?
REMY, CAN YOU PLEASE KEEP YOUR MIND OUT OF THE GUTTER AND FOCUSED ON ESCAPE?
-GASP- DON' YOU DARE CALL OUR HONEYMOON *"THE GUTTER,"* ROGUE.

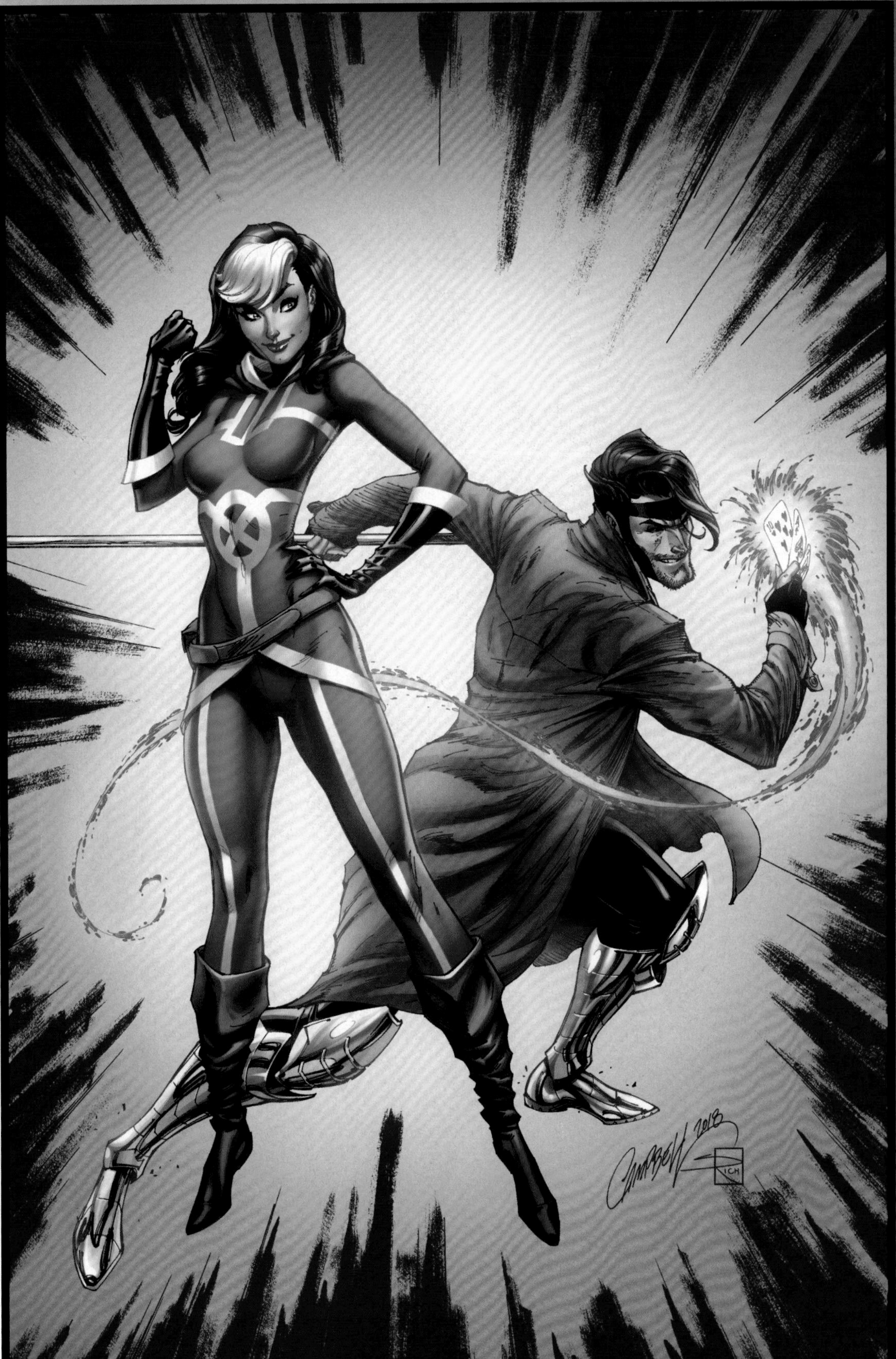

#1 VARIANT BY J. SCOTT CAMPBELL & SABINE RICH

4

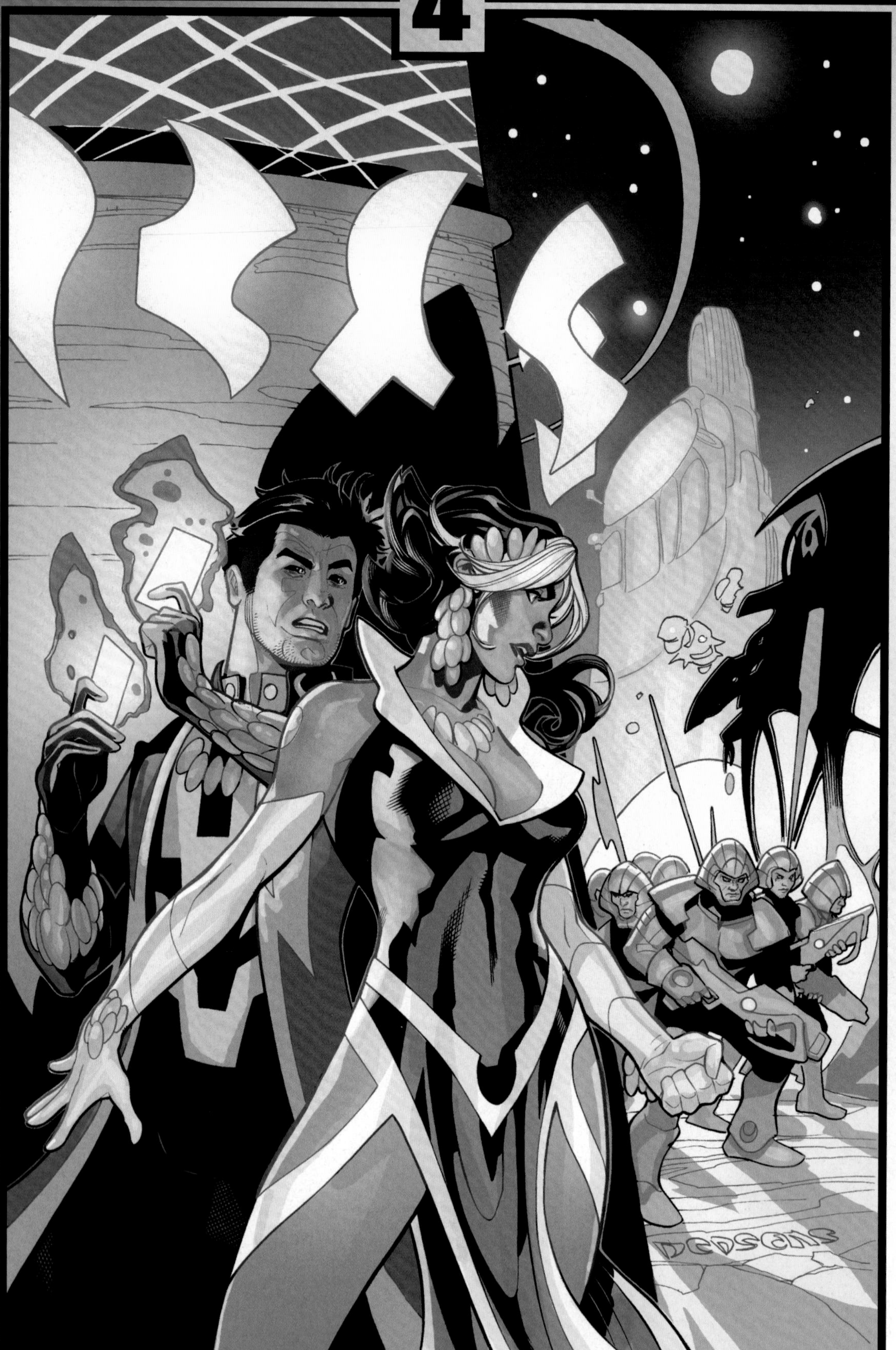

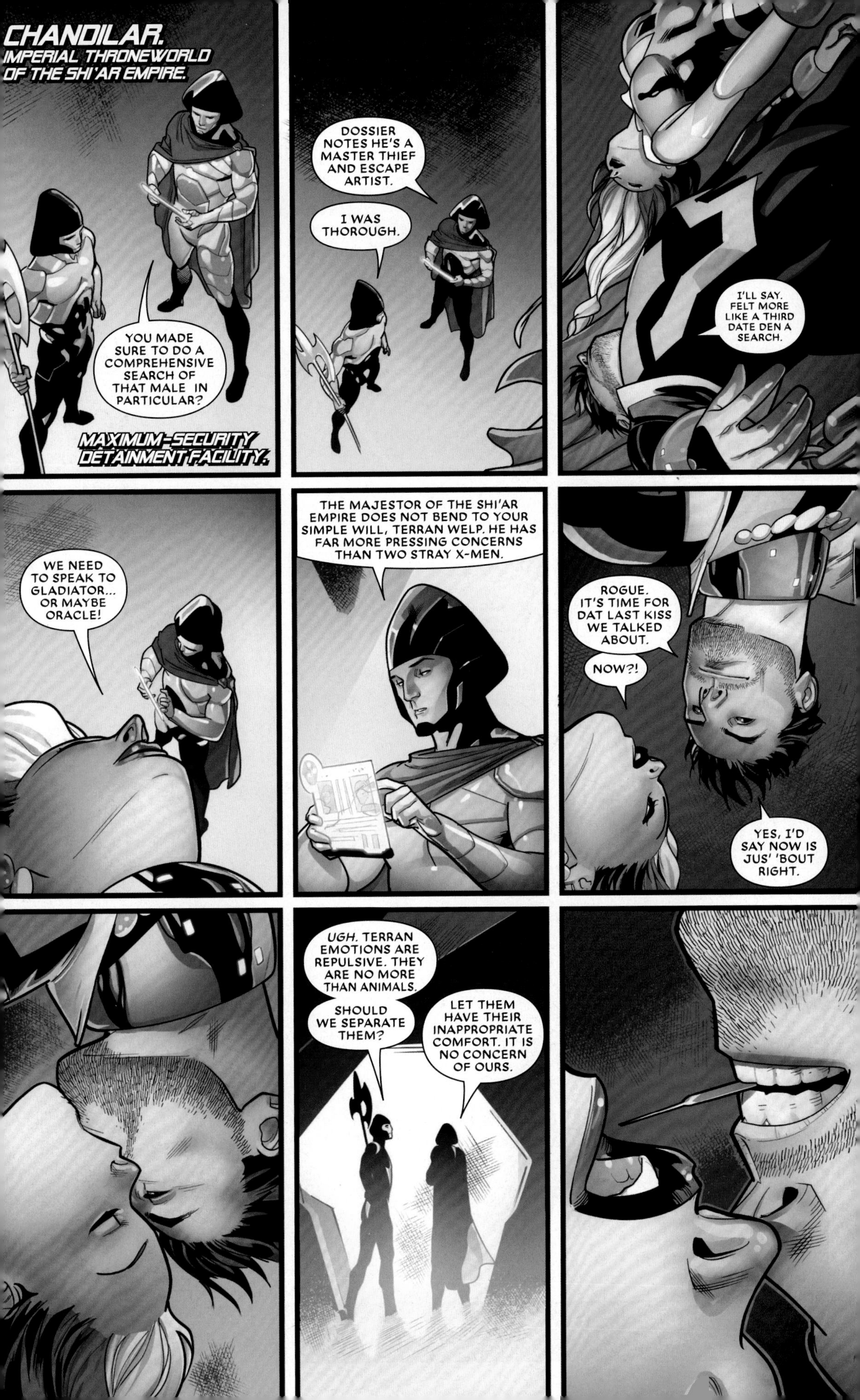
CHANDILAR. IMPERIAL THRONEWORLD OF THE SHI'AR EMPIRE.
YOU MADE SURE TO DO A COMPREHENSIVE SEARCH OF THAT MALE IN PARTICULAR?
MAXIMUM-SECURITY DETAINMENT FACILITY.
DOSSIER NOTES HE'S A MASTER THIEF AND ESCAPE ARTIST.
I WAS THOROUGH.
I'LL SAY. FELT MORE LIKE A THIRD DATE DEN A SEARCH.
WE NEED TO SPEAK TO GLADIATOR... OR MAYBE ORACLE!
THE MAJESTOR OF THE SHI'AR EMPIRE DOES NOT BEND TO YOUR SIMPLE WILL, TERRAN WELP. HE HAS FAR MORE PRESSING CONCERNS THAN TWO STRAY X-MEN.
ROGUE. IT'S TIME FOR DAT LAST KISS WE TALKED ABOUT.
NOW?!
YES, I'D SAY NOW IS JUS' 'BOUT RIGHT.
UGH. TERRAN EMOTIONS ARE REPULSIVE. THEY ARE NO MORE THAN ANIMALS.
SHOULD WE SEPARATE THEM?
LET THEM HAVE THEIR INAPPROPRIATE COMFORT. IT IS NO CONCERN OF OURS.

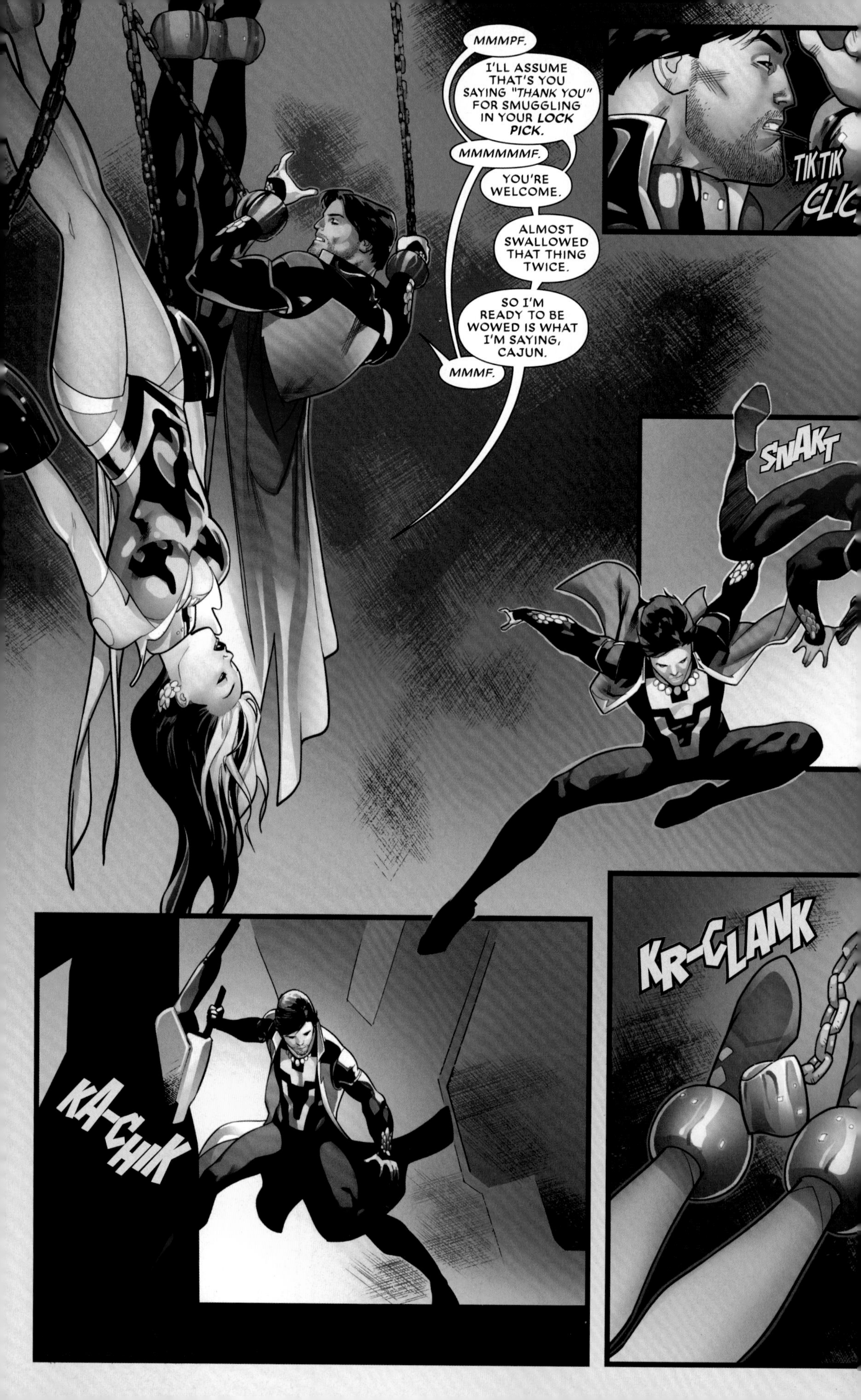

MMMPF.
I'LL ASSUME THAT'S YOU SAYING "THANK YOU" FOR SMUGGLING IN YOUR LOCK PICK.
MMMMMMF.
YOU'RE WELCOME.
ALMOST SWALLOWED THAT THING TWICE.
SO I'M READY TO BE WOWED IS WHAT I'M SAYING, CAJUN.
MMMF.
TIK TIK
SNAKT
KA-CHIK
KR-CLANK

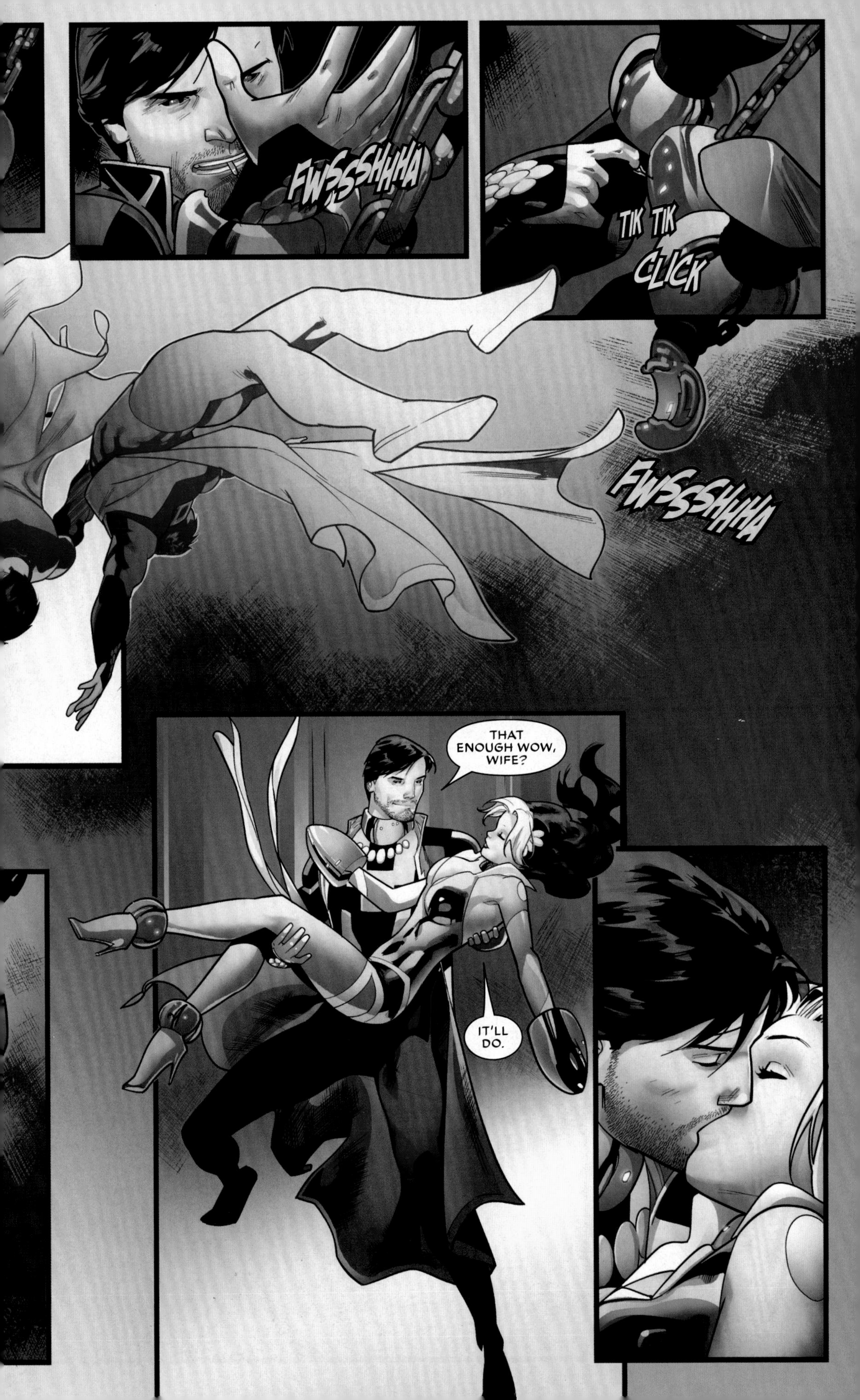
FWSSSHHA
TIK TIK
CLICK
FWSSSHHA
THAT ENOUGH WOW, WIFE?
IT'LL DO.

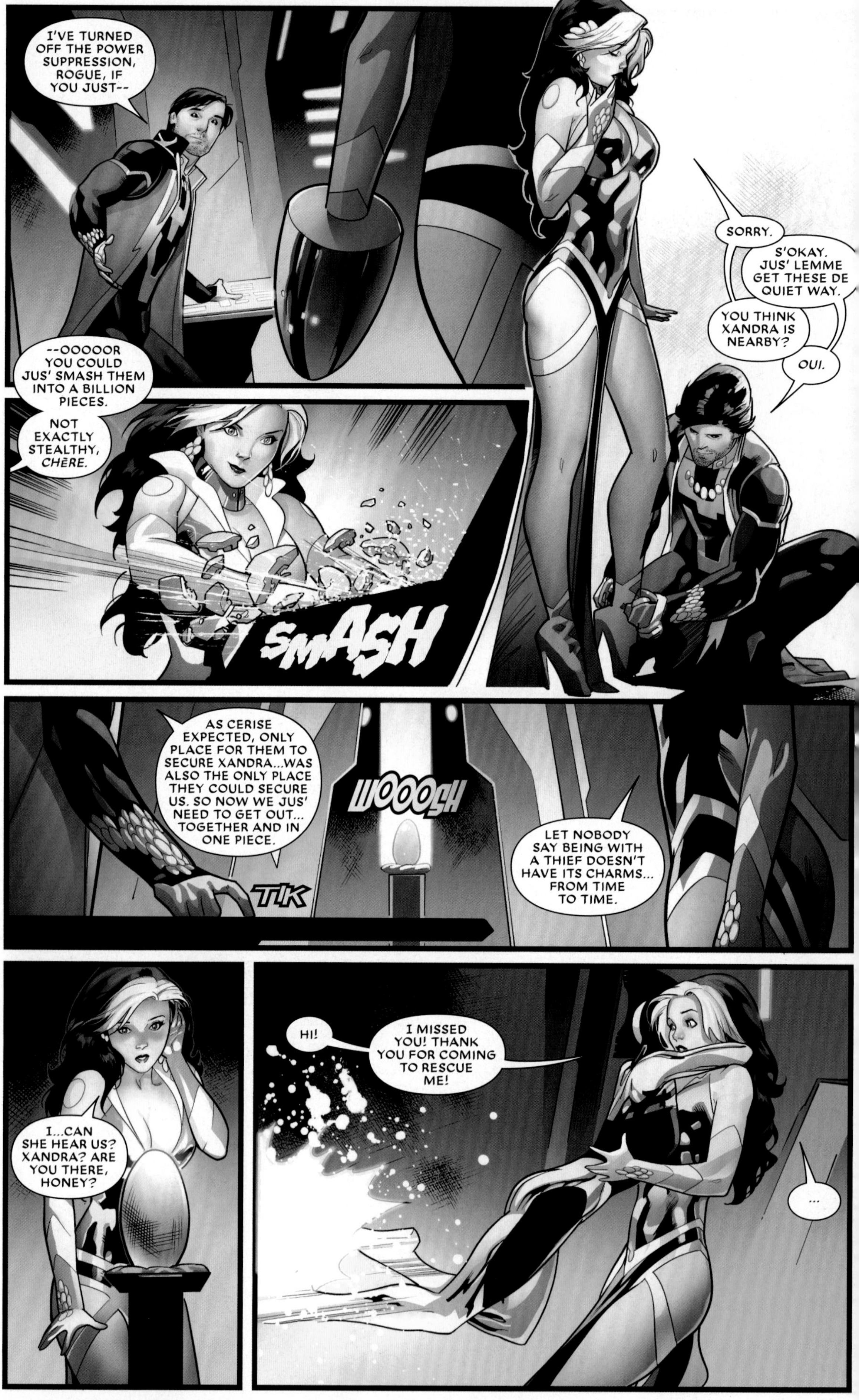

I'VE TURNED OFF THE POWER SUPPRESSION, ROGUE, IF YOU JUST--
--OOOOOR YOU COULD JUS' SMASH THEM INTO A BILLION PIECES.
NOT EXACTLY STEALTHY, *CHÈRE.*
SMASH
SORRY.
S'OKAY. JUS' LEMME GET THESE DE QUIET WAY.
YOU THINK XANDRA IS NEARBY?
OUI.
AS CERISE EXPECTED, ONLY PLACE FOR THEM TO SECURE XANDRA...WAS ALSO THE ONLY PLACE THEY COULD SECURE US. SO NOW WE JUS' NEED TO GET OUT... TOGETHER AND IN ONE PIECE.
WOOOSH
TIK
LET NOBODY SAY BEING WITH A THIEF DOESN'T HAVE ITS CHARMS... FROM TIME TO TIME.
I...CAN SHE HEAR US? XANDRA? ARE YOU THERE, HONEY?
HI!
I MISSED YOU! THANK YOU FOR COMING TO RESCUE ME!
...

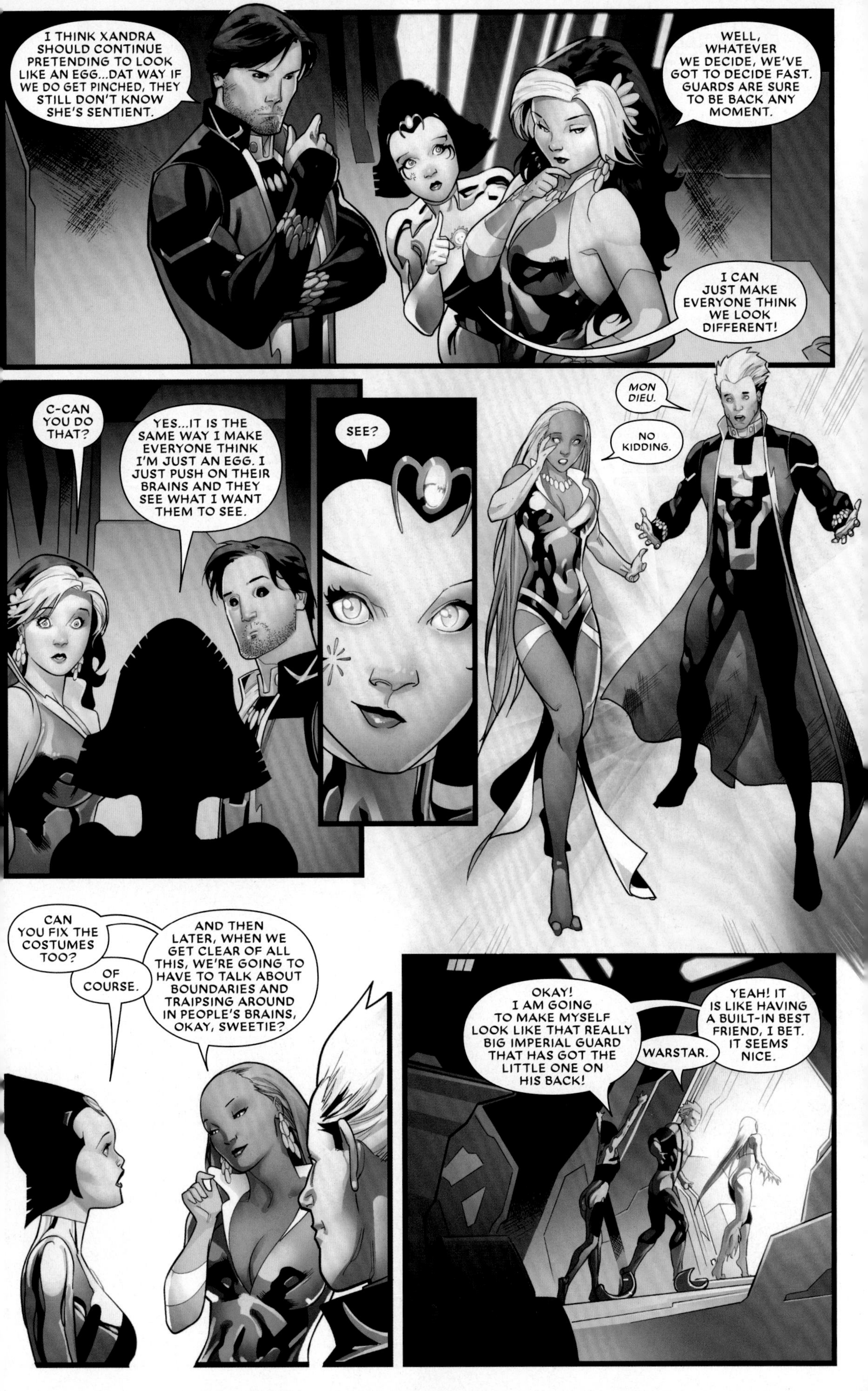
I THINK XANDRA SHOULD CONTINUE PRETENDING TO LOOK LIKE AN EGG...DAT WAY IF WE DO GET PINCHED, THEY STILL DON'T KNOW SHE'S SENTIENT.
WELL, WHATEVER WE DECIDE, WE'VE GOT TO DECIDE FAST. GUARDS ARE SURE TO BE BACK ANY MOMENT.
I CAN JUST MAKE EVERYONE THINK WE LOOK DIFFERENT!
C-CAN YOU DO THAT?
YES...IT IS THE SAME WAY I MAKE EVERYONE THINK I'M JUST AN EGG. I JUST PUSH ON THEIR BRAINS AND THEY SEE WHAT I WANT THEM TO SEE.
SEE?
MON DIEU.
NO KIDDING.
CAN YOU FIX THE COSTUMES TOO?
OF COURSE.
AND THEN LATER, WHEN WE GET CLEAR OF ALL THIS, WE'RE GOING TO HAVE TO TALK ABOUT BOUNDARIES AND TRAPSING AROUND IN PEOPLE'S BRAINS, OKAY, SWEETIE?
OKAY! I AM GOING TO MAKE MYSELF LOOK LIKE THAT REALLY BIG IMPERIAL GUARD THAT HAS GOT THE LITTLE ONE ON HIS BACK!
WARSTAR.
YEAH! IT IS LIKE HAVING A BUILT-IN BEST FRIEND, I BET. IT SEEMS NICE.

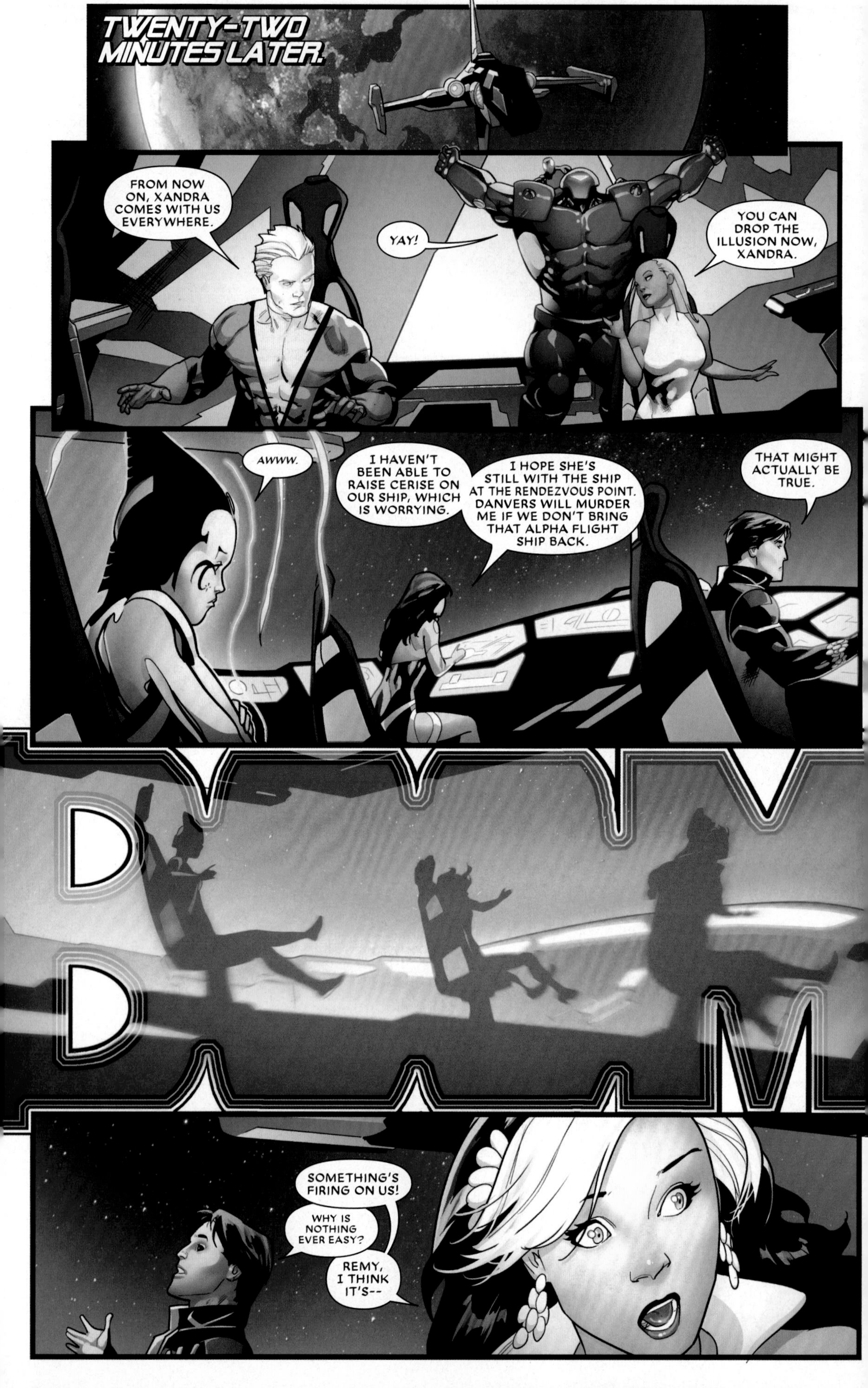
TWENTY-TWO MINUTES LATER.
FROM NOW ON, XANDRA COMES WITH US EVERYWHERE.
YAY!
YOU CAN DROP THE ILLUSION NOW, XANDRA.
AWWW.
I HAVEN'T BEEN ABLE TO RAISE CERISE ON OUR SHIP, WHICH IS WORRYING.
I HOPE SHE'S STILL WITH THE SHIP AT THE RENDEZVOUS POINT. DANVERS WILL MURDER ME IF WE DON'T BRING THAT ALPHA FLIGHT SHIP BACK.
THAT MIGHT ACTUALLY BE TRUE.
DDVVAAMM
SOMETHING'S FIRING ON US!
WHY IS NOTHING EVER EASY?
REMY, I THINK IT'S--

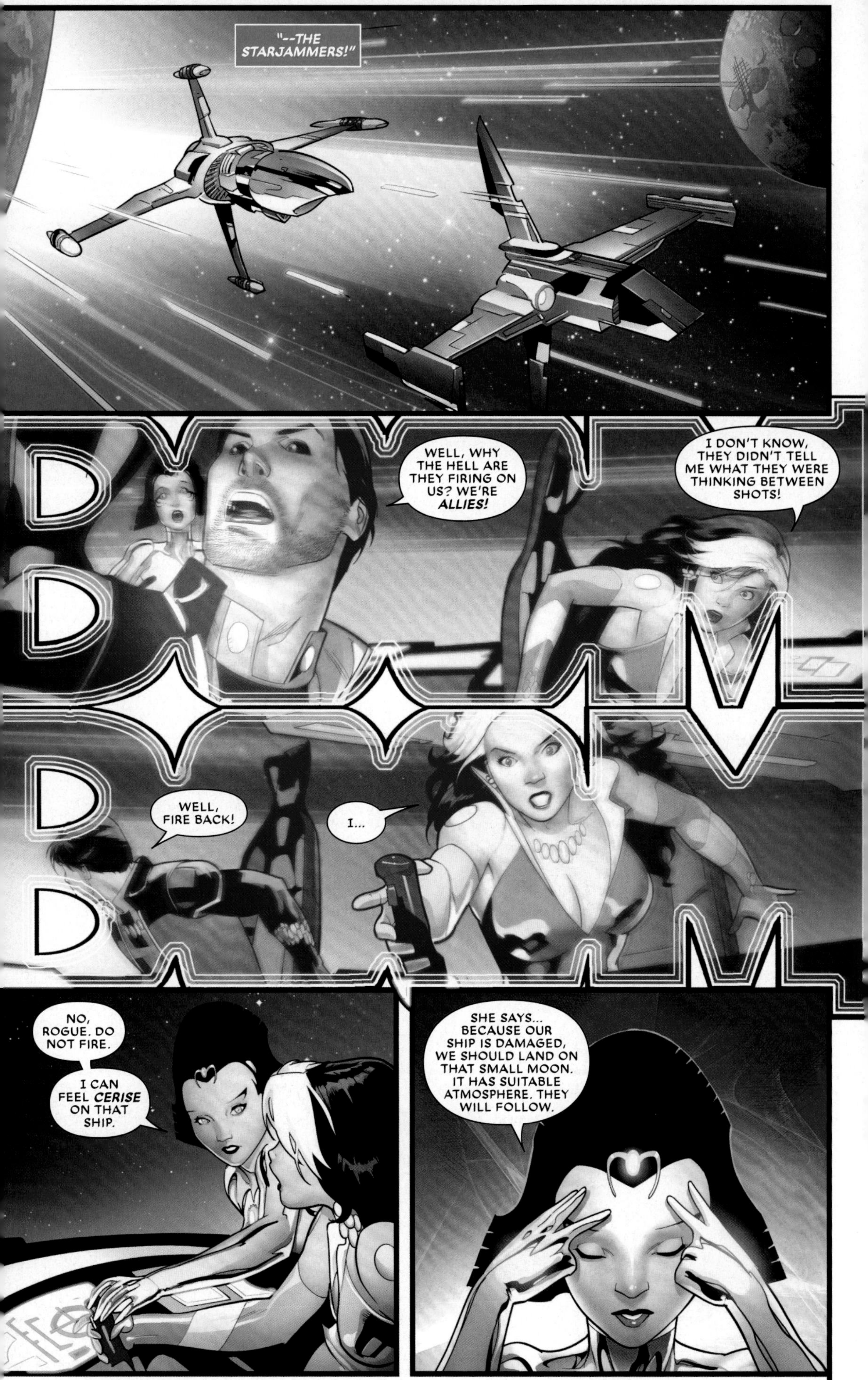
"--THE STARJAMMERS!"
WELL, WHY THE HELL ARE THEY FIRING ON US? WE'RE ALLIES!
I DON'T KNOW, THEY DIDN'T TELL ME WHAT THEY WERE THINKING BETWEEN SHOTS!
DOOM
DOOM
WELL, FIRE BACK!
I...
NO, ROGUE. DO NOT FIRE.
I CAN FEEL CERISE ON THAT SHIP.
SHE SAYS... BECAUSE OUR SHIP IS DAMAGED, WE SHOULD LAND ON THAT SMALL MOON. IT HAS SUITABLE ATMOSPHERE. THEY WILL FOLLOW.

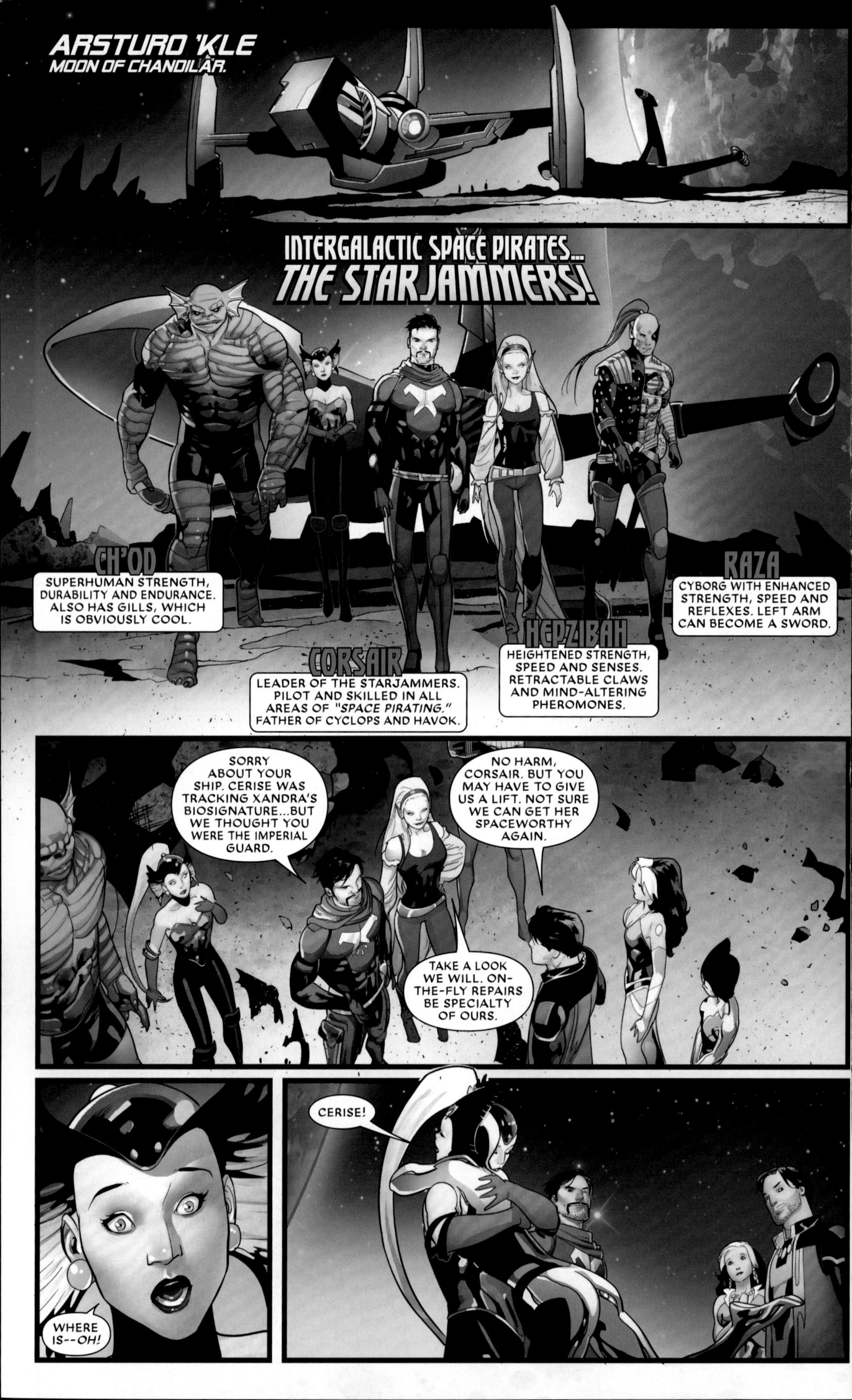
ARSTURO 'KLE
MOON OF CHANDILAR.
INTERGALACTIC SPACE PIRATES... THE STARJAMMERS!
CH'OD
SUPERHUMAN STRENGTH, DURABILITY AND ENDURANCE. ALSO HAS GILLS, WHICH IS OBVIOUSLY COOL.
CORSAIR
LEADER OF THE STARJAMMERS. PILOT AND SKILLED IN ALL AREAS OF "SPACE PIRATING." FATHER OF CYCLOPS AND HAVOK.
HEPZIBAH
HEIGHTENED STRENGTH, SPEED AND SENSES. RETRACTABLE CLAWS AND MIND-ALTERING PHEROMONES.
RAZA
CYBORG WITH ENHANCED STRENGTH, SPEED AND REFLEXES. LEFT ARM CAN BECOME A SWORD.
SORRY ABOUT YOUR SHIP. CERISE WAS TRACKING XANDRA'S BIOSIGNATURE...BUT WE THOUGHT YOU WERE THE IMPERIAL GUARD.
NO HARM, CORSAIR. BUT YOU MAY HAVE TO GIVE US A LIFT. NOT SURE WE CAN GET HER SPACEWORTHY AGAIN.
TAKE A LOOK WE WILL. ON-THE-FLY REPAIRS BE SPECIALTY OF OURS.
WHERE IS--OH!
CERISE!

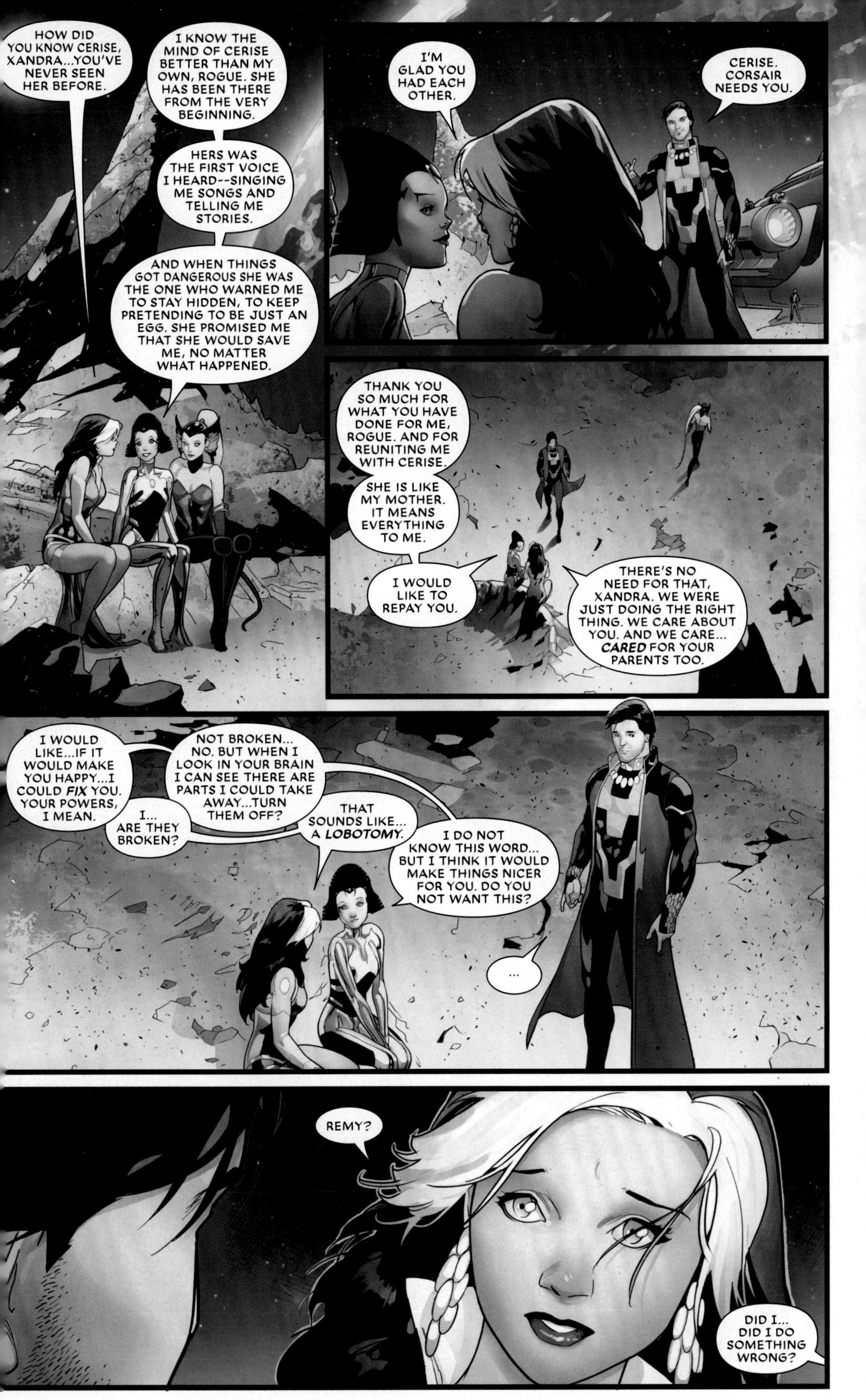
HOW DID YOU KNOW CERISE, XANDRA...YOU'VE NEVER SEEN HER BEFORE.
I KNOW THE MIND OF CERISE BETTER THAN MY OWN, ROGUE. SHE HAS BEEN THERE FROM THE VERY BEGINNING.
HERS WAS THE FIRST VOICE I HEARD--SINGING ME SONGS AND TELLING ME STORIES.
AND WHEN THINGS GOT DANGEROUS SHE WAS THE ONE WHO WARNED ME TO STAY HIDDEN, TO KEEP PRETENDING TO BE JUST AN EGG. SHE PROMISED ME THAT SHE WOULD SAVE ME, NO MATTER WHAT HAPPENED.
I'M GLAD YOU HAD EACH OTHER.
CERISE. CORSAIR NEEDS YOU.
THANK YOU SO MUCH FOR WHAT YOU HAVE DONE FOR ME, ROGUE. AND FOR REUNITING ME WITH CERISE.
SHE IS LIKE MY MOTHER. IT MEANS EVERYTHING TO ME.
I WOULD LIKE TO REPAY YOU.
THERE'S NO NEED FOR THAT, XANDRA. WE WERE JUST DOING THE RIGHT THING. WE CARE ABOUT YOU. AND WE CARE... *CARED* FOR YOUR PARENTS TOO.
I WOULD LIKE...IF IT WOULD MAKE YOU HAPPY...I COULD *FIX* YOU. YOUR POWERS, I MEAN.
I... ARE THEY BROKEN?
NOT BROKEN... NO. BUT WHEN I LOOK IN YOUR BRAIN I CAN SEE THERE ARE PARTS I COULD TAKE AWAY...TURN THEM OFF?
THAT SOUNDS LIKE... A *LOBOTOMY*.
I DO NOT KNOW THIS WORD... BUT I THINK IT WOULD MAKE THINGS NICER FOR YOU. DO YOU NOT WANT THIS?
...
REMY?
DID I... DID I DO SOMETHING WRONG?

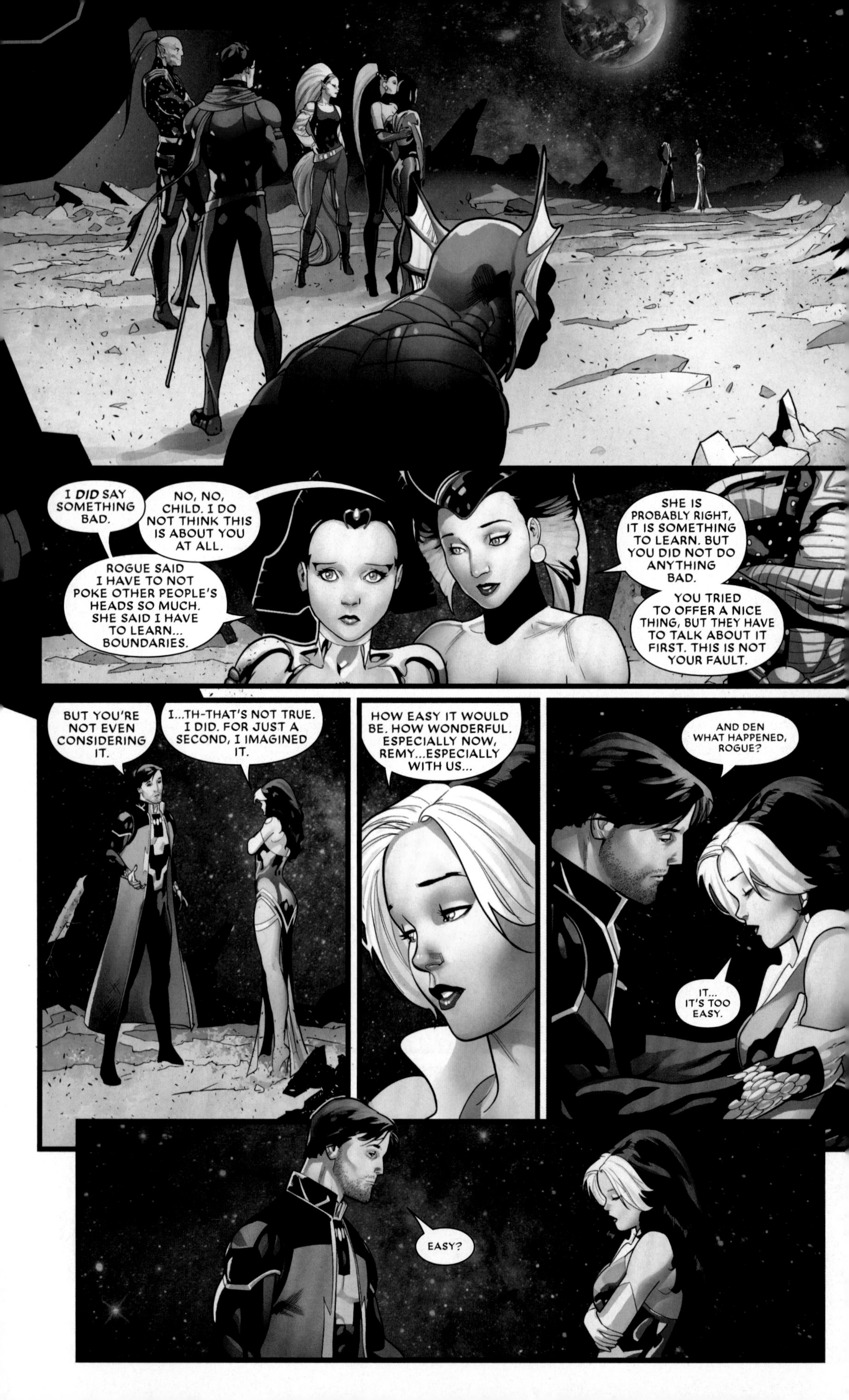
I DID SAY SOMETHING BAD.
NO, NO, CHILD. I DO NOT THINK THIS IS ABOUT YOU AT ALL.
ROGUE SAID I HAVE TO NOT POKE OTHER PEOPLE'S HEADS SO MUCH. SHE SAID I HAVE TO LEARN... BOUNDARIES.
SHE IS PROBABLY RIGHT, IT IS SOMETHING TO LEARN. BUT YOU DID NOT DO ANYTHING BAD.
YOU TRIED TO OFFER A NICE THING, BUT THEY HAVE TO TALK ABOUT IT FIRST. THIS IS NOT YOUR FAULT.
BUT YOU'RE NOT EVEN CONSIDERING IT.
I...TH-THAT'S NOT TRUE. I DID. FOR JUST A SECOND, I IMAGINED IT.
HOW EASY IT WOULD BE. HOW WONDERFUL. ESPECIALLY NOW, REMY...ESPECIALLY WITH US...
AND DEN WHAT HAPPENED, ROGUE?
IT... IT'S TOO EASY.
EASY?

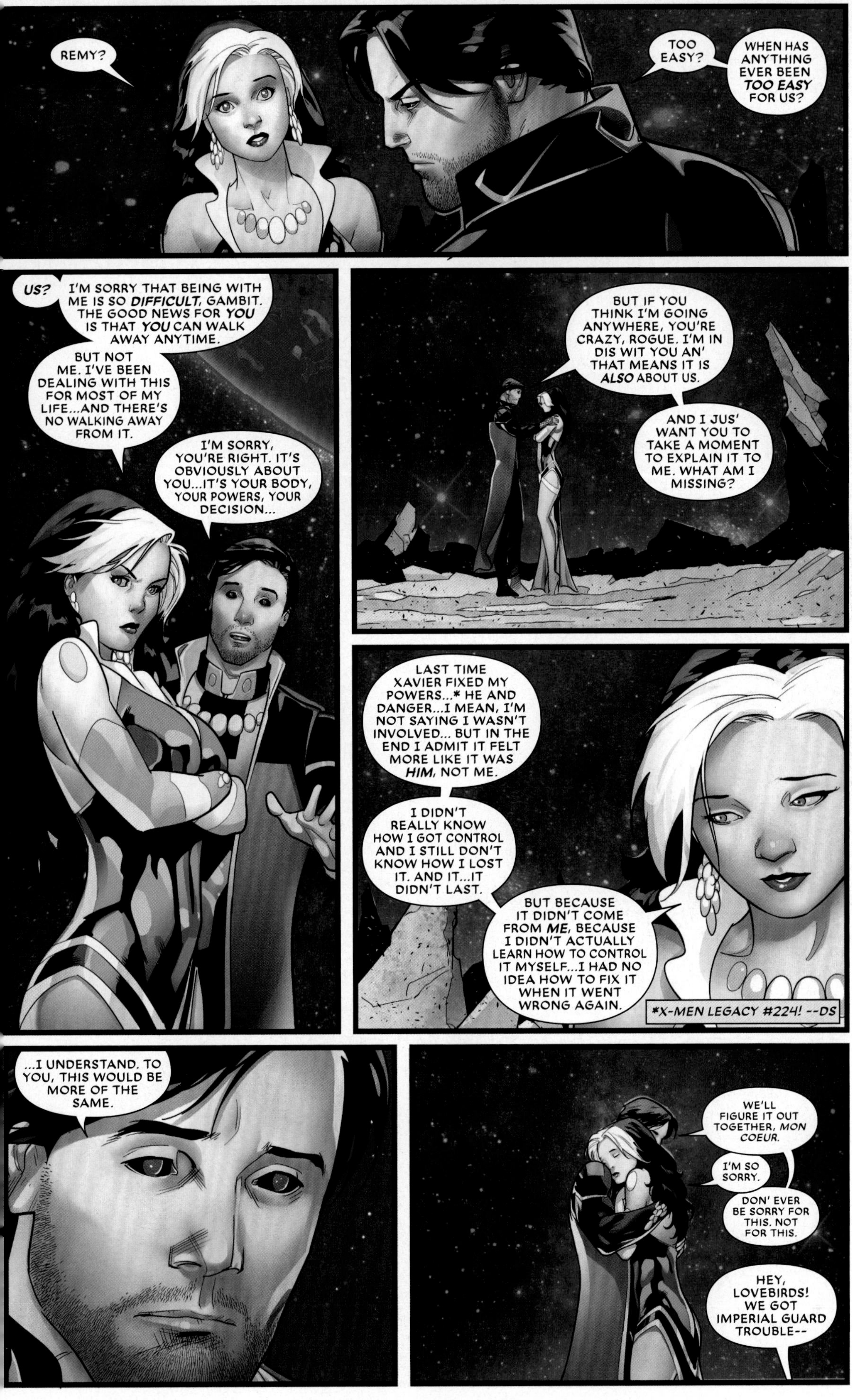
REMY?
TOO EASY?
WHEN HAS ANYTHING EVER BEEN TOO EASY FOR US?
US?
I'M SORRY THAT BEING WITH ME IS SO DIFFICULT, GAMBIT. THE GOOD NEWS FOR YOU IS THAT YOU CAN WALK AWAY ANYTIME.
BUT NOT ME. I'VE BEEN DEALING WITH THIS FOR MOST OF MY LIFE...AND THERE'S NO WALKING AWAY FROM IT.
I'M SORRY, YOU'RE RIGHT. IT'S OBVIOUSLY ABOUT YOU...IT'S YOUR BODY, YOUR POWERS, YOUR DECISION...
BUT IF YOU THINK I'M GOING ANYWHERE, YOU'RE CRAZY, ROGUE. I'M IN DIS WIT YOU AN' THAT MEANS IT IS ALSO ABOUT US.
AND I JUS' WANT YOU TO TAKE A MOMENT TO EXPLAIN IT TO ME. WHAT AM I MISSING?
LAST TIME XAVIER FIXED MY POWERS...* HE AND DANGER...I MEAN, I'M NOT SAYING I WASN'T INVOLVED... BUT IN THE END I ADMIT IT FELT MORE LIKE IT WAS HIM, NOT ME.
I DIDN'T REALLY KNOW HOW I GOT CONTROL AND I STILL DON'T KNOW HOW I LOST IT. AND IT...IT DIDN'T LAST.
BUT BECAUSE IT DIDN'T COME FROM ME, BECAUSE I DIDN'T ACTUALLY LEARN HOW TO CONTROL IT MYSELF...I HAD NO IDEA HOW TO FIX IT WHEN IT WENT WRONG AGAIN.
*X-MEN LEGACY #224! --DS
...I UNDERSTAND. TO YOU, THIS WOULD BE MORE OF THE SAME.
WE'LL FIGURE IT OUT TOGETHER, MON COEUR.
I'M SO SORRY.
DON' EVER BE SORRY FOR THIS. NOT FOR THIS.
HEY, LOVEBIRDS! WE GOT IMPERIAL GUARD TROUBLE--

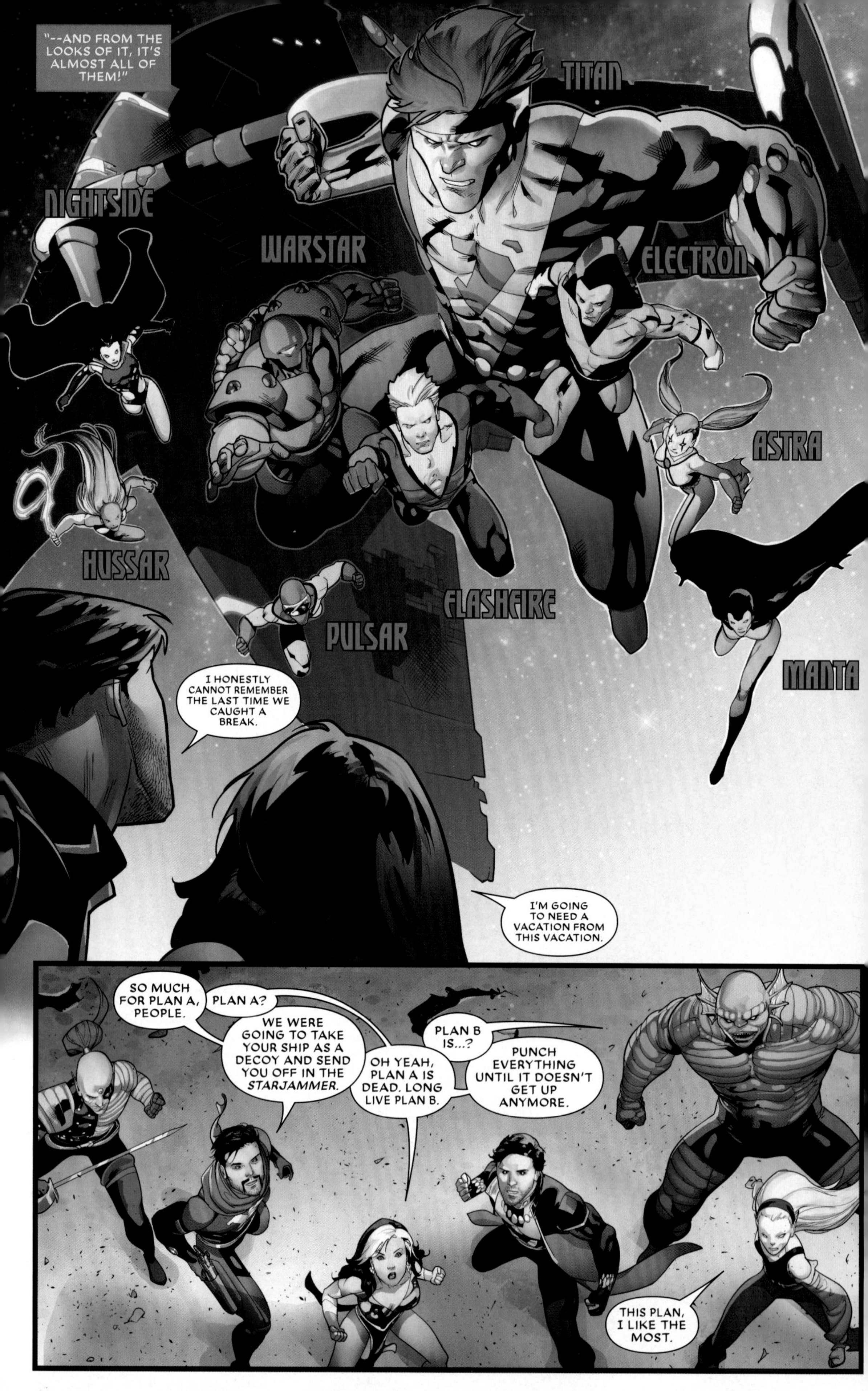
"--AND FROM THE LOOKS OF IT, IT'S ALMOST ALL OF THEM!"
TITAN
NIGHTSIDE
WARSTAR
ELECTRON
ASTRA
HUSSAR
FLASHFIRE
PULSAR
MANTA
I HONESTLY CANNOT REMEMBER THE LAST TIME WE CAUGHT A BREAK.
I'M GOING TO NEED A VACATION FROM THIS VACATION.
SO MUCH FOR PLAN A, PEOPLE.
PLAN A?
WE WERE GOING TO TAKE YOUR SHIP AS A DECOY AND SEND YOU OFF IN THE *STARJAMMER.*
OH YEAH, PLAN A IS DEAD. LONG LIVE PLAN B.
PLAN B IS...?
PUNCH EVERYTHING UNTIL IT DOESN'T GET UP ANYMORE.
THIS PLAN, I LIKE THE MOST.

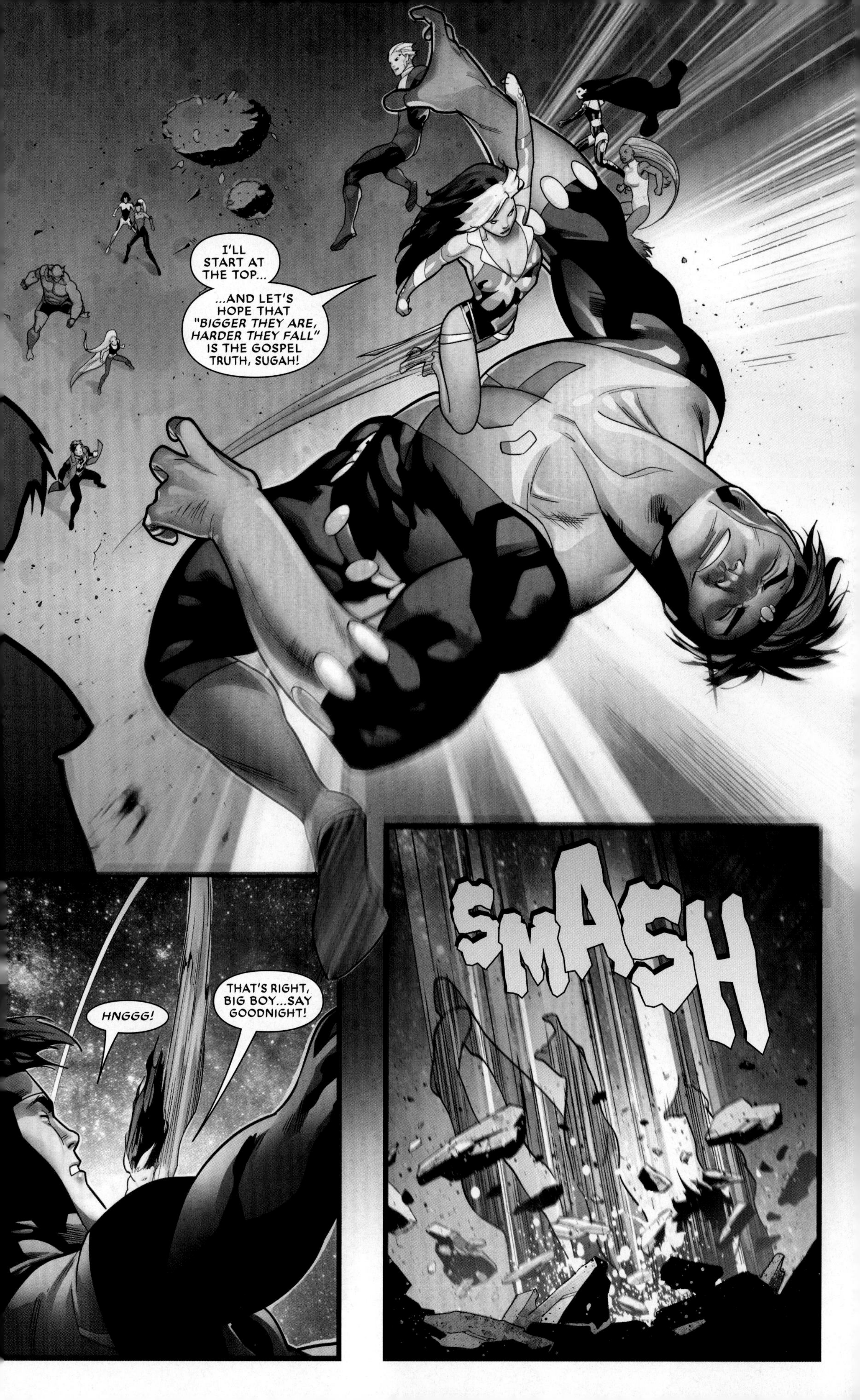
I'LL START AT THE TOP...
...AND LET'S HOPE THAT "BIGGER THEY ARE, HARDER THEY FALL" IS THE GOSPEL TRUTH, SUGAH!
HNGGG!
THAT'S RIGHT, BIG BOY...SAY GOODNIGHT!
SMASH

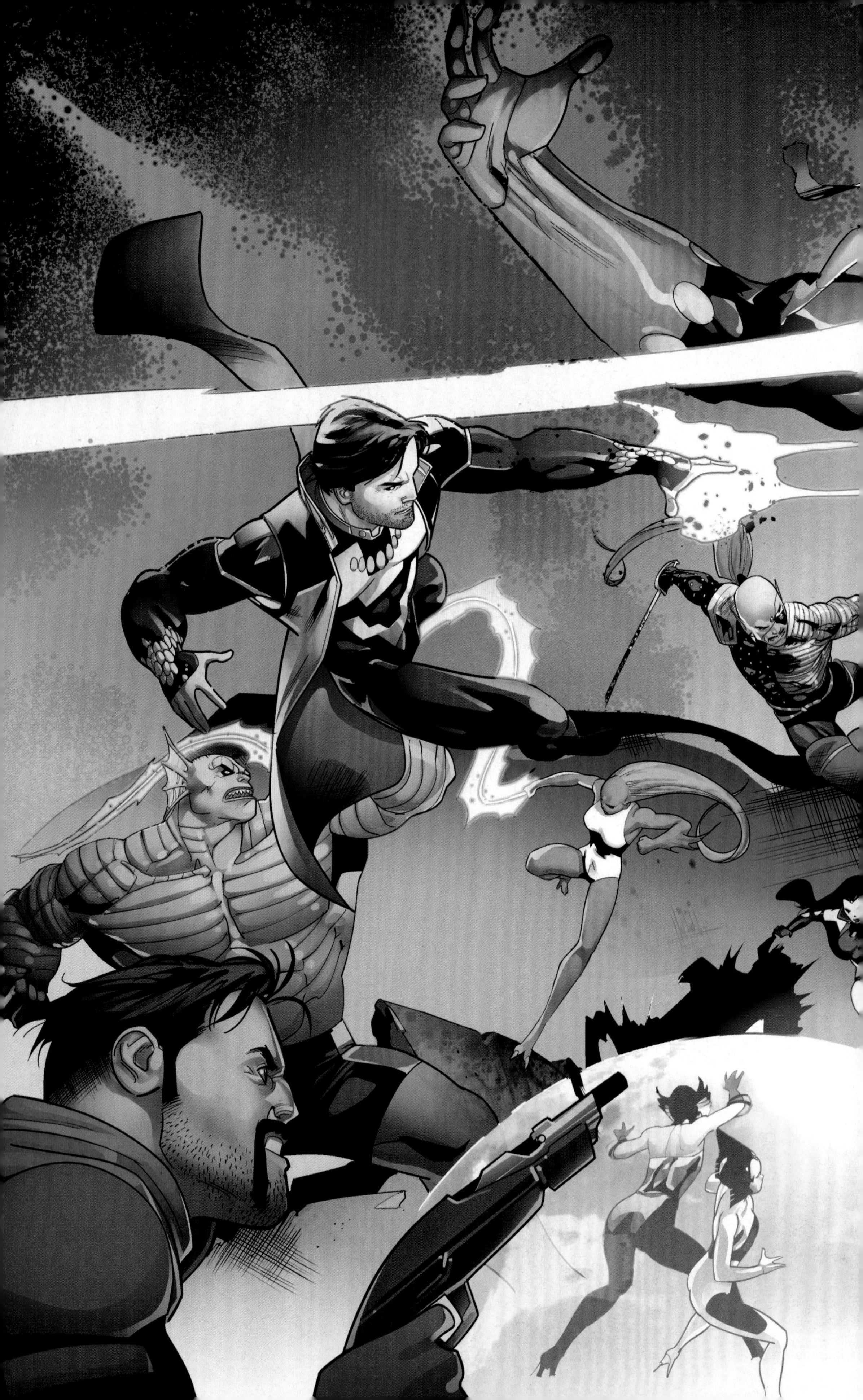

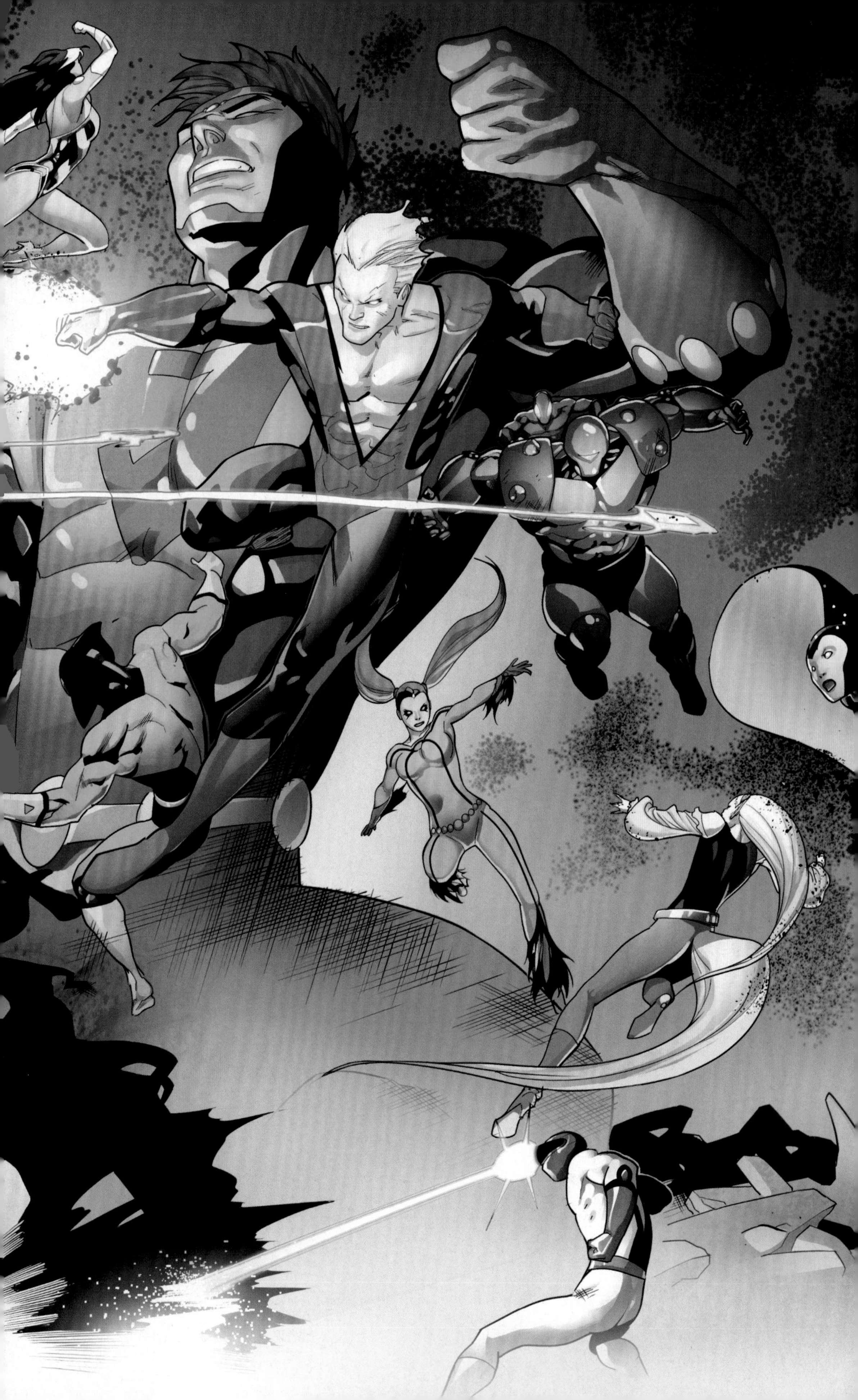

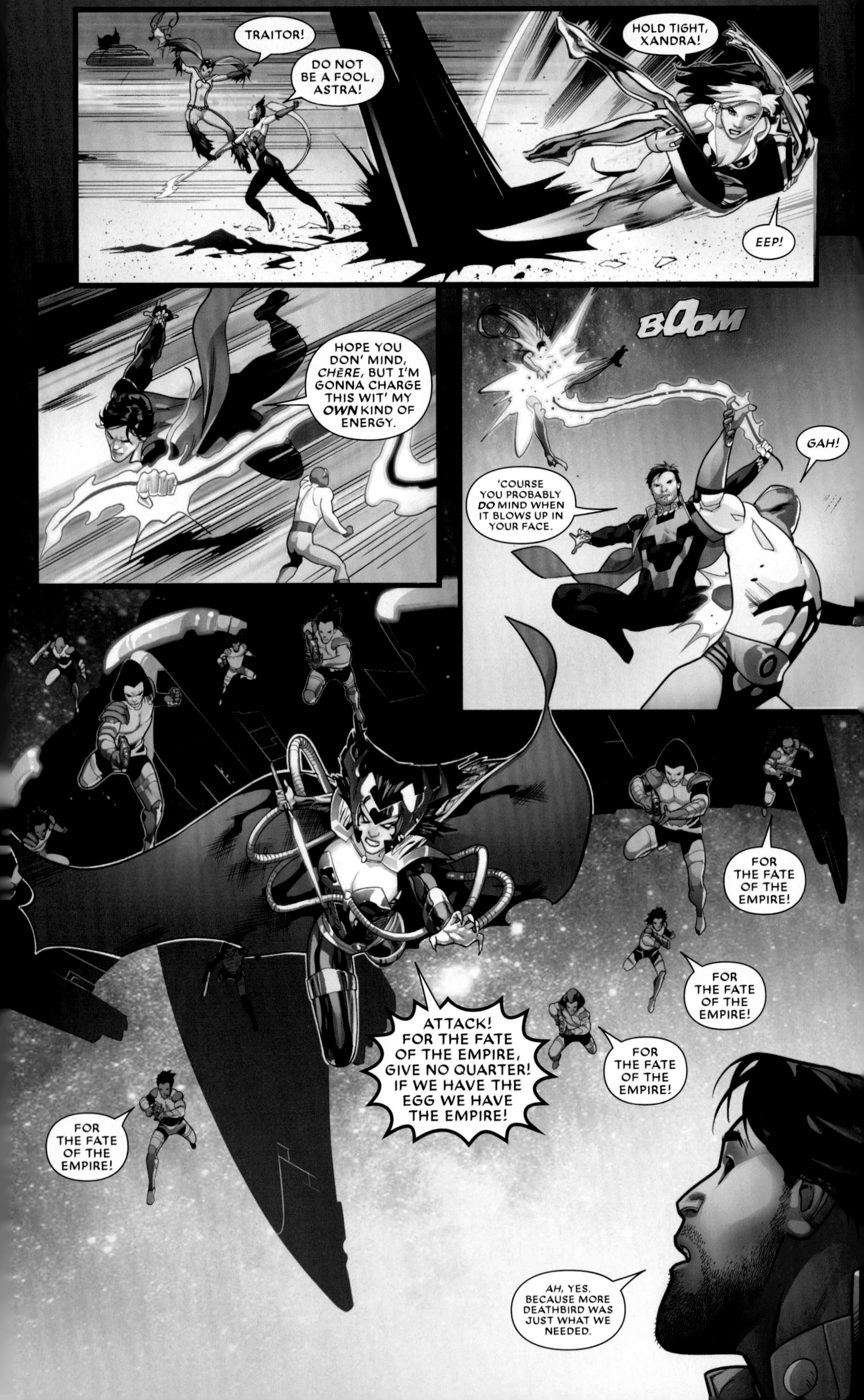
TRAITOR!
DO NOT BE A FOOL, ASTRA!
HOLD TIGHT, XANDRA!
EEP!
HOPE YOU DON' MIND, *CHÈRE*, BUT I'M GONNA CHARGE THIS WIT' MY **OWN** KIND OF ENERGY.
BOOM
GAH!
'COURSE YOU PROBABLY **DO** MIND WHEN IT BLOWS UP IN YOUR FACE.
FOR THE FATE OF THE EMPIRE!
FOR THE FATE OF THE EMPIRE!
ATTACK! FOR THE FATE OF THE EMPIRE, GIVE NO QUARTER! IF WE HAVE THE EGG WE HAVE THE EMPIRE!
FOR THE FATE OF THE EMPIRE!
FOR THE FATE OF THE EMPIRE!
AH, YES. BECAUSE MORE DEATHBIRD WAS JUST WHAT WE NEEDED.

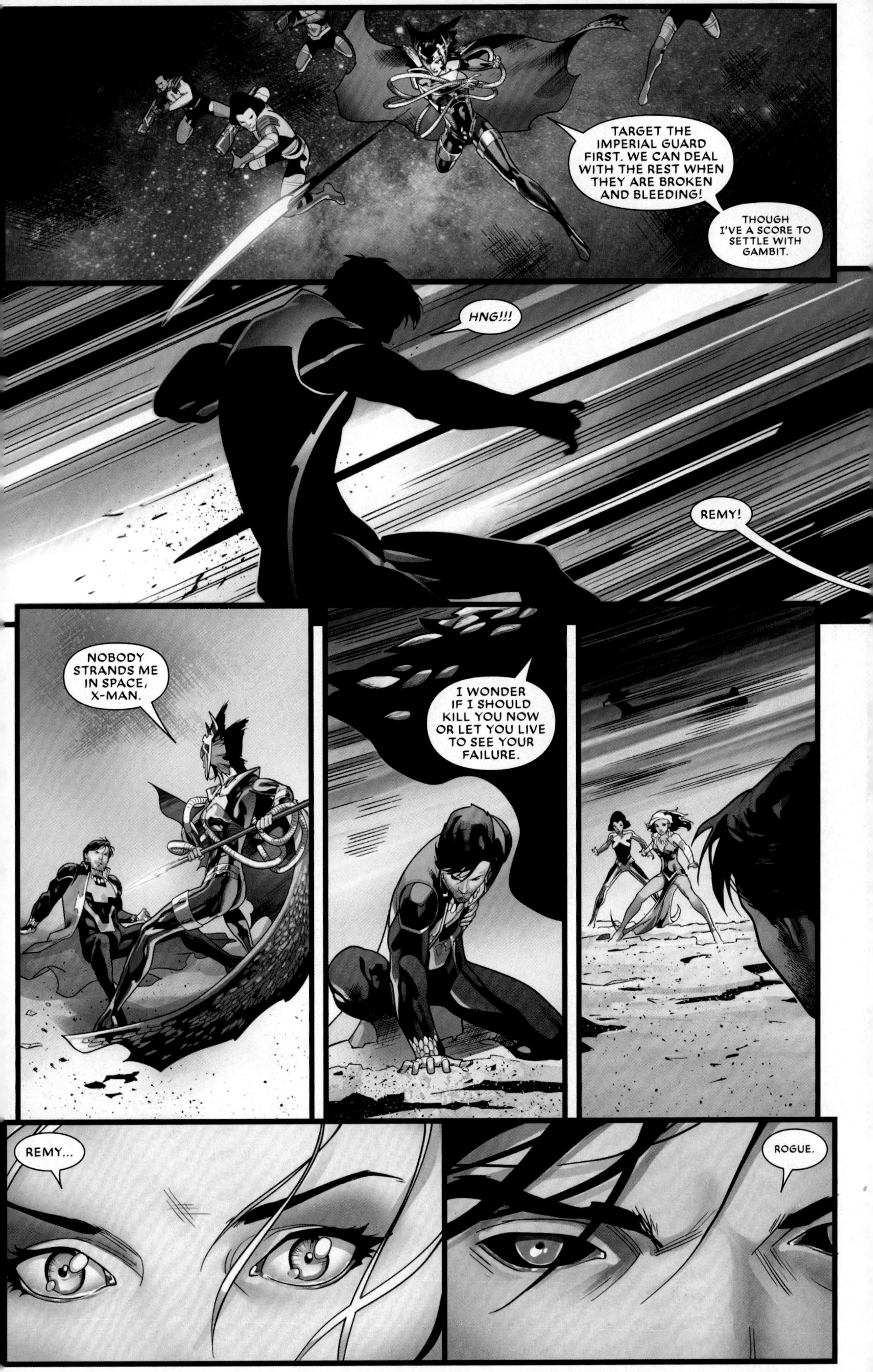
TARGET THE IMPERIAL GUARD FIRST. WE CAN DEAL WITH THE REST WHEN THEY ARE BROKEN AND BLEEDING!
THOUGH I'VE A SCORE TO SETTLE WITH GAMBIT.
HNG!!!
REMY!
NOBODY STRANDS ME IN SPACE, X-MAN.
I WONDER IF I SHOULD KILL YOU NOW OR LET YOU LIVE TO SEE YOUR FAILURE.
REMY...
ROGUE.

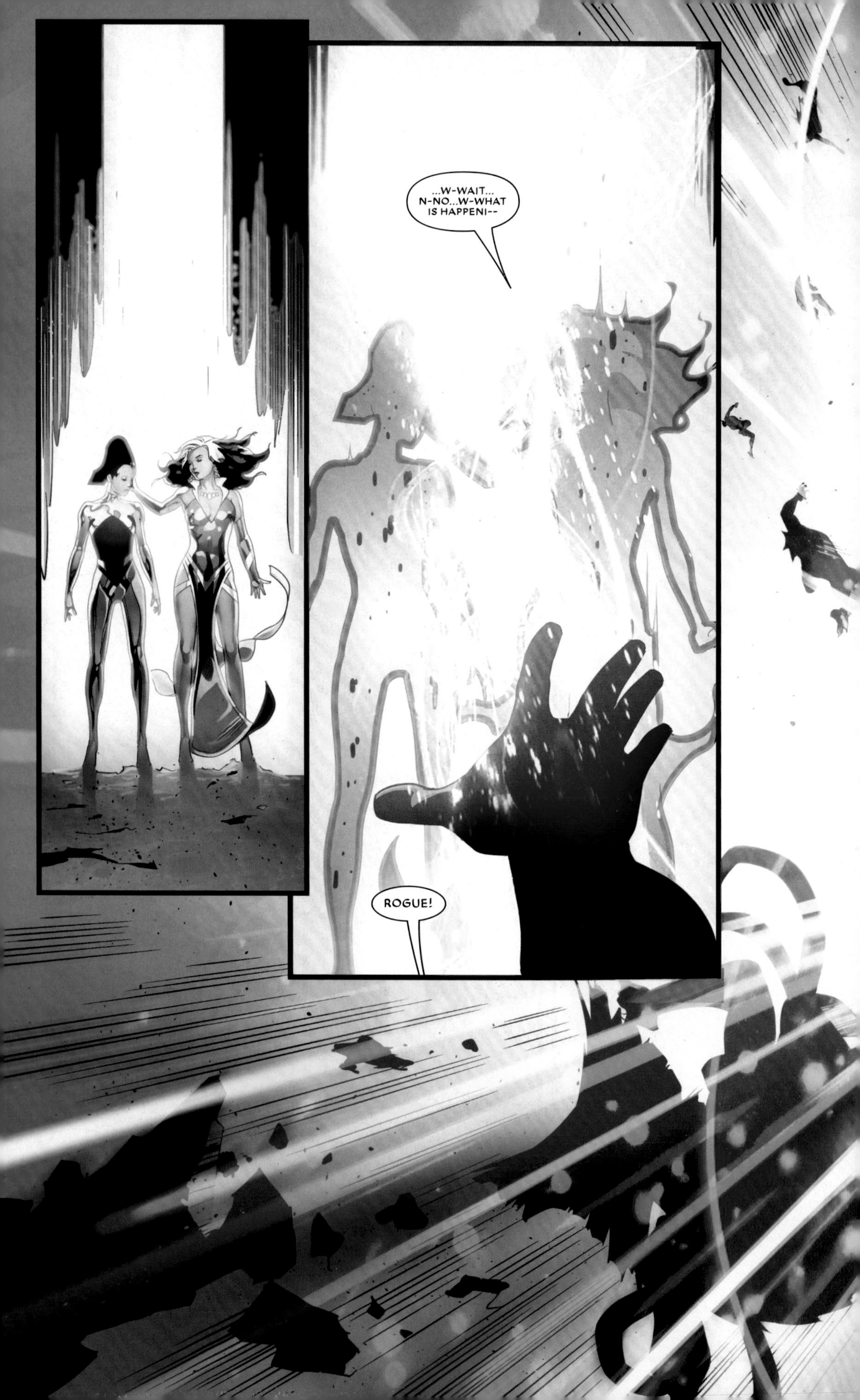
...W-WAIT... N-NO...W-WHAT IS HAPPENI--
ROGUE!

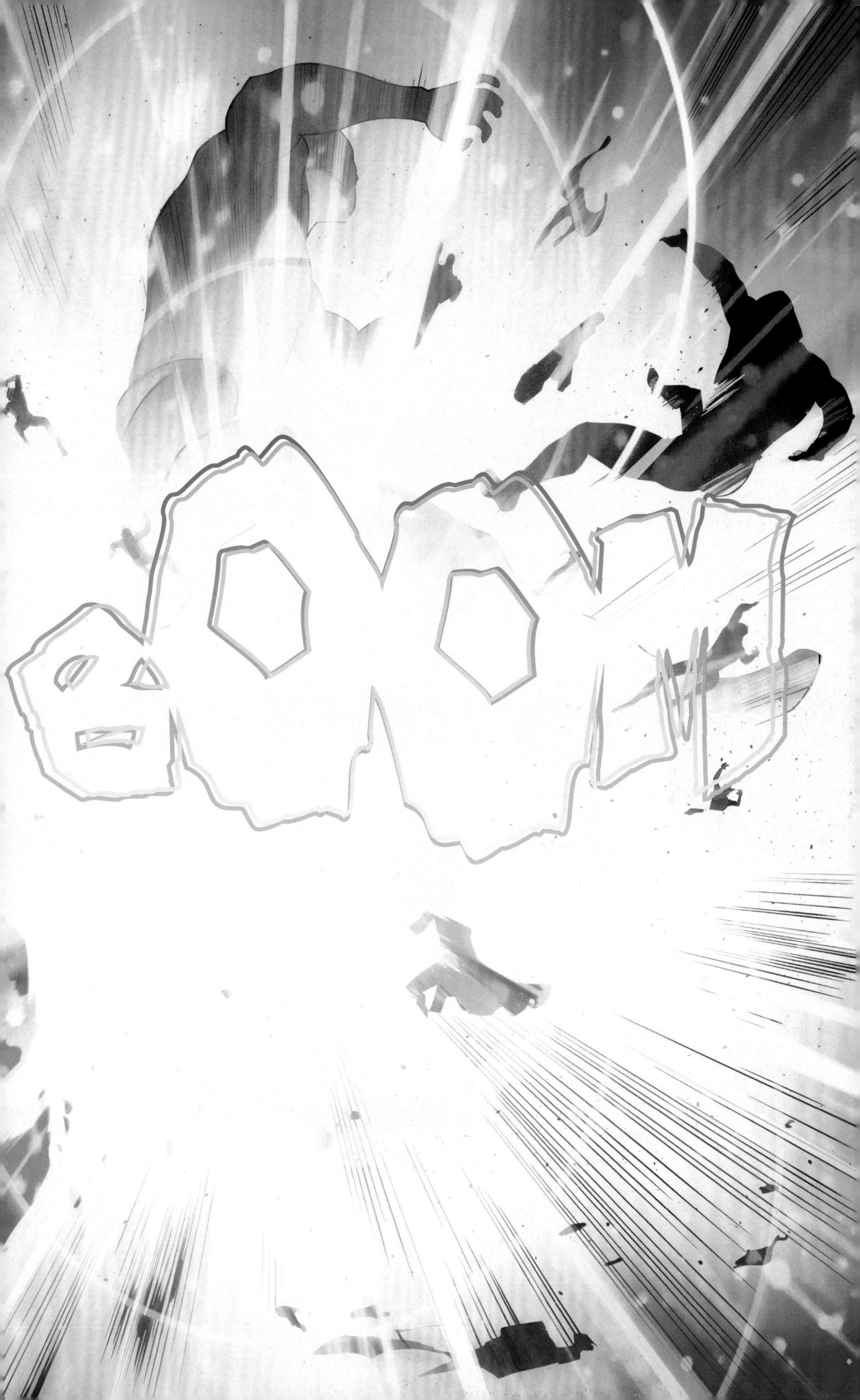
BOOM

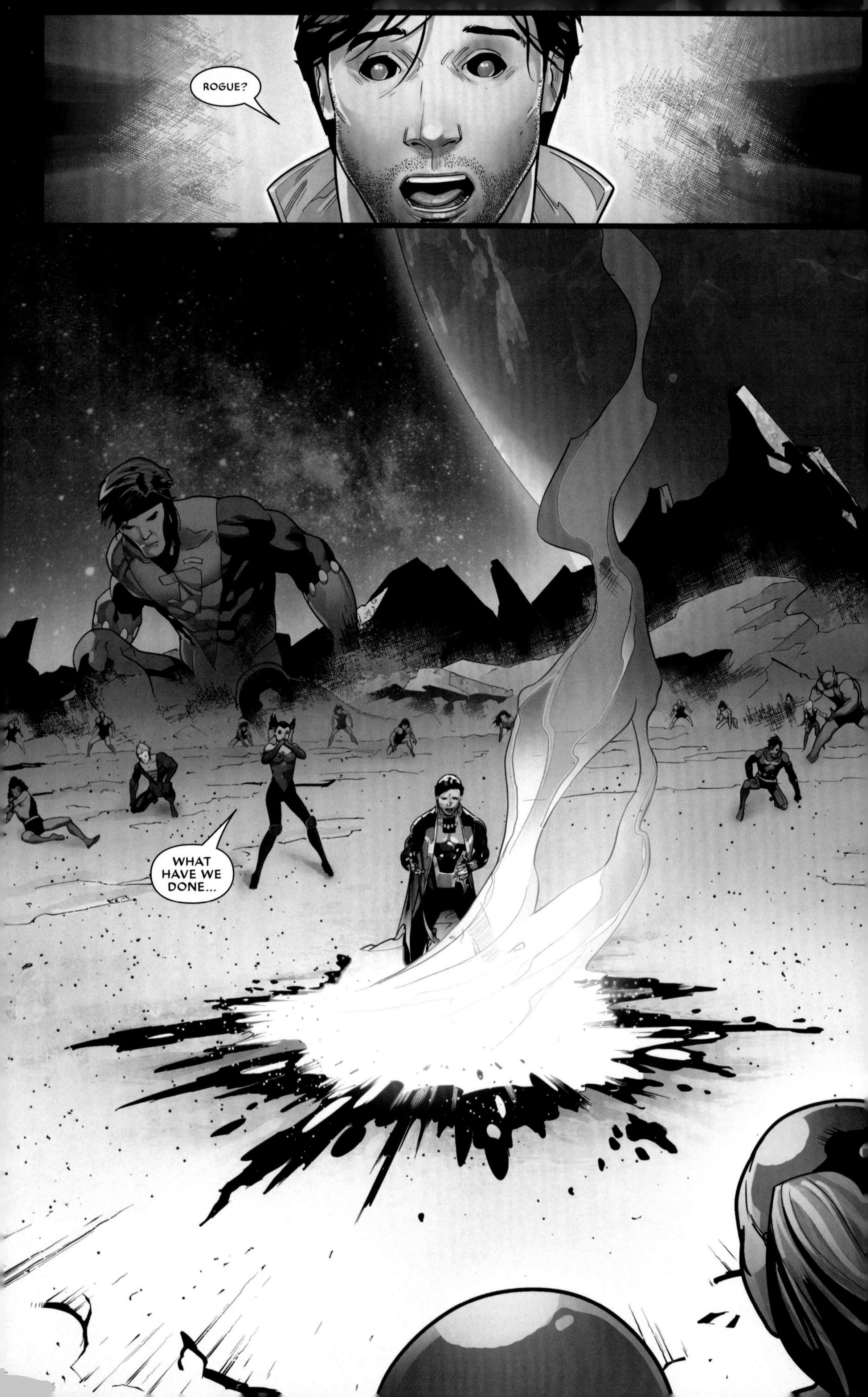
ROGUE?
WHAT HAVE WE DONE...

#1 VARIANT BY HUMBERTO RAMOS & EDGAR DELGADO

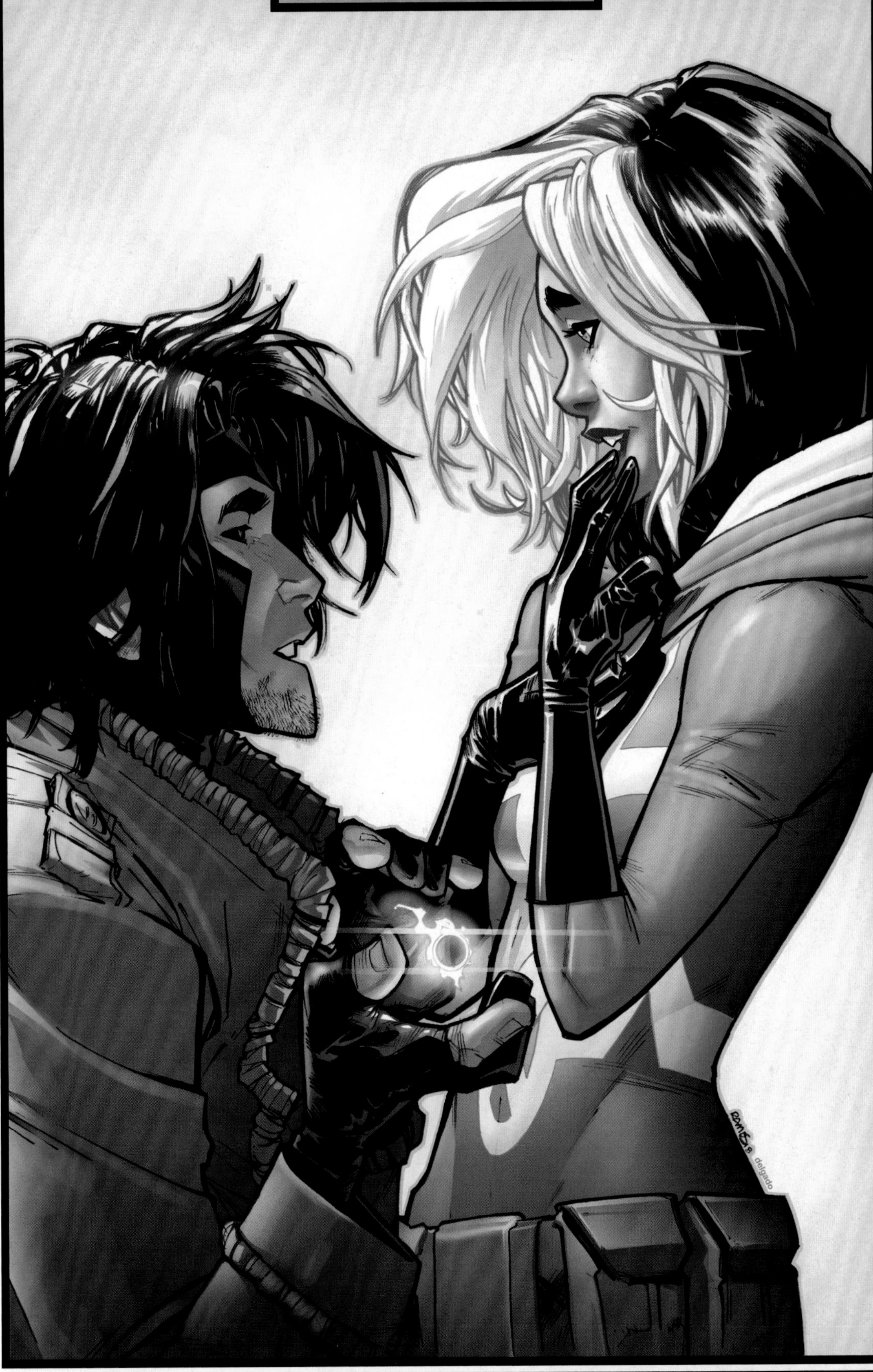

delgado

5

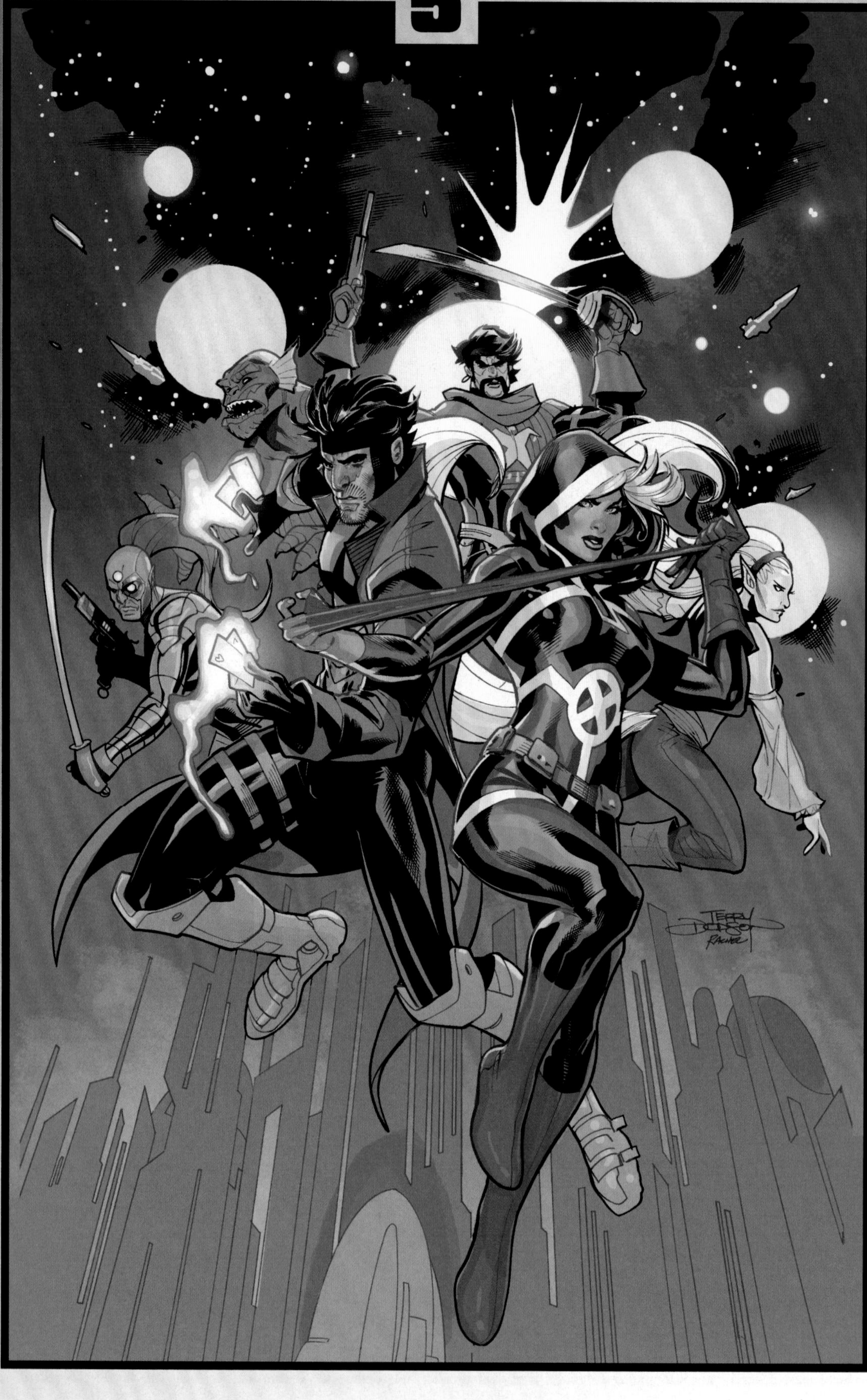

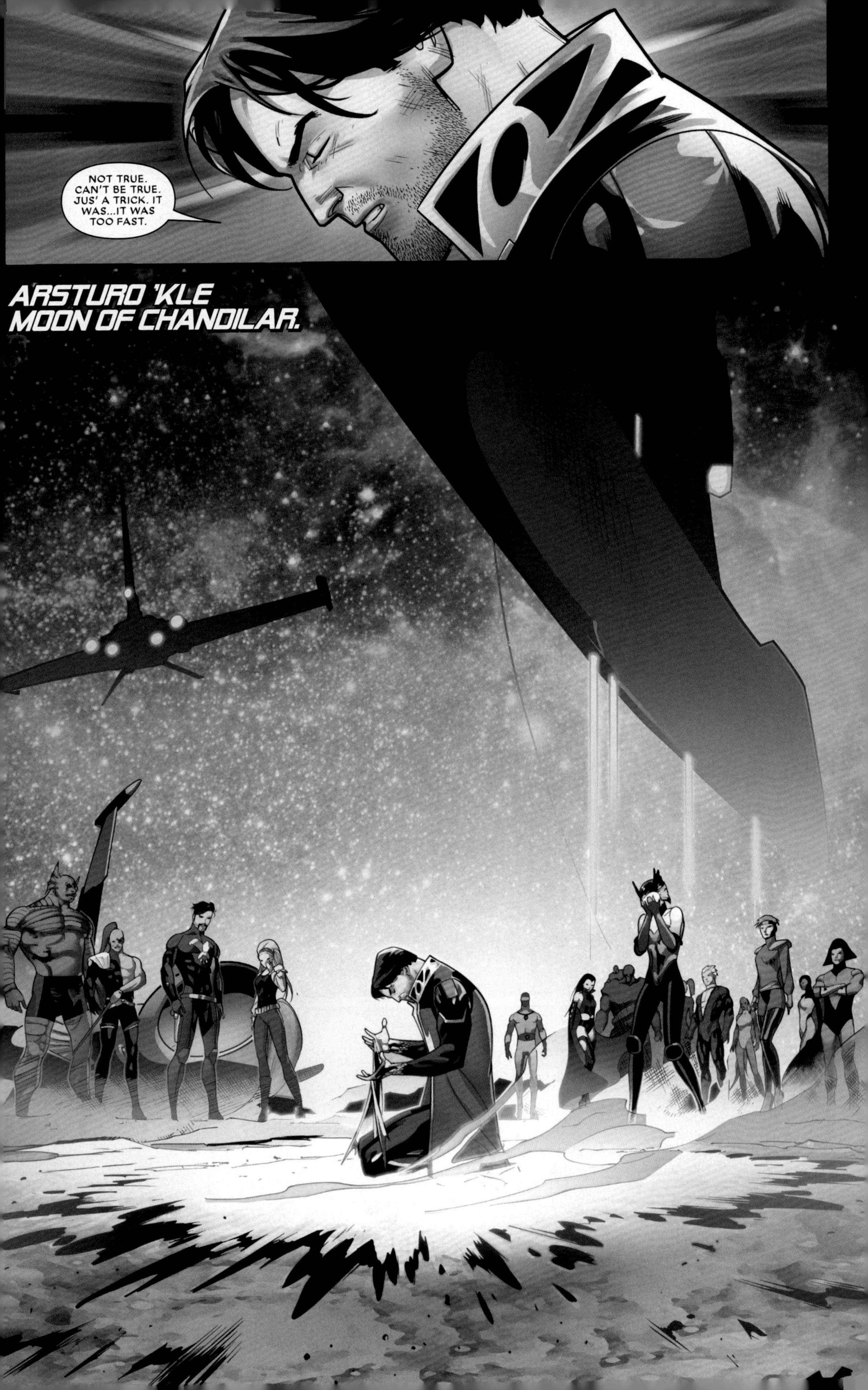
NOT TRUE. CAN'T BE TRUE. JUS' A TRICK. IT WAS...IT WAS TOO FAST.
ARSTURO 'KLE
MOON OF CHANDILAR.

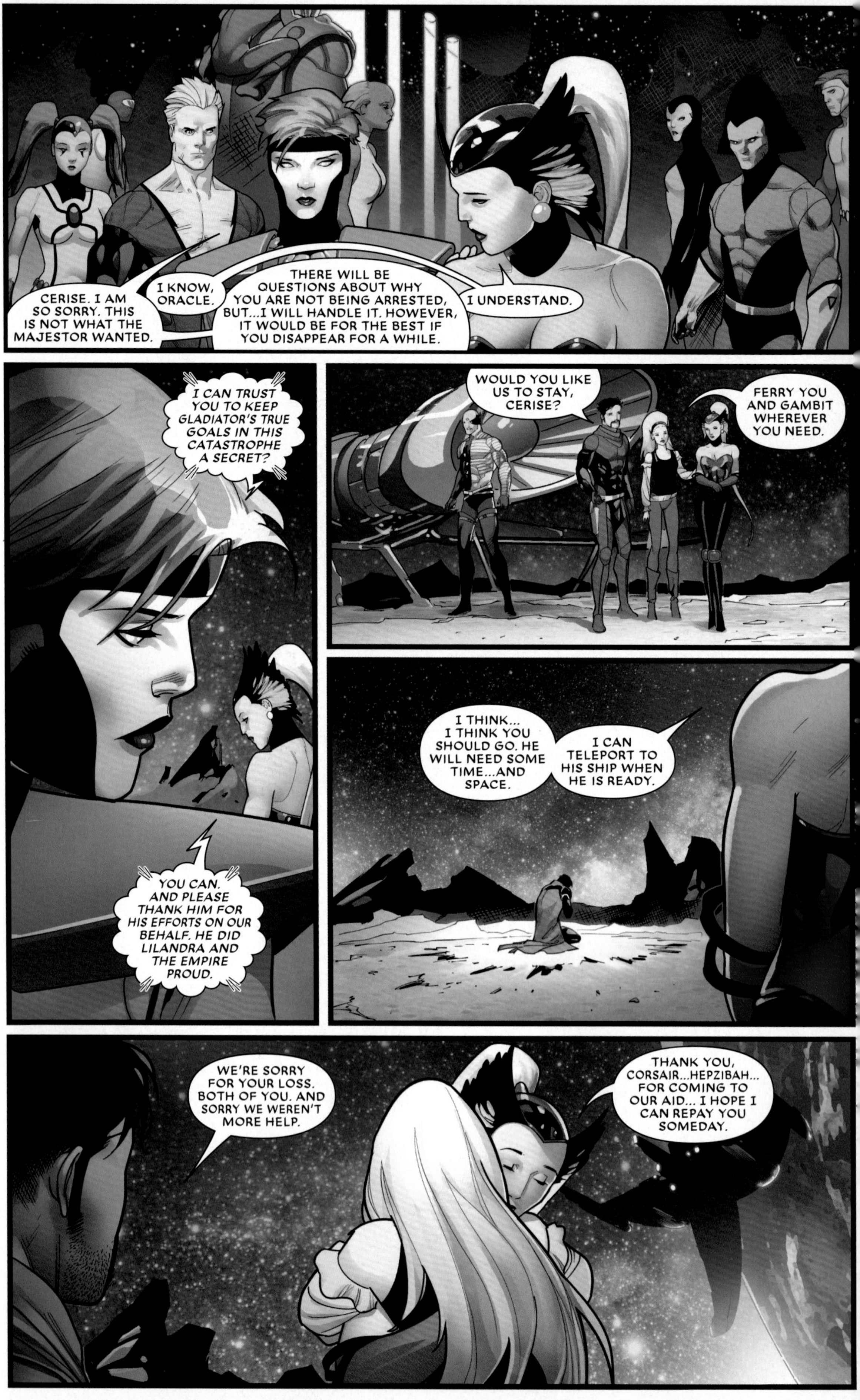
CERISE. I AM SO SORRY. THIS IS NOT WHAT THE MAJESTOR WANTED.
I KNOW, ORACLE.
THERE WILL BE QUESTIONS ABOUT WHY YOU ARE NOT BEING ARRESTED, BUT...I WILL HANDLE IT. HOWEVER, IT WOULD BE FOR THE BEST IF YOU DISAPPEAR FOR A WHILE.
I UNDERSTAND.
I CAN TRUST YOU TO KEEP GLADIATOR'S TRUE GOALS IN THIS CATASTROPHE A SECRET?
YOU CAN. AND PLEASE THANK HIM FOR HIS EFFORTS ON OUR BEHALF. HE DID LILANDRA AND THE EMPIRE PROUD.
WOULD YOU LIKE US TO STAY, CERISE?
FERRY YOU AND GAMBIT WHEREVER YOU NEED.
I THINK... I THINK YOU SHOULD GO. HE WILL NEED SOME TIME...AND SPACE.
I CAN TELEPORT TO HIS SHIP WHEN HE IS READY.
WE'RE SORRY FOR YOUR LOSS. BOTH OF YOU. AND SORRY WE WEREN'T MORE HELP.
THANK YOU, CORSAIR...HEPZIBAH... FOR COMING TO OUR AID... I HOPE I CAN REPAY YOU SOMEDAY.

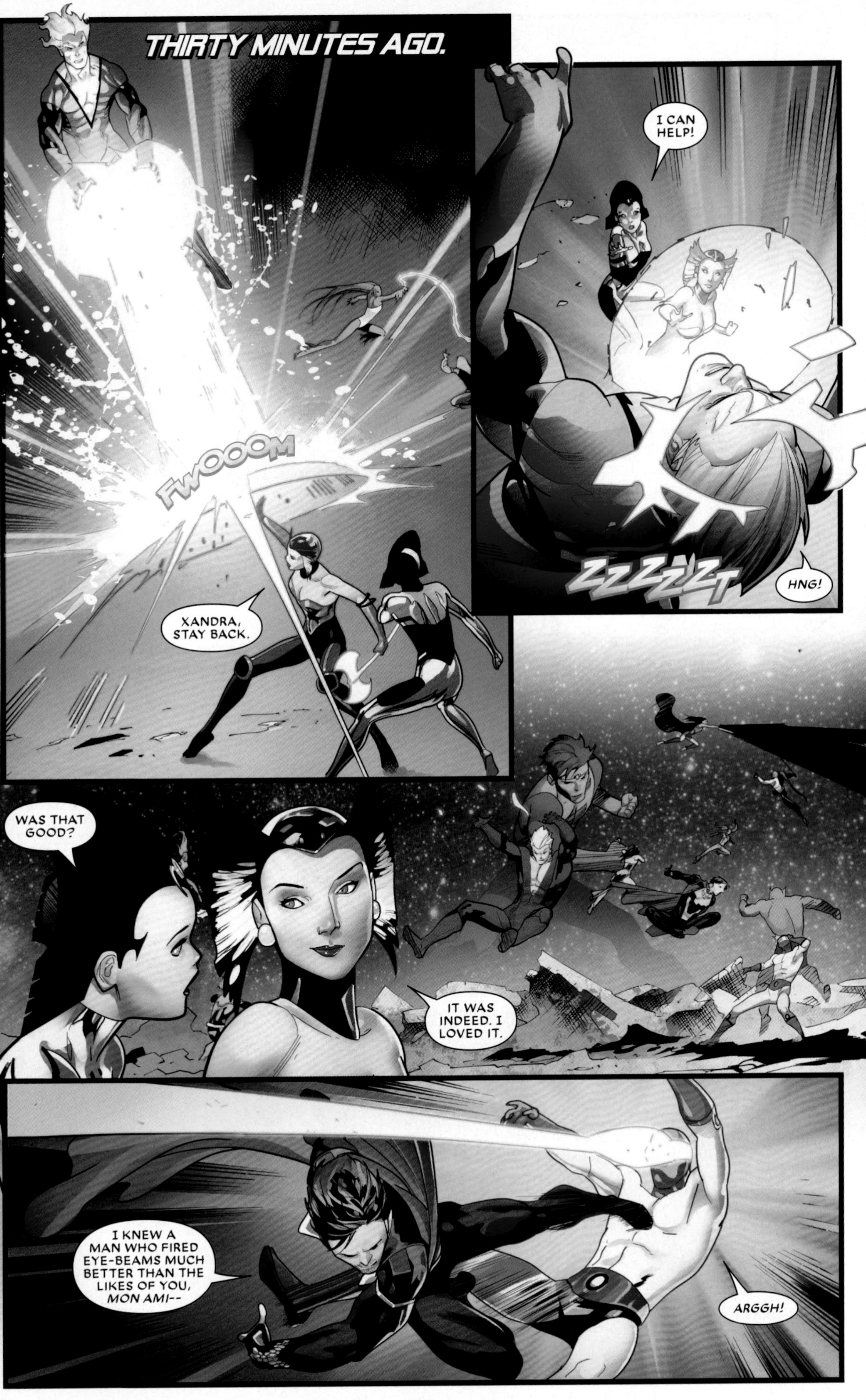
THIRTY MINUTES AGO.
FWOOOM
XANDRA, STAY BACK.
I CAN HELP!
ZZZZZZT
HNG!
WAS THAT GOOD?
IT WAS INDEED. I LOVED IT.
I KNEW A MAN WHO FIRED EYE-BEAMS MUCH BETTER THAN THE LIKES OF YOU, MON AMI--
ARGGH!

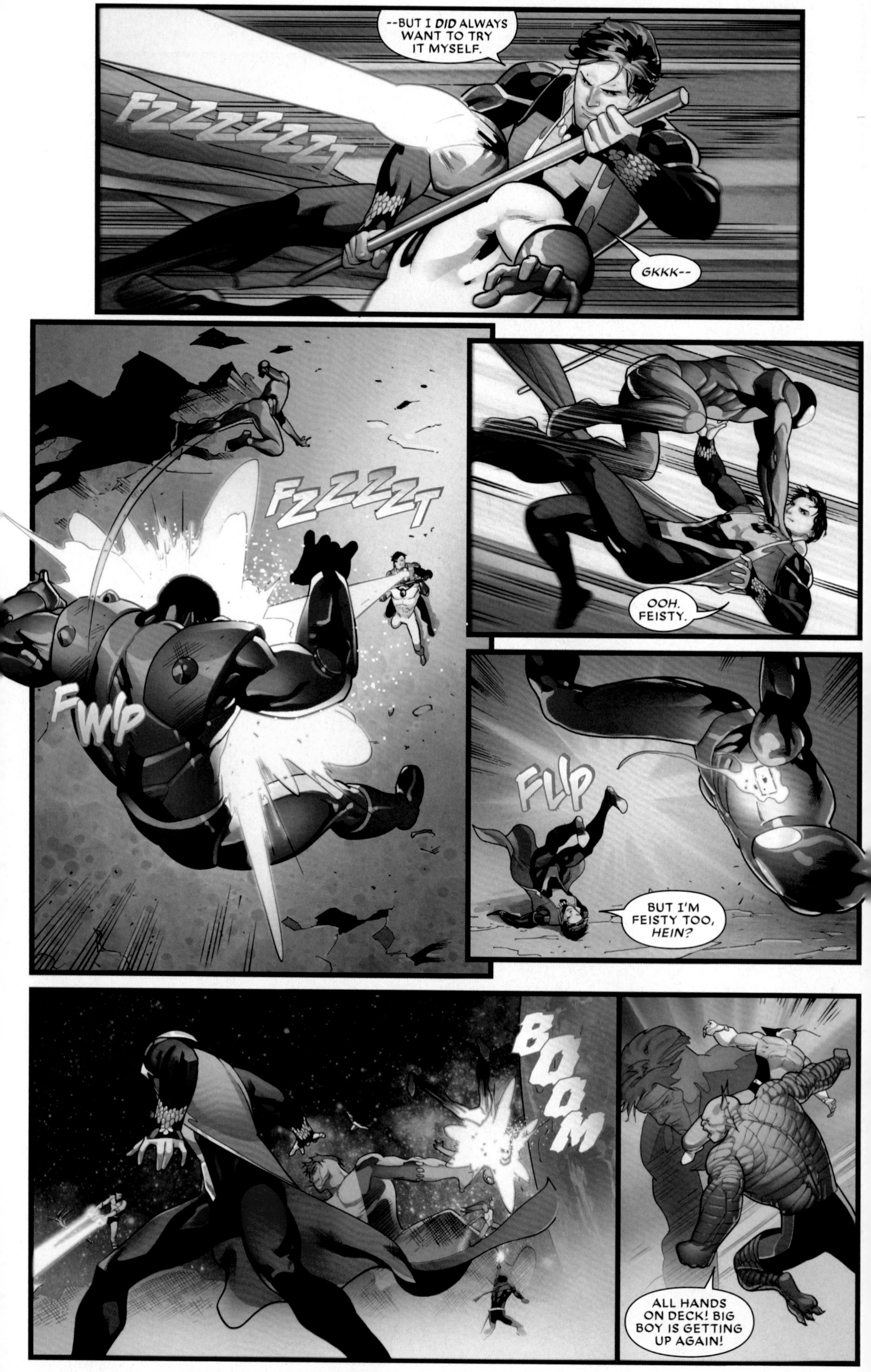
--BUT I DID ALWAYS WANT TO TRY IT MYSELF.
FZZZZZZZT
GKKK--
FZZZZZT
FWIP
OOH. FEISTY.
FLIP
BUT I'M FEISTY TOO, HEIN?
BOOM
ALL HANDS ON DECK! BIG BOY IS GETTING UP AGAIN!

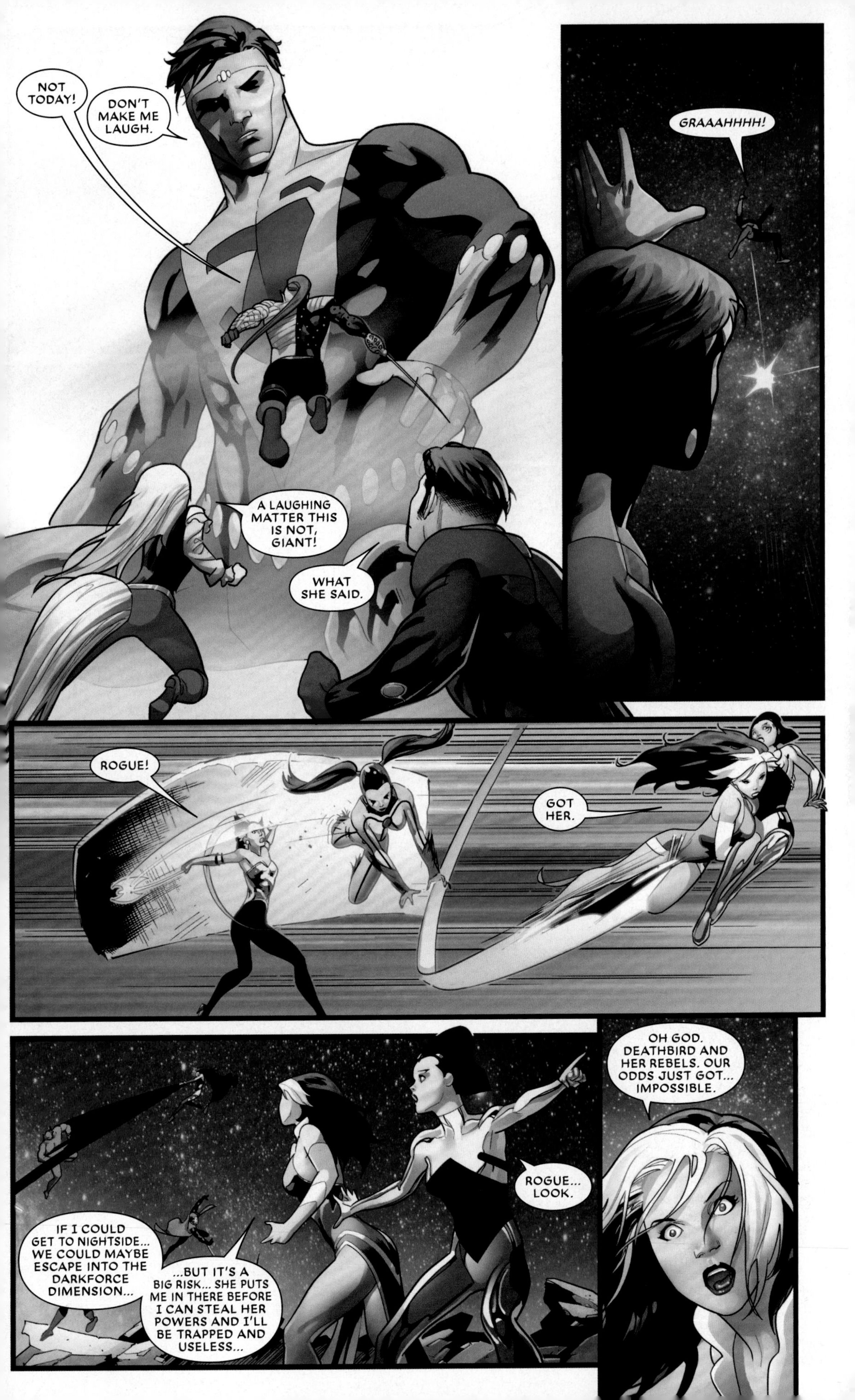
NOT TODAY!
DON'T MAKE ME LAUGH.
A LAUGHING MATTER THIS IS NOT, GIANT!
WHAT SHE SAID.
GRAAAHHHH!
ROGUE!
GOT HER.
ROGUE... LOOK.
IF I COULD GET TO NIGHTSIDE... WE COULD MAYBE ESCAPE INTO THE DARKFORCE DIMENSION...
...BUT IT'S A BIG RISK... SHE PUTS ME IN THERE BEFORE I CAN STEAL HER POWERS AND I'LL BE TRAPPED AND USELESS...
OH GOD. DEATHBIRD AND HER REBELS. OUR ODDS JUST GOT... IMPOSSIBLE.

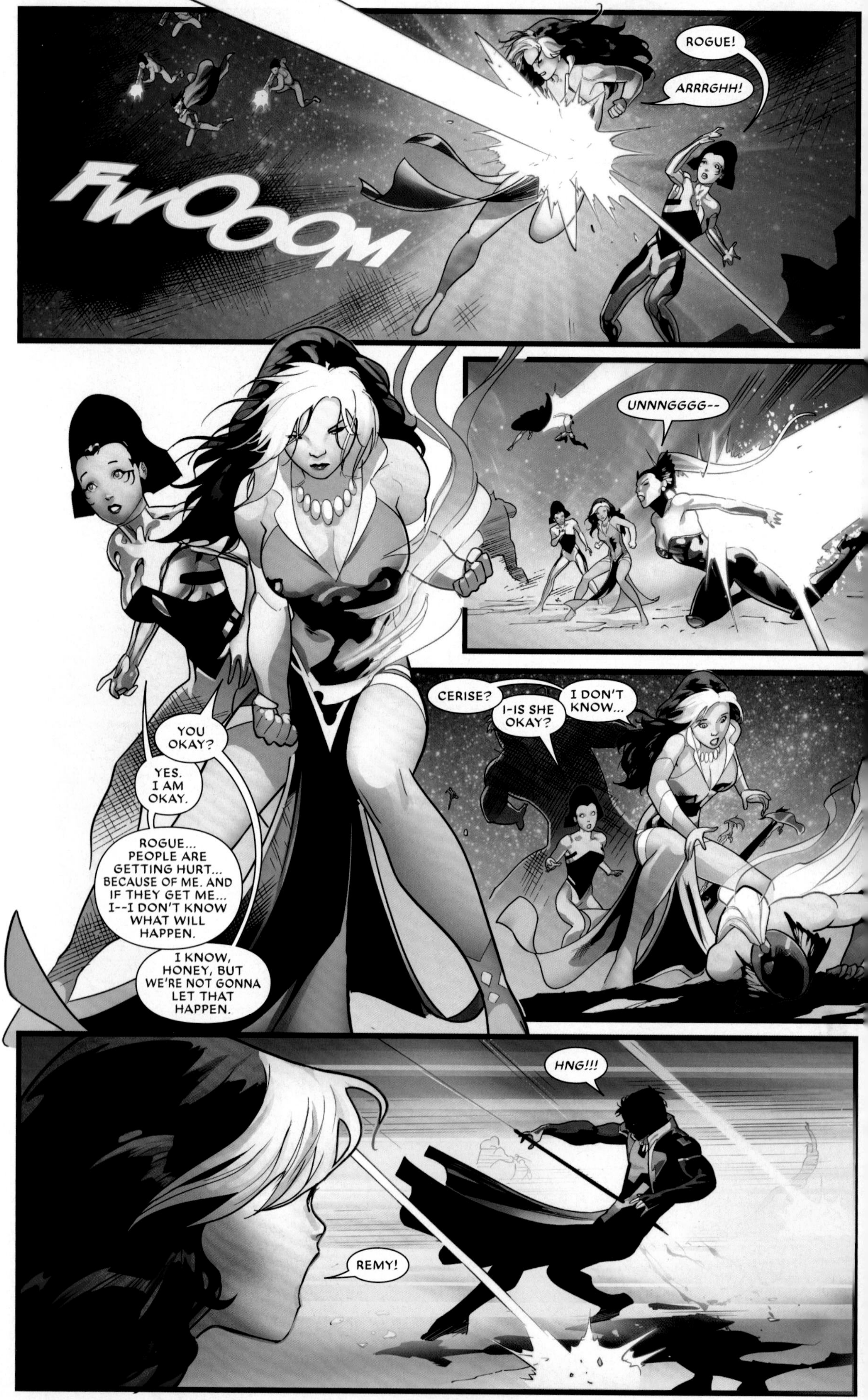
ROGUE!
ARRRGHH!
FWOOOM
UNNNGGGG--
YOU OKAY?
YES. I AM OKAY.
ROGUE... PEOPLE ARE GETTING HURT... BECAUSE OF ME. AND IF THEY GET ME... I--I DON'T KNOW WHAT WILL HAPPEN.
I KNOW, HONEY, BUT WE'RE NOT GONNA LET THAT HAPPEN.
CERISE?
I-IS SHE OKAY?
I DON'T KNOW...
HNG!!!
REMY!

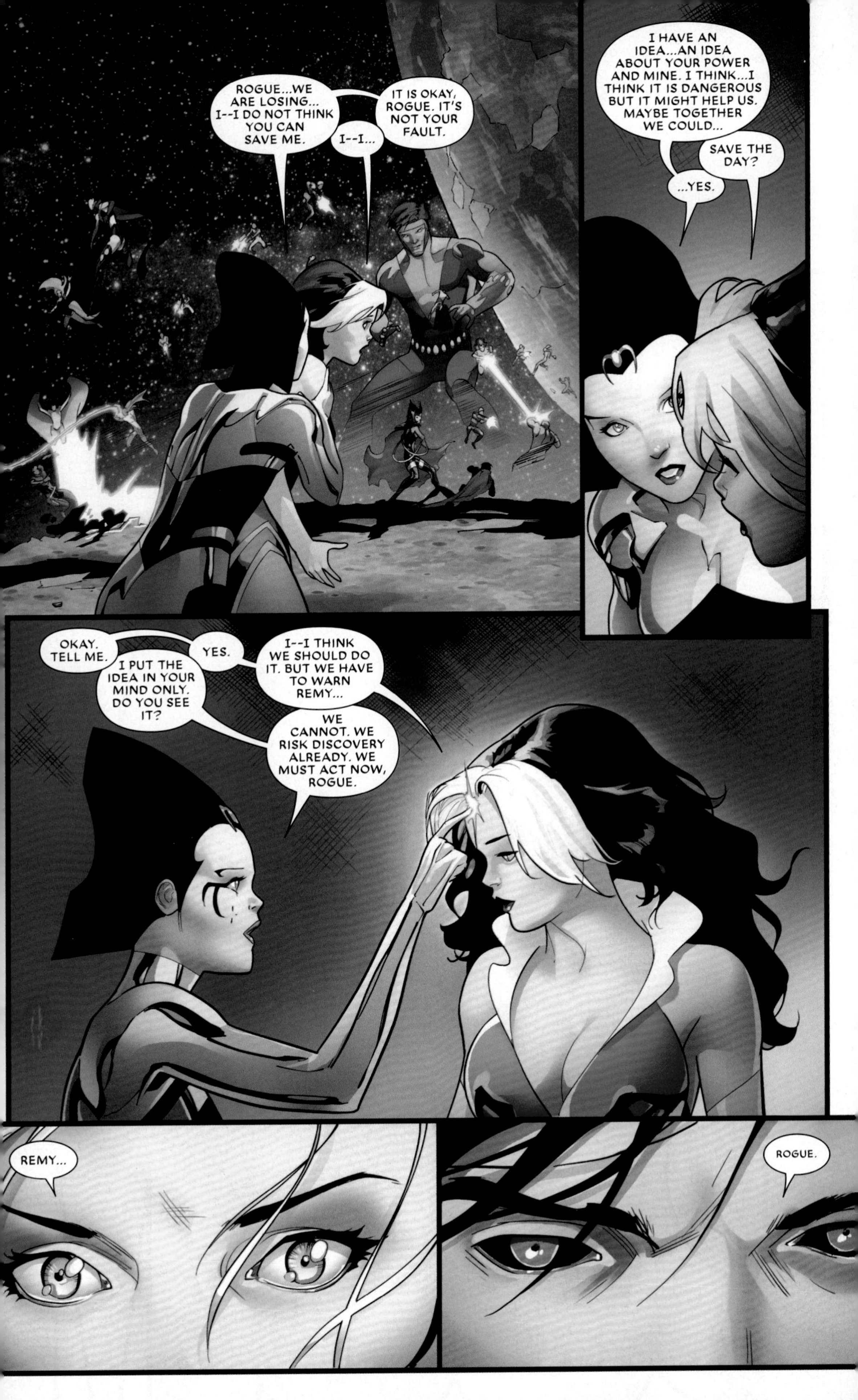
ROGUE...WE ARE LOSING... I--I DO NOT THINK YOU CAN SAVE ME.
I--I...
IT IS OKAY, ROGUE. IT'S NOT YOUR FAULT.
I HAVE AN IDEA...AN IDEA ABOUT YOUR POWER AND MINE. I THINK...I THINK IT IS DANGEROUS BUT IT MIGHT HELP US. MAYBE TOGETHER WE COULD...
SAVE THE DAY?
...YES.
OKAY. TELL ME.
I PUT THE IDEA IN YOUR MIND ONLY. DO YOU SEE IT?
YES.
I--I THINK WE SHOULD DO IT. BUT WE HAVE TO WARN REMY...
WE CANNOT. WE RISK DISCOVERY ALREADY. WE MUST ACT NOW, ROGUE.
REMY...
ROGUE.

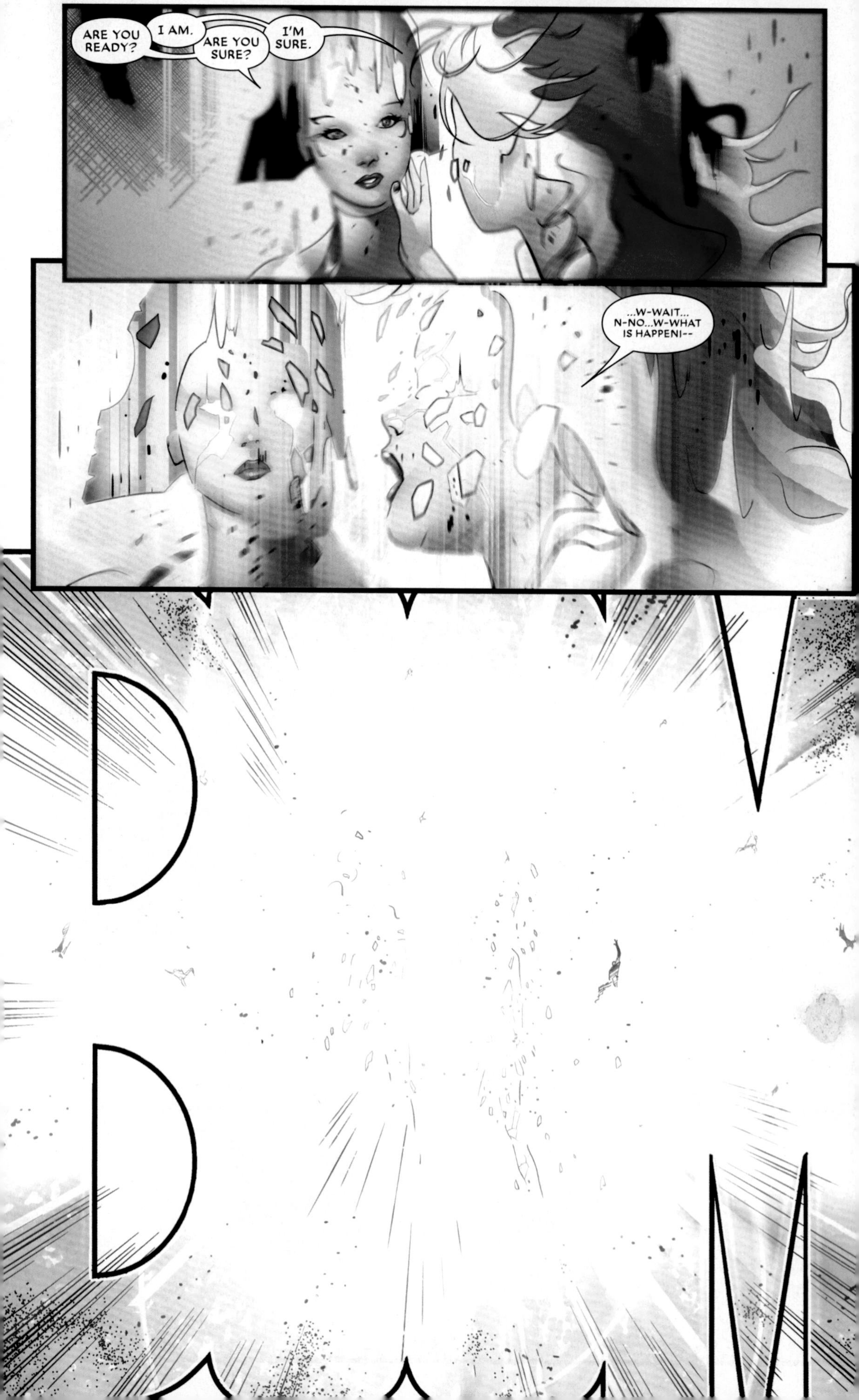
ARE YOU READY?
I AM.
ARE YOU SURE?
I'M SURE.
...W-WAIT... N-NO...W-WHAT IS HAPPENI--
DOOM

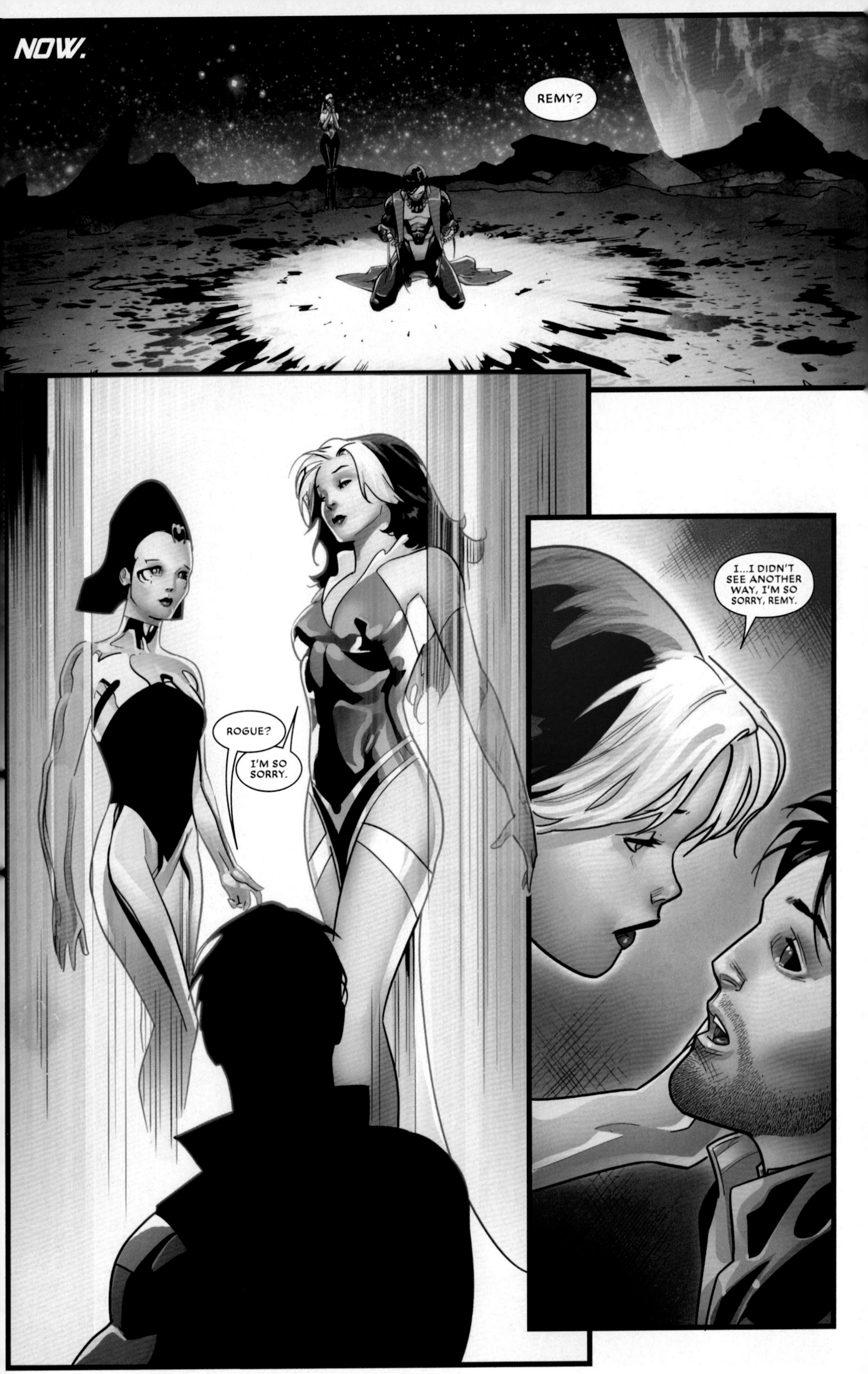
NOW.
REMY?
ROGUE?
I'M SO SORRY.
I...I DIDN'T SEE ANOTHER WAY, I'M SO SORRY, REMY.

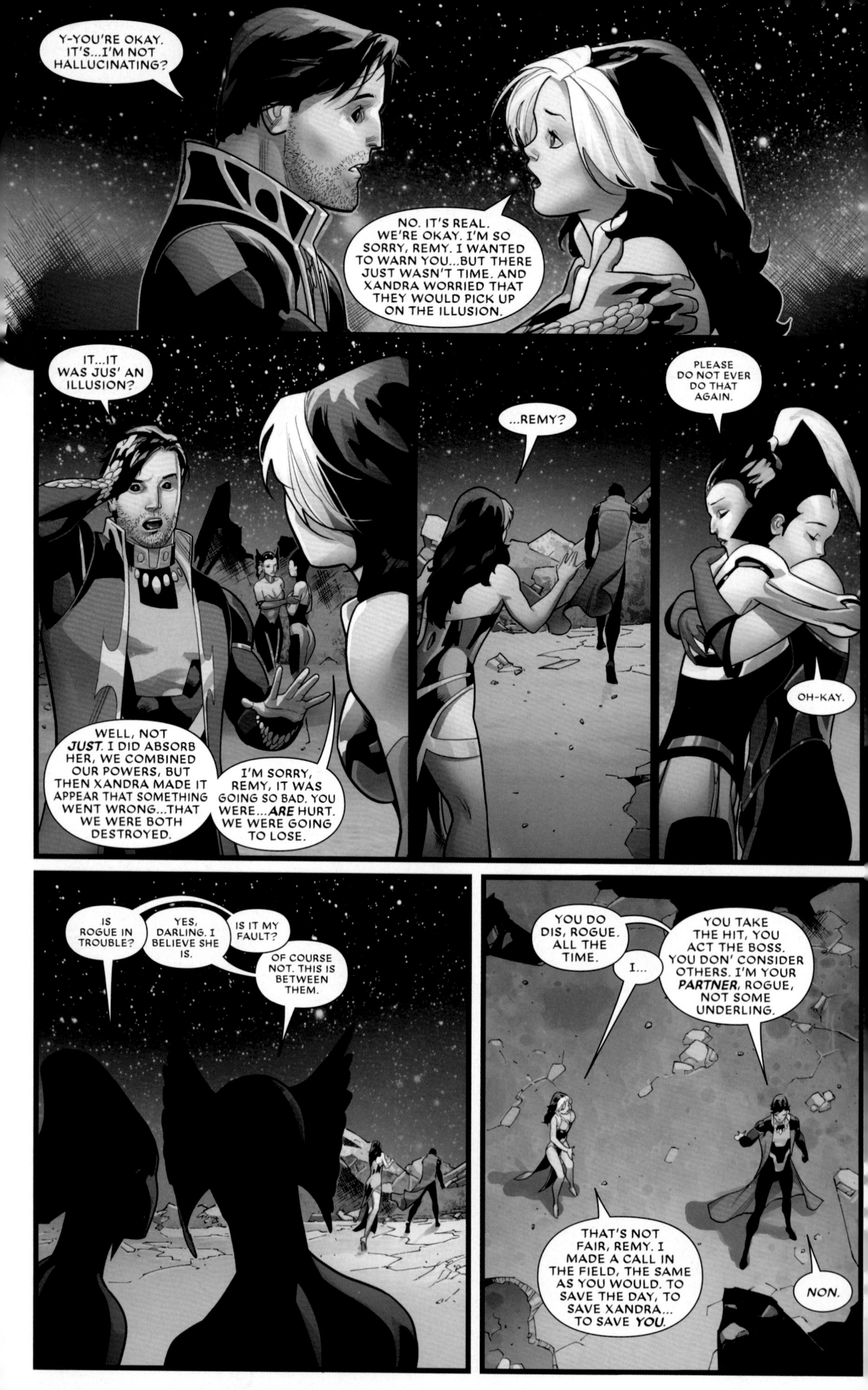
Y-YOU'RE OKAY. IT'S...I'M NOT HALLUCINATING?
NO. IT'S REAL. WE'RE OKAY. I'M SO SORRY, REMY. I WANTED TO WARN YOU...BUT THERE JUST WASN'T TIME. AND XANDRA WORRIED THAT THEY WOULD PICK UP ON THE ILLUSION.
IT...IT WAS JUS' AN ILLUSION?
WELL, NOT *JUST*. I DID ABSORB HER, WE COMBINED OUR POWERS, BUT THEN XANDRA MADE IT APPEAR THAT SOMETHING WENT WRONG...THAT WE WERE BOTH DESTROYED.
I'M SORRY, REMY, IT WAS GOING SO BAD. YOU WERE...*ARE* HURT. WE WERE GOING TO LOSE.
...REMY?
PLEASE DO NOT EVER DO THAT AGAIN.
OH-KAY.
IS ROGUE IN TROUBLE?
YES, DARLING. I BELIEVE SHE IS.
IS IT MY FAULT?
OF COURSE NOT. THIS IS BETWEEN THEM.
YOU DO DIS, ROGUE. ALL THE TIME.
I...
YOU TAKE THE HIT, YOU ACT THE BOSS. YOU DON' CONSIDER OTHERS. I'M YOUR *PARTNER*, ROGUE, NOT SOME UNDERLING.
THAT'S NOT FAIR, REMY. I MADE A CALL IN THE FIELD, THE SAME AS YOU WOULD. TO SAVE THE DAY, TO SAVE XANDRA... TO SAVE *YOU*.
NON.

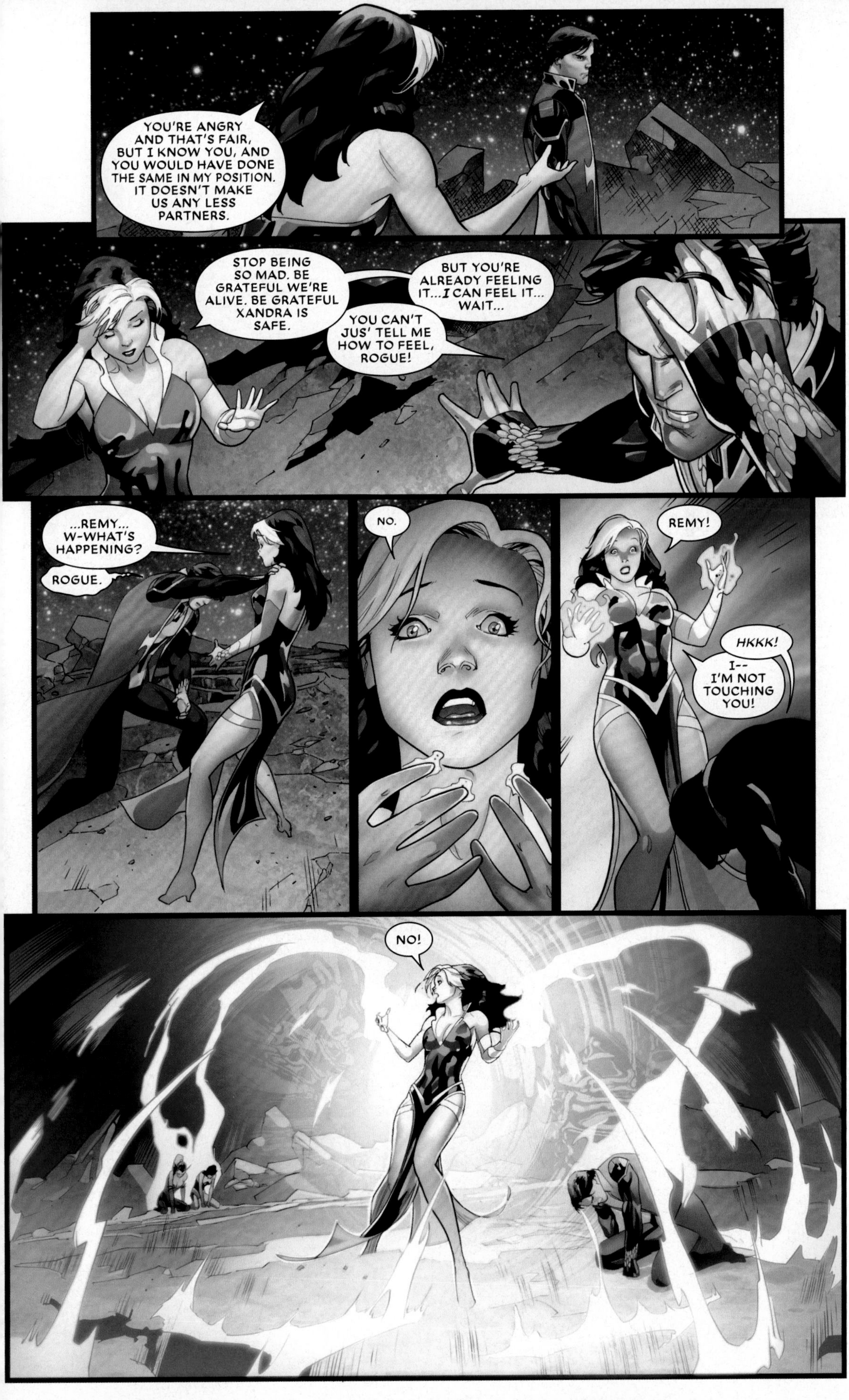
YOU'RE ANGRY AND THAT'S FAIR, BUT I KNOW YOU, AND YOU WOULD HAVE DONE THE SAME IN MY POSITION. IT DOESN'T MAKE US ANY LESS PARTNERS.
STOP BEING SO MAD. BE GRATEFUL WE'RE ALIVE. BE GRATEFUL XANDRA IS SAFE.
YOU CAN'T JUS' TELL ME HOW TO FEEL, ROGUE!
BUT YOU'RE ALREADY FEELING IT...*I* CAN FEEL IT... WAIT...
...REMY... W-WHAT'S HAPPENING?
ROGUE.
NO.
REMY!
HKKK!
I-- I'M NOT TOUCHING YOU!
NO!

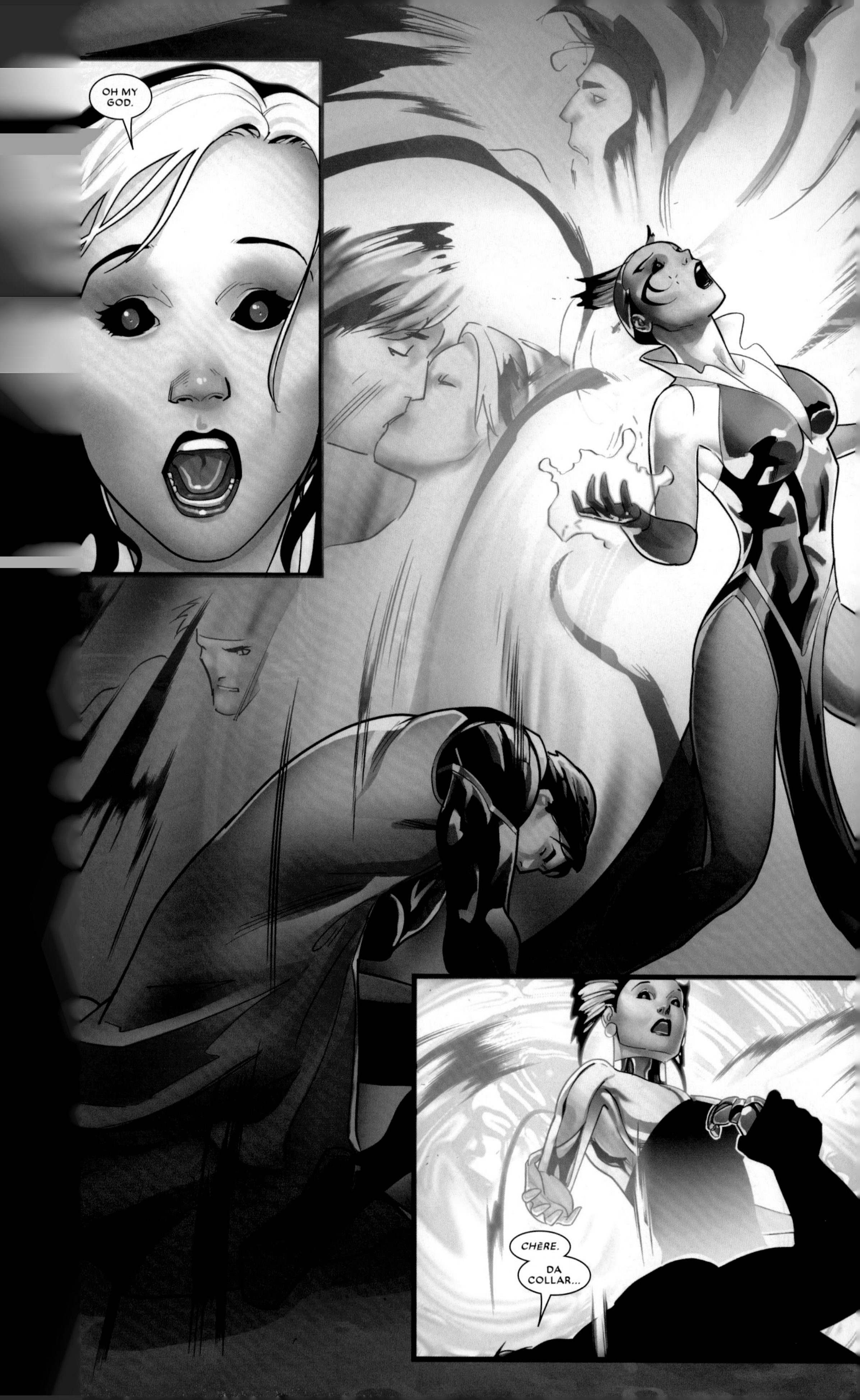
OH MY GOD.
CHÈRE.
DA COLLAR...

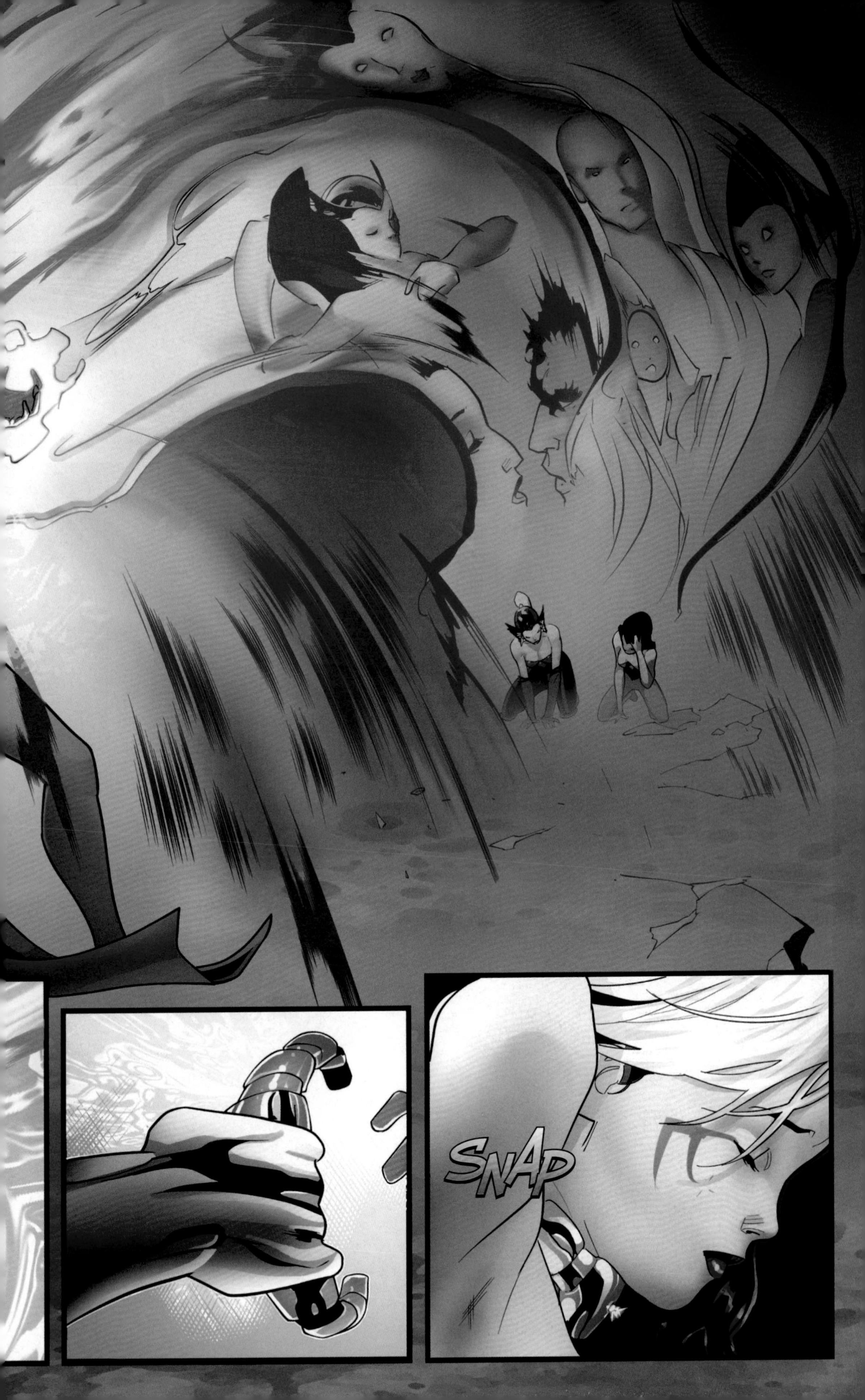
SNAP

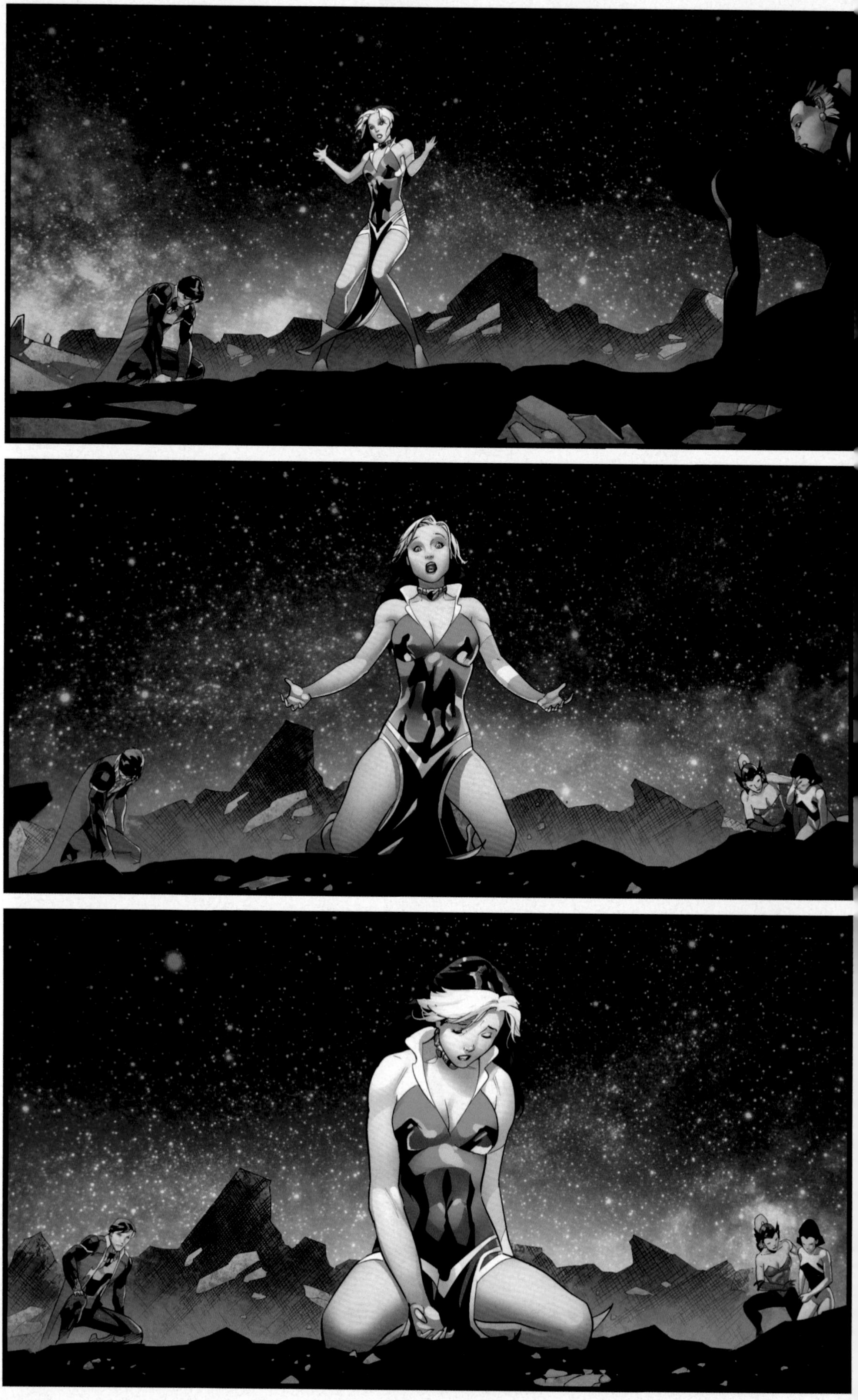

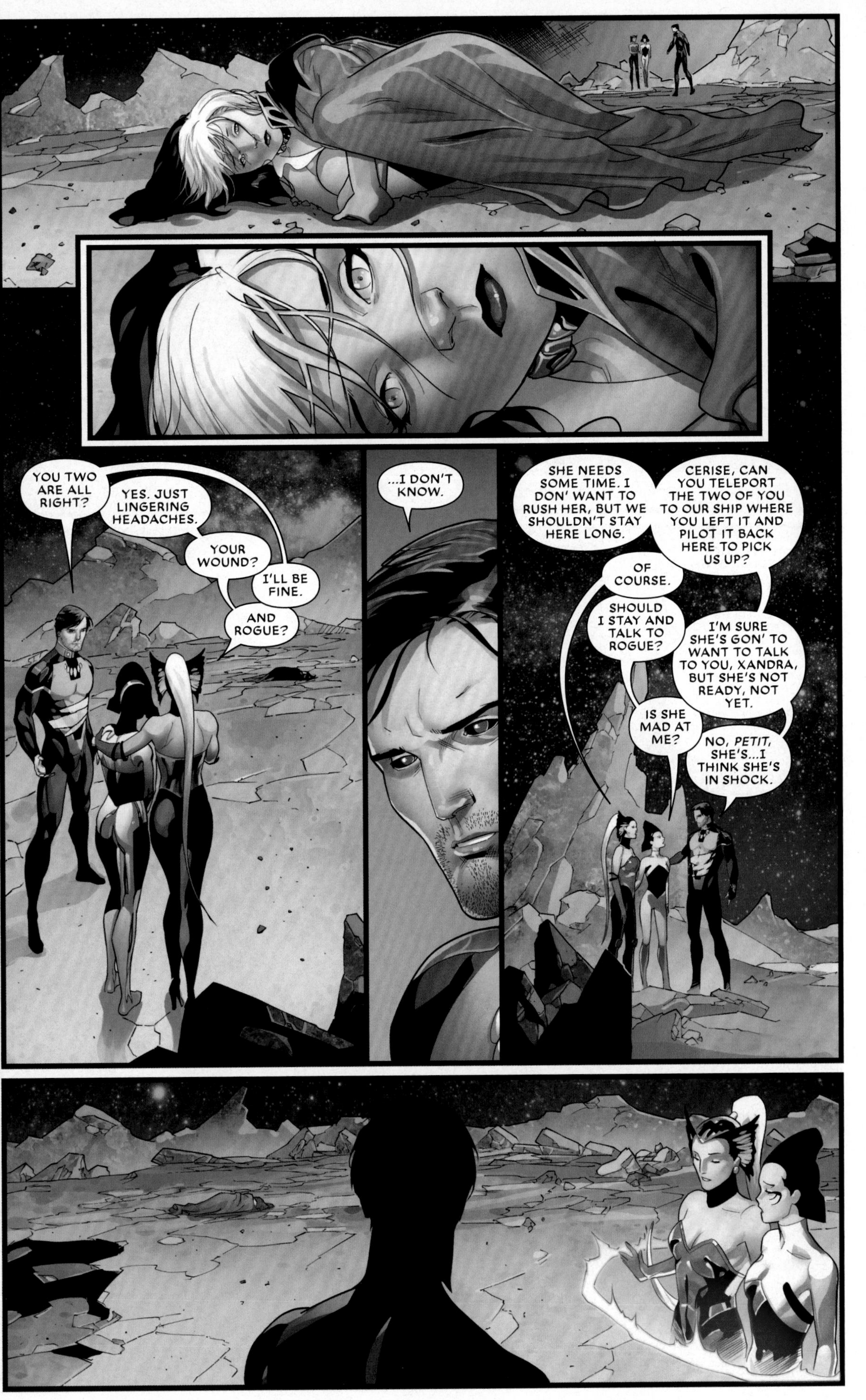
YOU TWO ARE ALL RIGHT?
YES. JUST LINGERING HEADACHES.
YOUR WOUND?
I'LL BE FINE.
AND ROGUE?
...I DON'T KNOW.
SHE NEEDS SOME TIME. I DON' WANT TO RUSH HER, BUT WE SHOULDN'T STAY HERE LONG.
CERISE, CAN YOU TELEPORT THE TWO OF YOU TO OUR SHIP WHERE YOU LEFT IT AND PILOT IT BACK HERE TO PICK US UP?
OF COURSE.
SHOULD I STAY AND TALK TO ROGUE?
I'M SURE SHE'S GON' TO WANT TO TALK TO YOU, XANDRA, BUT SHE'S NOT READY, NOT YET.
IS SHE MAD AT ME?
NO, *PETIT*, SHE'S...I THINK SHE'S IN SHOCK.

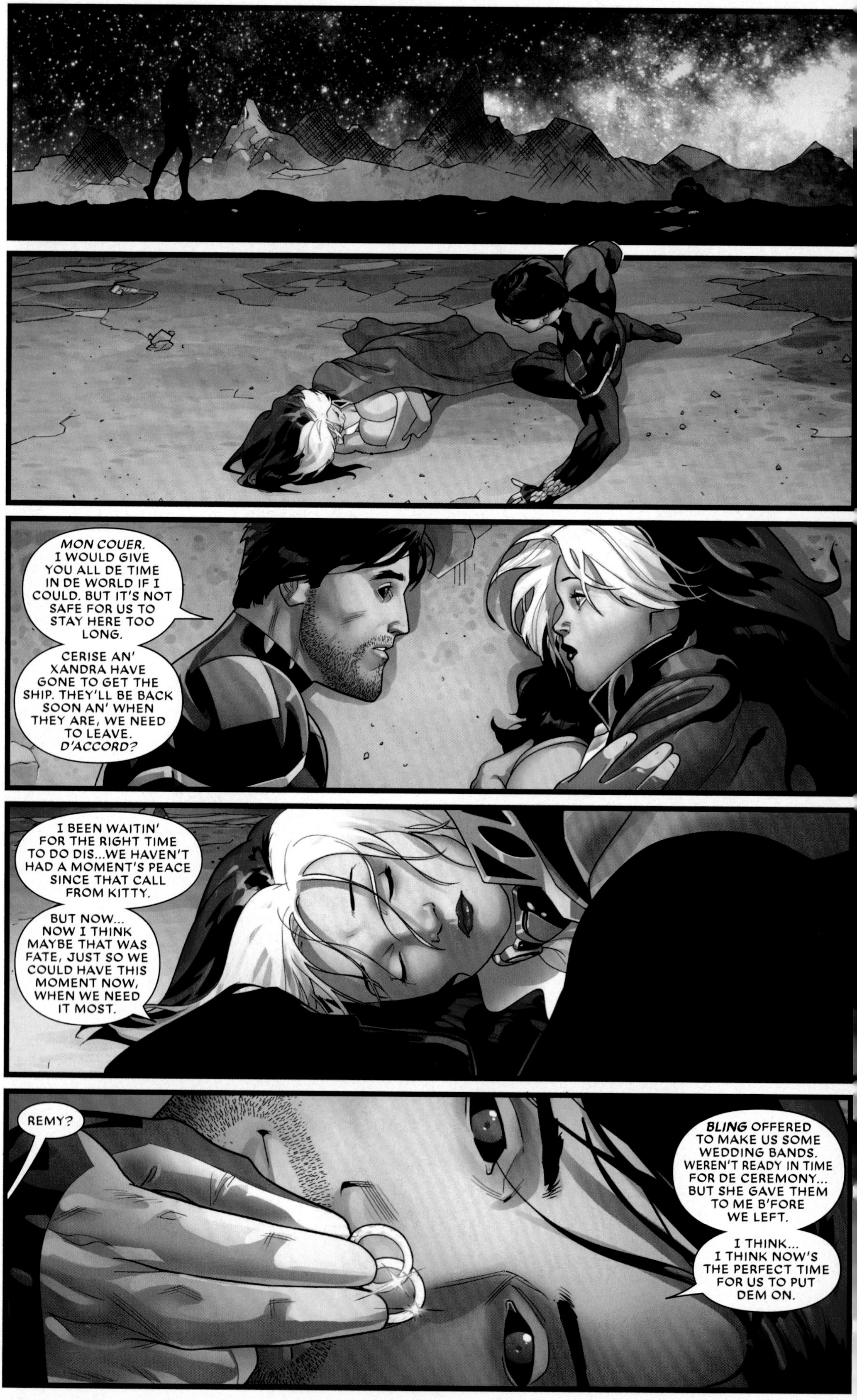
MON COUER. I WOULD GIVE YOU ALL DE TIME IN DE WORLD IF I COULD. BUT IT'S NOT SAFE FOR US TO STAY HERE TOO LONG.
CERISE AN' XANDRA HAVE GONE TO GET THE SHIP. THEY'LL BE BACK SOON AN' WHEN THEY ARE, WE NEED TO LEAVE. D'ACCORD?
I BEEN WAITIN' FOR THE RIGHT TIME TO DO DIS...WE HAVEN'T HAD A MOMENT'S PEACE SINCE THAT CALL FROM KITTY.
BUT NOW... NOW I THINK MAYBE THAT WAS FATE, JUST SO WE COULD HAVE THIS MOMENT NOW, WHEN WE NEED IT MOST.
REMY?
BLING OFFERED TO MAKE US SOME WEDDING BANDS. WEREN'T READY IN TIME FOR DE CEREMONY... BUT SHE GAVE THEM TO ME B'FORE WE LEFT.
I THINK... I THINK NOW'S THE PERFECT TIME FOR US TO PUT DEM ON.

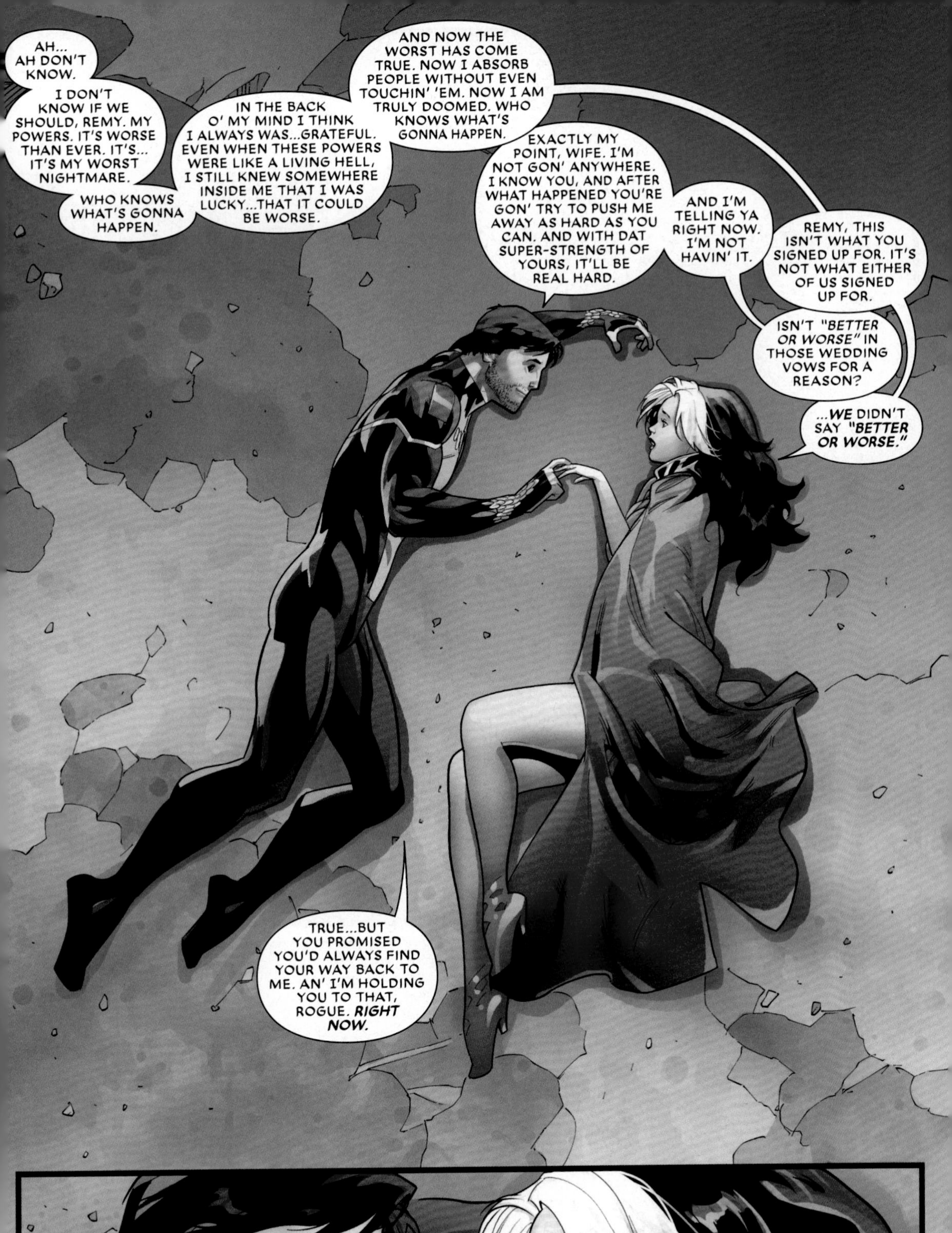
AH... AH DON'T KNOW.
I DON'T KNOW IF WE SHOULD, REMY. MY POWERS. IT'S WORSE THAN EVER. IT'S... IT'S MY WORST NIGHTMARE.
WHO KNOWS WHAT'S GONNA HAPPEN.
IN THE BACK O' MY MIND I THINK I ALWAYS WAS...GRATEFUL. EVEN WHEN THESE POWERS WERE LIKE A LIVING HELL, I STILL KNEW SOMEWHERE INSIDE ME THAT I WAS LUCKY...THAT IT COULD BE WORSE.
AND NOW THE WORST HAS COME TRUE. NOW I ABSORB PEOPLE WITHOUT EVEN TOUCHIN' 'EM. NOW I AM TRULY DOOMED. WHO KNOWS WHAT'S GONNA HAPPEN.
EXACTLY MY POINT, WIFE. I'M NOT GON' ANYWHERE. I KNOW YOU, AND AFTER WHAT HAPPENED YOU'RE GON' TRY TO PUSH ME AWAY AS HARD AS YOU CAN. AND WITH DAT SUPER-STRENGTH OF YOURS, IT'LL BE REAL HARD.
AND I'M TELLING YA RIGHT NOW. I'M NOT HAVIN' IT.
REMY, THIS ISN'T WHAT YOU SIGNED UP FOR. IT'S NOT WHAT EITHER OF US SIGNED UP FOR.
ISN'T *"BETTER OR WORSE"* IN THOSE WEDDING VOWS FOR A REASON?
...***WE*** DIDN'T SAY ***"BETTER OR WORSE."***
TRUE...BUT YOU PROMISED YOU'D ALWAYS FIND YOUR WAY BACK TO ME. AN' I'M HOLDING YOU TO THAT, ROGUE. ***RIGHT NOW.***
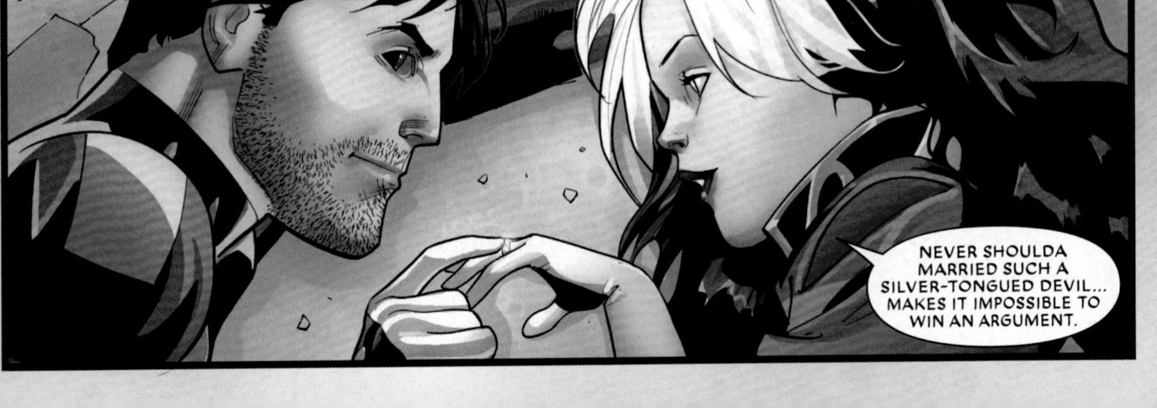
NEVER SHOULDA MARRIED SUCH A SILVER-TONGUED DEVIL... MAKES IT IMPOSSIBLE TO WIN AN ARGUMENT.

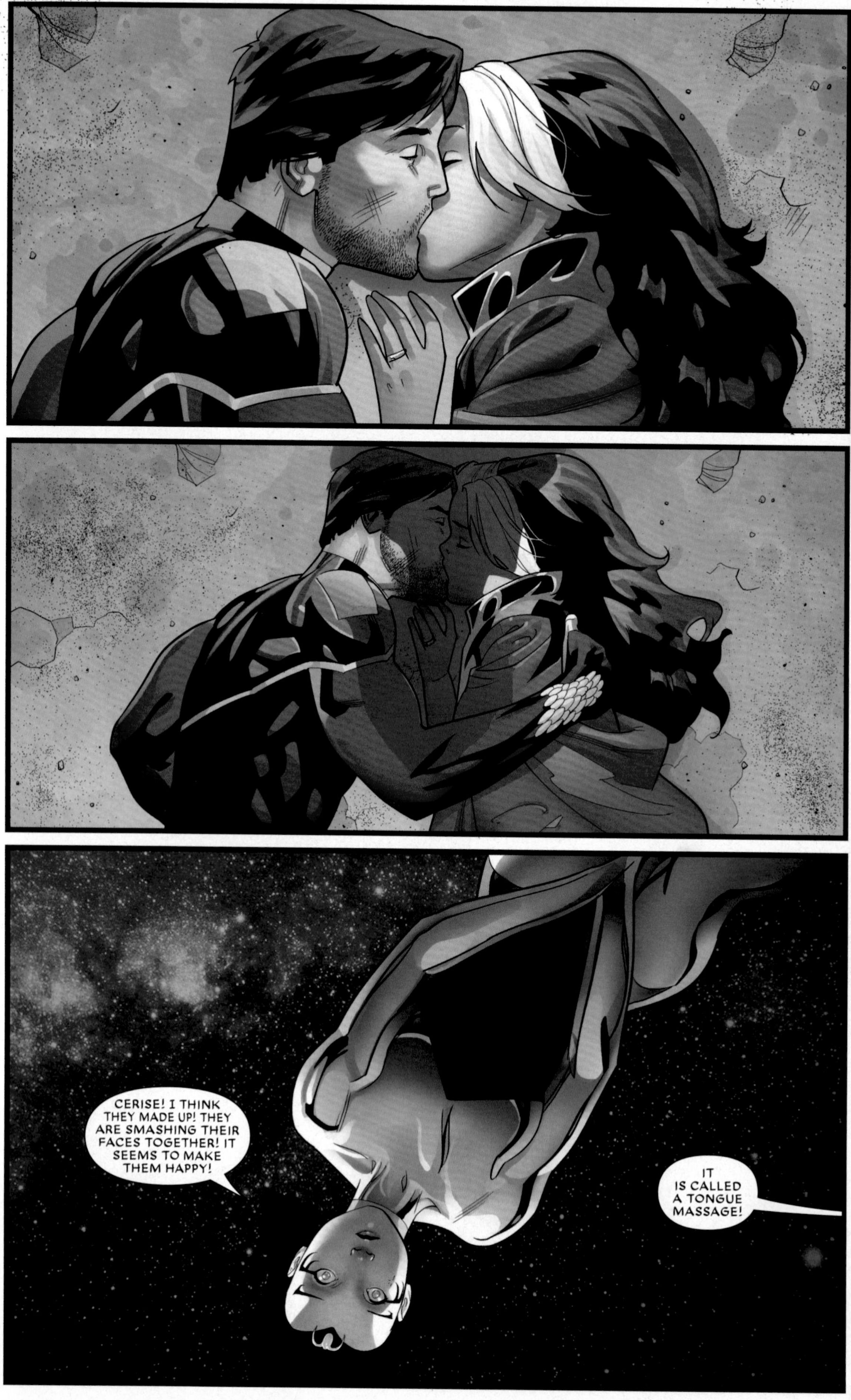
CERISE! I THINK THEY MADE UP! THEY ARE SMASHING THEIR FACES TOGETHER! IT SEEMS TO MAKE THEM HAPPY!
IT IS CALLED A TONGUE MASSAGE!

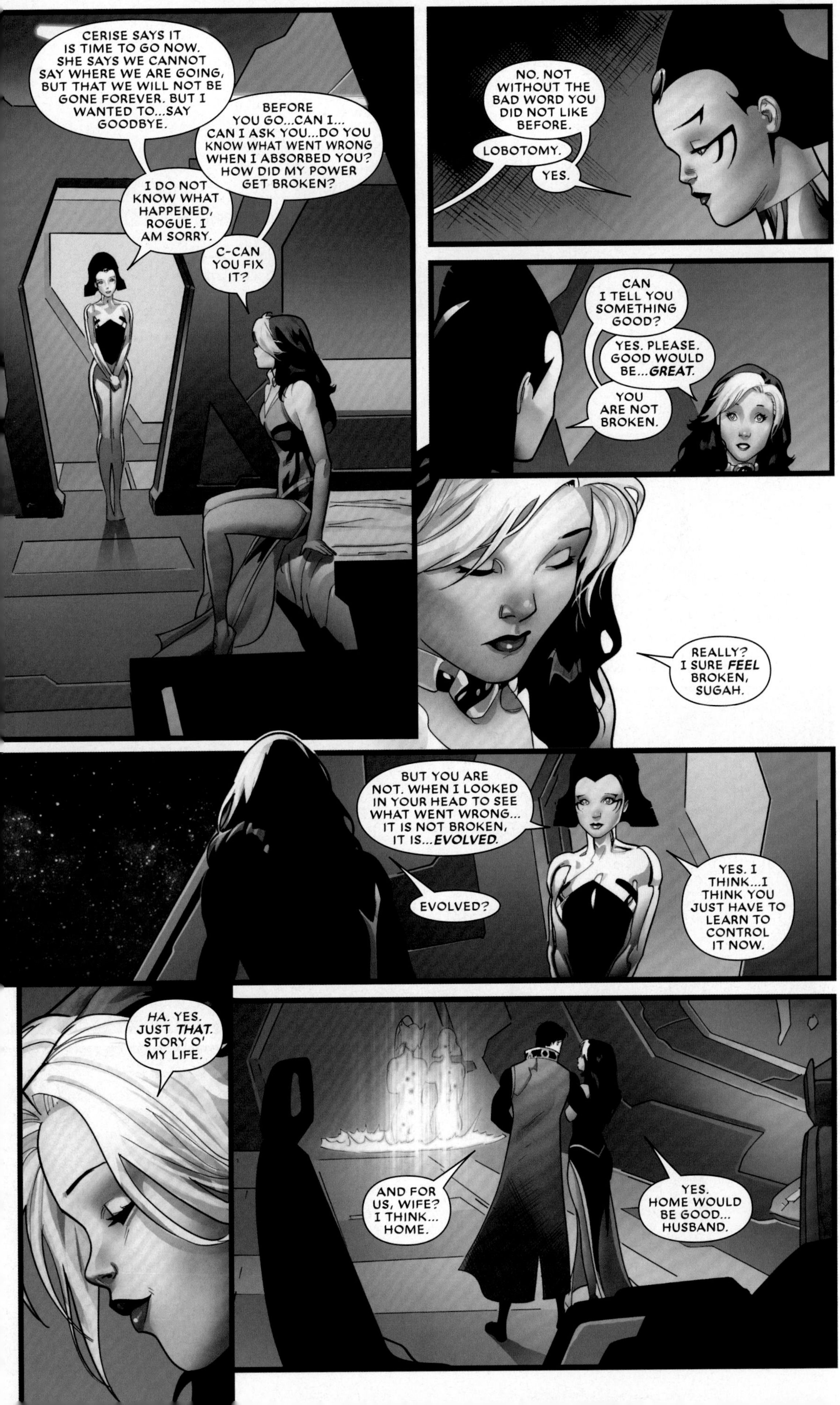
CERISE SAYS IT IS TIME TO GO NOW. SHE SAYS WE CANNOT SAY WHERE WE ARE GOING, BUT THAT WE WILL NOT BE GONE FOREVER. BUT I WANTED TO...SAY GOODBYE.
BEFORE YOU GO...CAN I... CAN I ASK YOU...DO YOU KNOW WHAT WENT WRONG WHEN I ABSORBED YOU? HOW DID MY POWER GET BROKEN?
I DO NOT KNOW WHAT HAPPENED, ROGUE. I AM SORRY.
C-CAN YOU FIX IT?
NO. NOT WITHOUT THE BAD WORD YOU DID NOT LIKE BEFORE.
LOBOTOMY.
YES.
CAN I TELL YOU SOMETHING GOOD?
YES. PLEASE. GOOD WOULD BE...*GREAT*.
YOU ARE NOT BROKEN.
REALLY? I SURE *FEEL* BROKEN, SUGAH.
BUT YOU ARE NOT. WHEN I LOOKED IN YOUR HEAD TO SEE WHAT WENT WRONG... IT IS NOT BROKEN, IT IS...*EVOLVED*.
EVOLVED?
YES. I THINK...I THINK YOU JUST HAVE TO LEARN TO CONTROL IT NOW.
HA. YES. JUST *THAT*. STORY O' MY LIFE.
AND FOR US, WIFE? I THINK... HOME.
YES. HOME WOULD BE GOOD... HUSBAND.

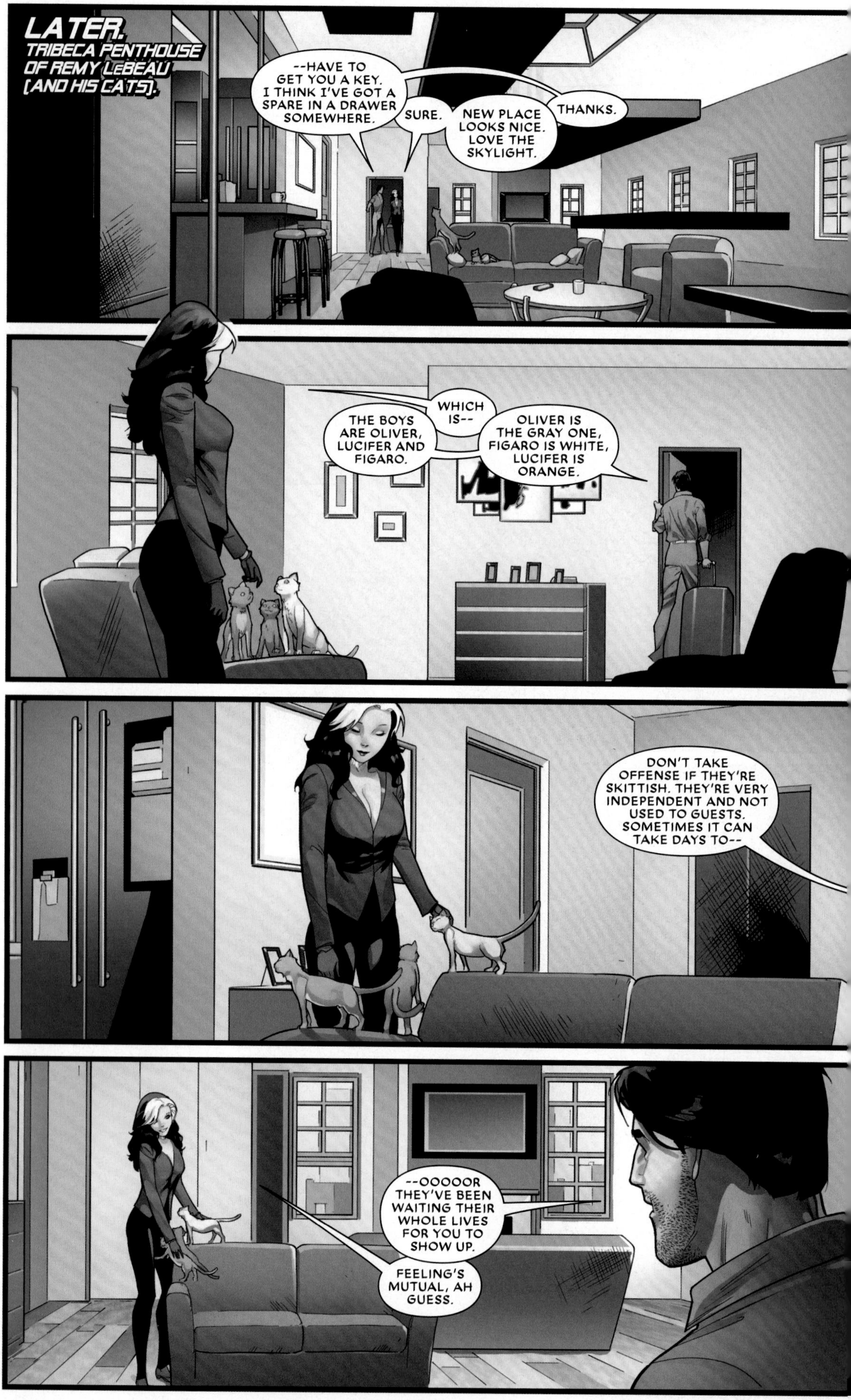
LATER. TRIBECA PENTHOUSE OF REMY LeBEAU [AND HIS CATS].
--HAVE TO GET YOU A KEY. I THINK I'VE GOT A SPARE IN A DRAWER SOMEWHERE.
THANKS.
SURE.
NEW PLACE LOOKS NICE. LOVE THE SKYLIGHT.
THE BOYS ARE OLIVER, LUCIFER AND FIGARO.
WHICH IS--
OLIVER IS THE GRAY ONE, FIGARO IS WHITE, LUCIFER IS ORANGE.
DON'T TAKE OFFENSE IF THEY'RE SKITTISH. THEY'RE VERY INDEPENDENT AND NOT USED TO GUESTS. SOMETIMES IT CAN TAKE DAYS TO--
--OOOOOR THEY'VE BEEN WAITING THEIR WHOLE LIVES FOR YOU TO SHOW UP.
FEELING'S MUTUAL, AH GUESS.

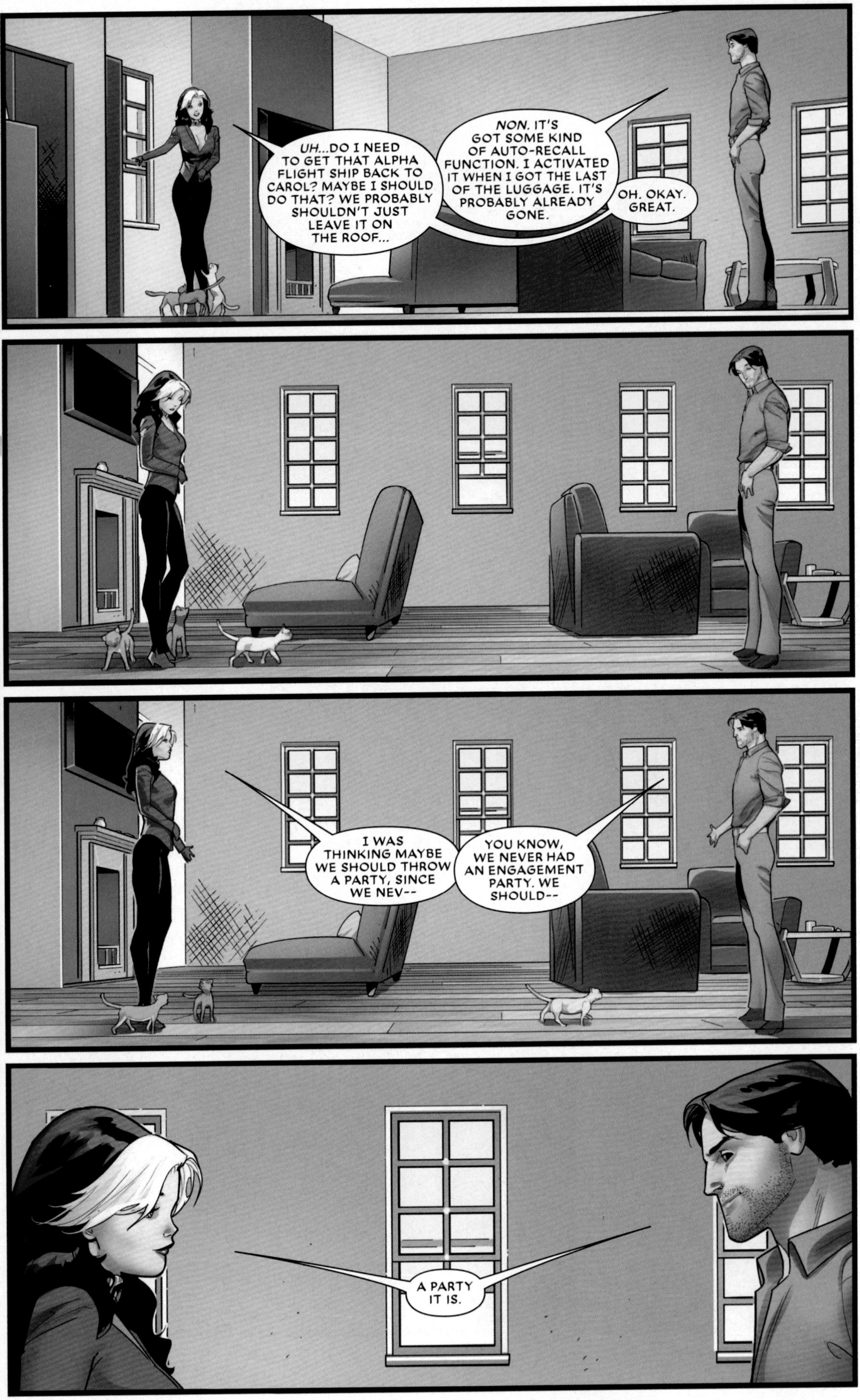
UH...DO I NEED TO GET THAT ALPHA FLIGHT SHIP BACK TO CAROL? MAYBE I SHOULD DO THAT? WE PROBABLY SHOULDN'T JUST LEAVE IT ON THE ROOF...
NON. IT'S GOT SOME KIND OF AUTO-RECALL FUNCTION. I ACTIVATED IT WHEN I GOT THE LAST OF THE LUGGAGE. IT'S PROBABLY ALREADY GONE.
OH. OKAY. GREAT.
I WAS THINKING MAYBE WE SHOULD THROW A PARTY, SINCE WE NEV--
YOU KNOW, WE NEVER HAD AN ENGAGEMENT PARTY. WE SHOULD--
A PARTY IT IS.

6

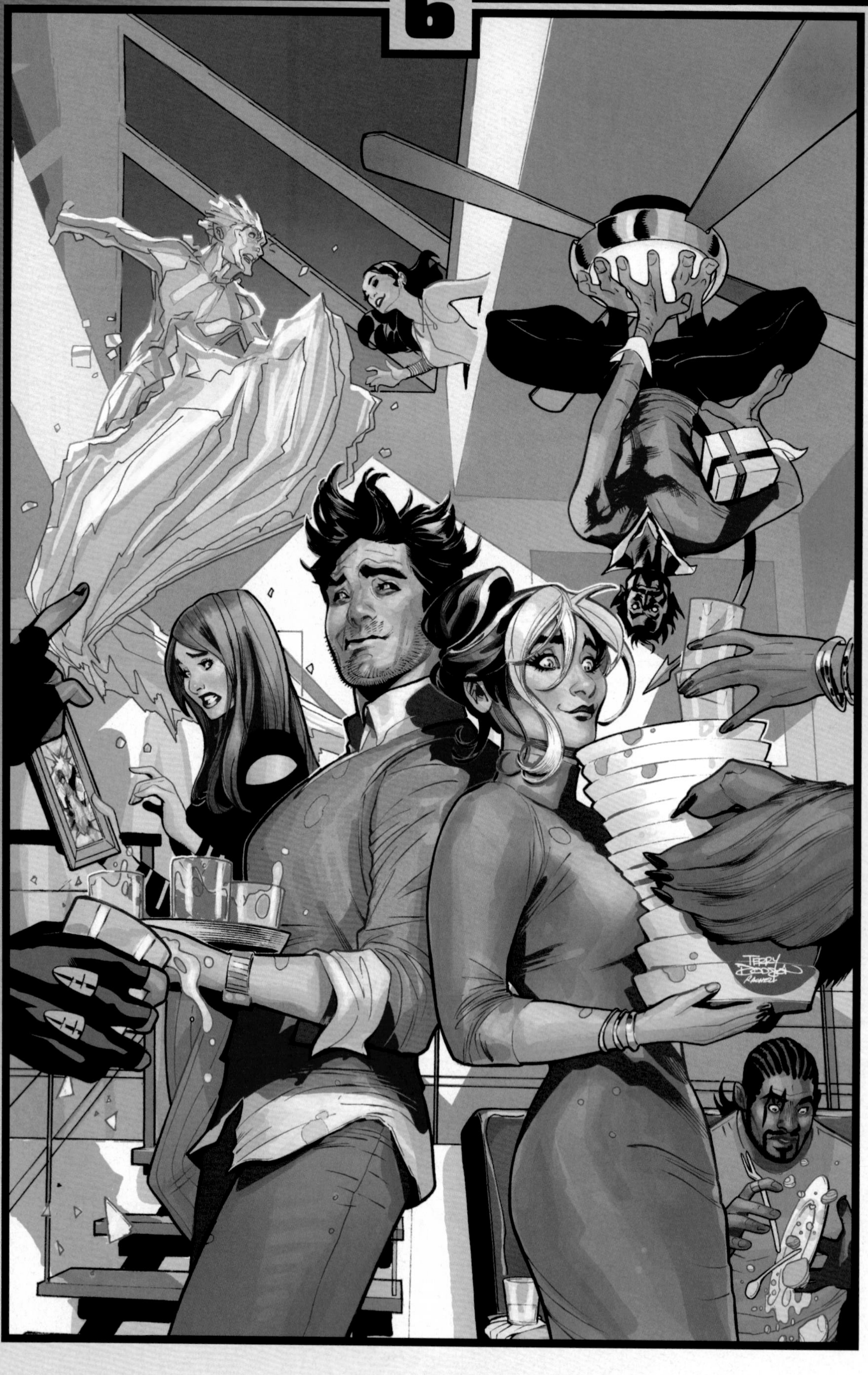

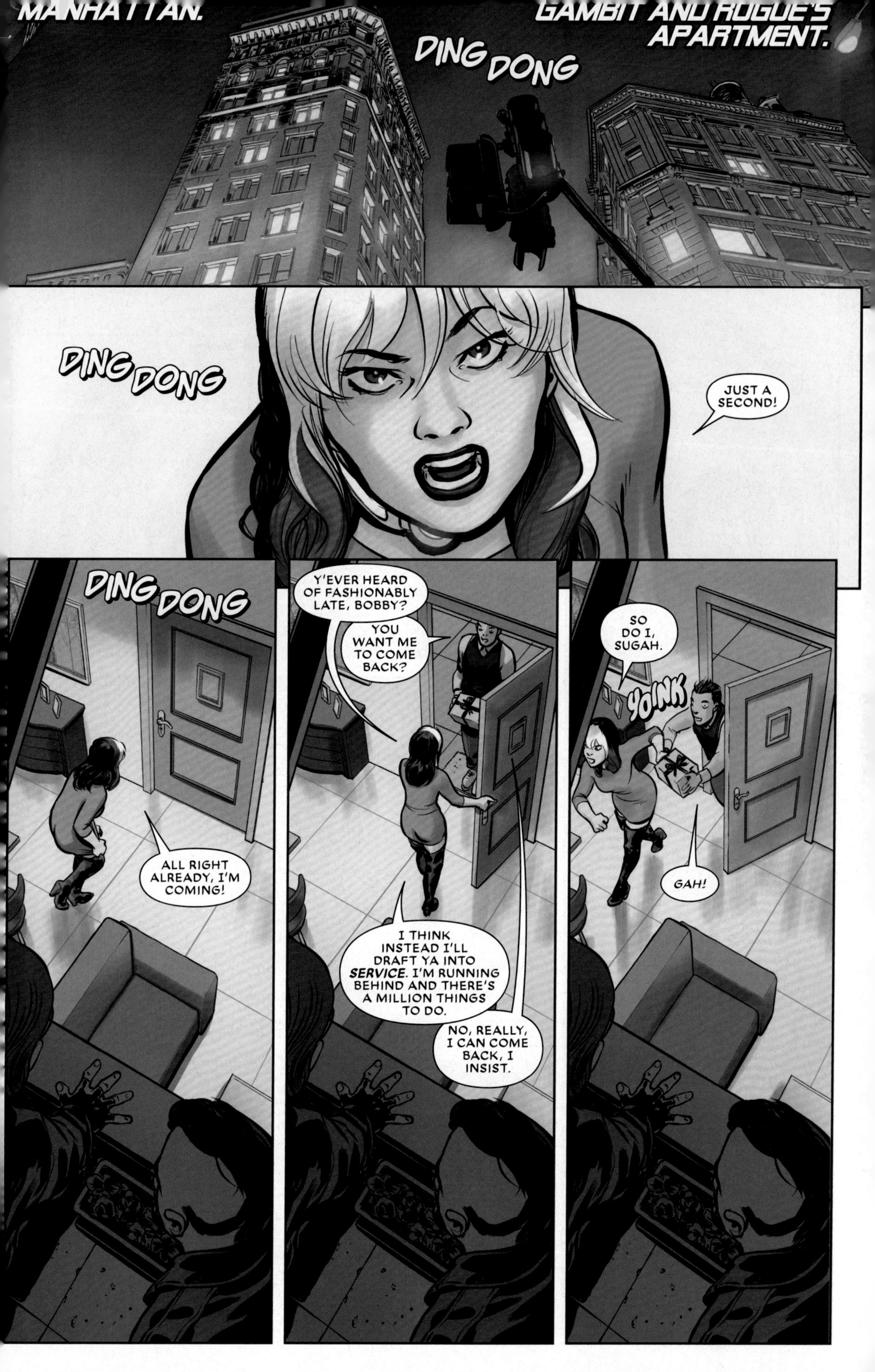

MANHATTAN.
GAMBIT AND ROGUE'S APARTMENT.
DING DONG
DING DONG
JUST A SECOND!
DING DONG
ALL RIGHT ALREADY, I'M COMING!
Y'EVER HEARD OF FASHIONABLY LATE, BOBBY?
YOU WANT ME TO COME BACK?
I THINK INSTEAD I'LL DRAFT YA INTO SERVICE. I'M RUNNING BEHIND AND THERE'S A MILLION THINGS TO DO.
NO, REALLY, I CAN COME BACK, I INSIST.
SO DO I, SUGAH.
YOINK
GAH!

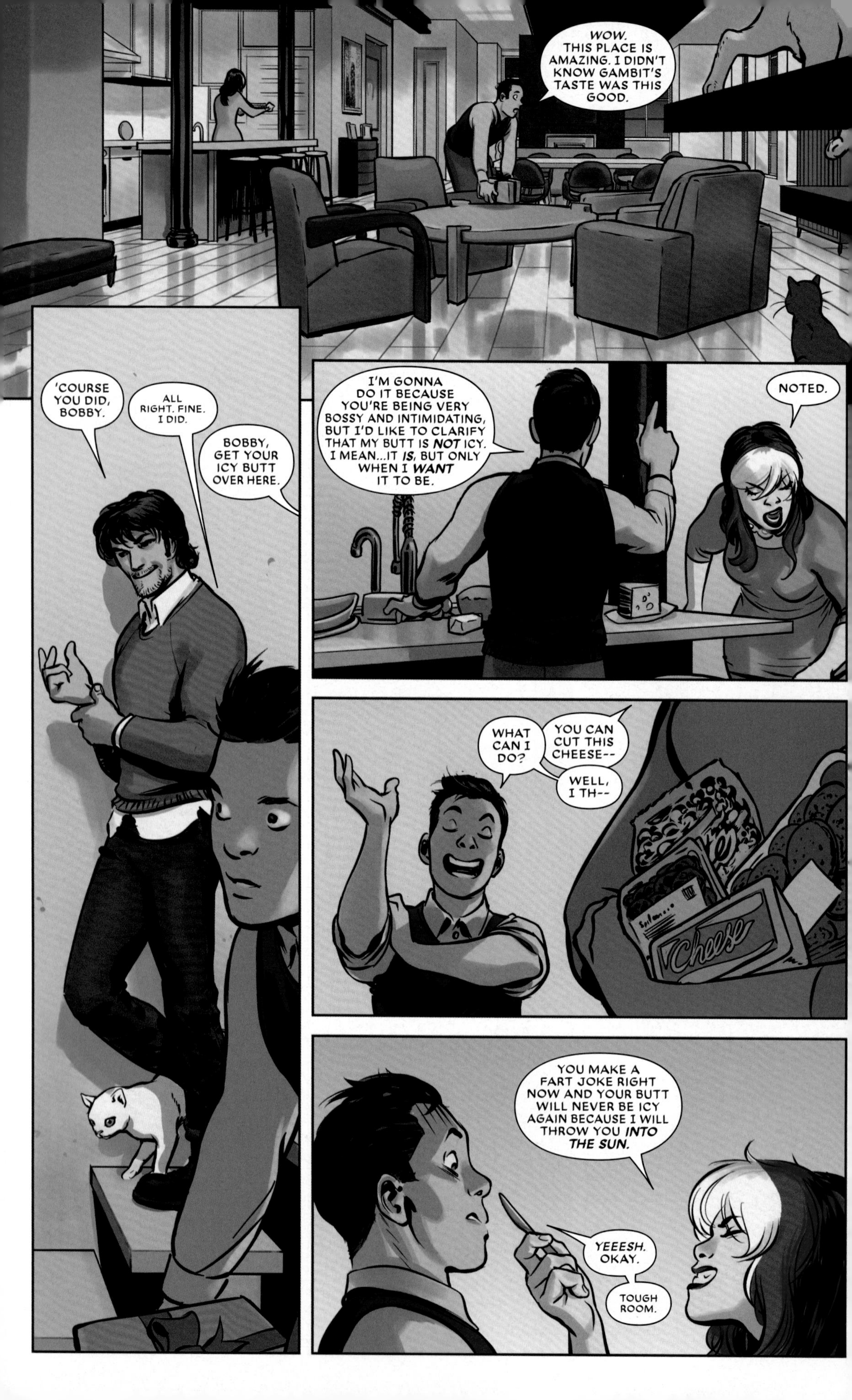
WOW. THIS PLACE IS AMAZING. I DIDN'T KNOW GAMBIT'S TASTE WAS THIS GOOD.
'COURSE YOU DID, BOBBY.
ALL RIGHT. FINE. I DID.
BOBBY, GET YOUR ICY BUTT OVER HERE.
I'M GONNA DO IT BECAUSE YOU'RE BEING VERY BOSSY AND INTIMIDATING, BUT I'D LIKE TO CLARIFY THAT MY BUTT IS *NOT* ICY. I MEAN...IT *IS*, BUT ONLY WHEN I *WANT* IT TO BE.
NOTED.
WHAT CAN I DO?
YOU CAN CUT THIS CHEESE--
WELL, I TH--
Cheese
YOU MAKE A FART JOKE RIGHT NOW AND YOUR BUTT WILL NEVER BE ICY AGAIN BECAUSE I WILL THROW YOU *INTO THE SUN.*
YEEESH. OKAY.
TOUGH ROOM.

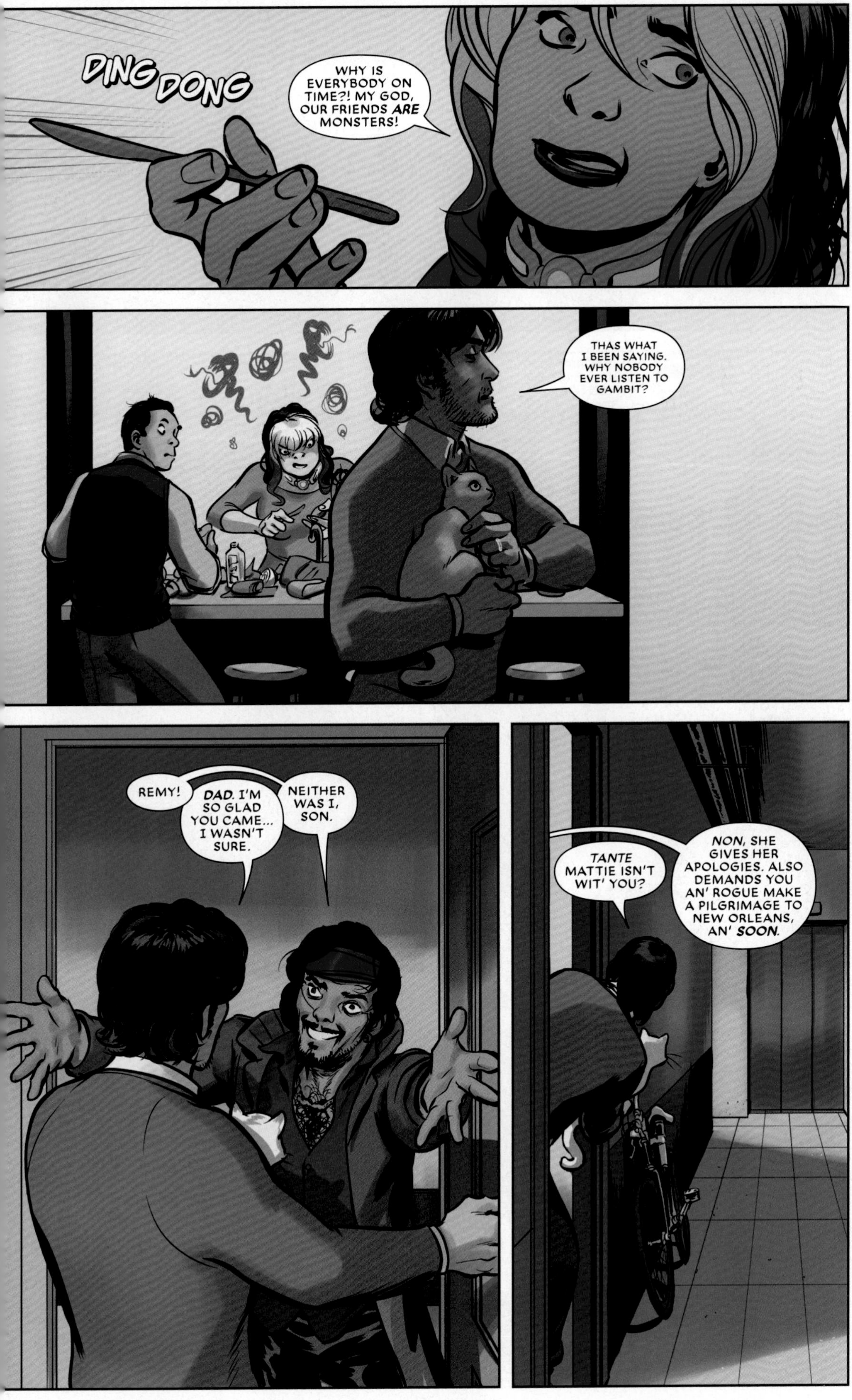
DING DONG
WHY IS EVERYBODY ON TIME?! MY GOD, OUR FRIENDS *ARE* MONSTERS!
THAS WHAT I BEEN SAYING. WHY NOBODY EVER LISTEN TO GAMBIT?
REMY!
DAD. I'M SO GLAD YOU CAME... I WASN'T SURE.
NEITHER WAS I, SON.
TANTE MATTIE ISN'T WIT' YOU?
NON, SHE GIVES HER APOLOGIES. ALSO DEMANDS YOU AN' ROGUE MAKE A PILGRIMAGE TO NEW ORLEANS, AN' ***SOON***.

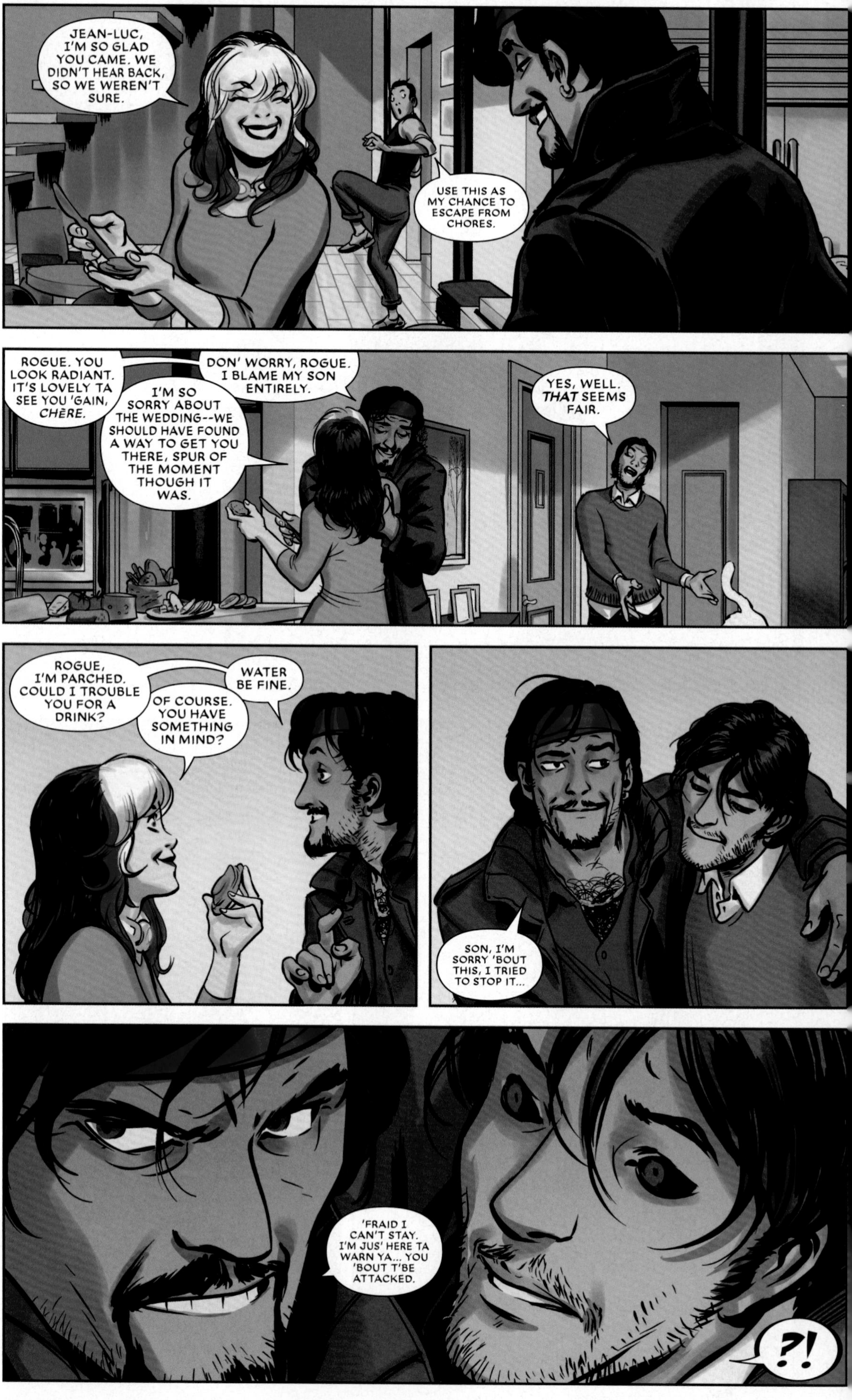
JEAN-LUC, I'M SO GLAD YOU CAME. WE DIDN'T HEAR BACK, SO WE WEREN'T SURE.
USE THIS AS MY CHANCE TO ESCAPE FROM CHORES.
ROGUE. YOU LOOK RADIANT. IT'S LOVELY TA SEE YOU 'GAIN, *CHÈRE.*
I'M SO SORRY ABOUT THE WEDDING--WE SHOULD HAVE FOUND A WAY TO GET YOU THERE, SPUR OF THE MOMENT THOUGH IT WAS.
DON' WORRY, ROGUE. I BLAME MY SON ENTIRELY.
YES, WELL. *THAT* SEEMS FAIR.
ROGUE, I'M PARCHED. COULD I TROUBLE YOU FOR A DRINK?
OF COURSE. YOU HAVE SOMETHING IN MIND?
WATER BE FINE.
SON, I'M SORRY 'BOUT THIS, I TRIED TO STOP IT...
'FRAID I CAN'T STAY. I'M JUS' HERE TA WARN YA... YOU 'BOUT T'BE ATTACKED.
?!

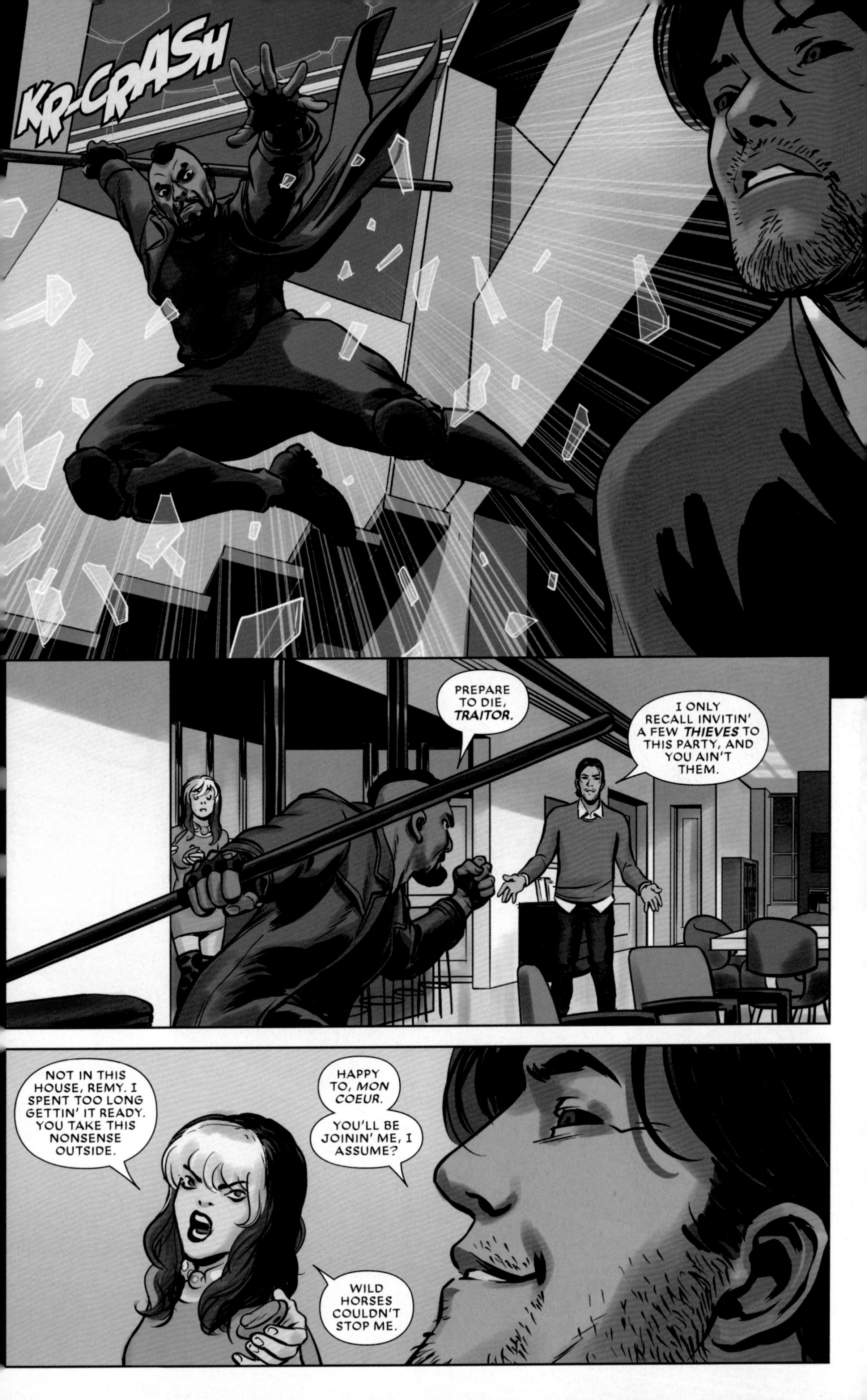
KR-CRASH
PREPARE TO DIE, *TRAITOR.*
I ONLY RECALL INVITIN' A FEW *THIEVES* TO THIS PARTY, AND YOU AIN'T THEM.
NOT IN THIS HOUSE, REMY. I SPENT TOO LONG GETTIN' IT READY. YOU TAKE THIS NONSENSE OUTSIDE.
HAPPY TO, *MON COEUR.*
YOU'LL BE JOININ' ME, I ASSUME?
WILD HORSES COULDN'T STOP ME.

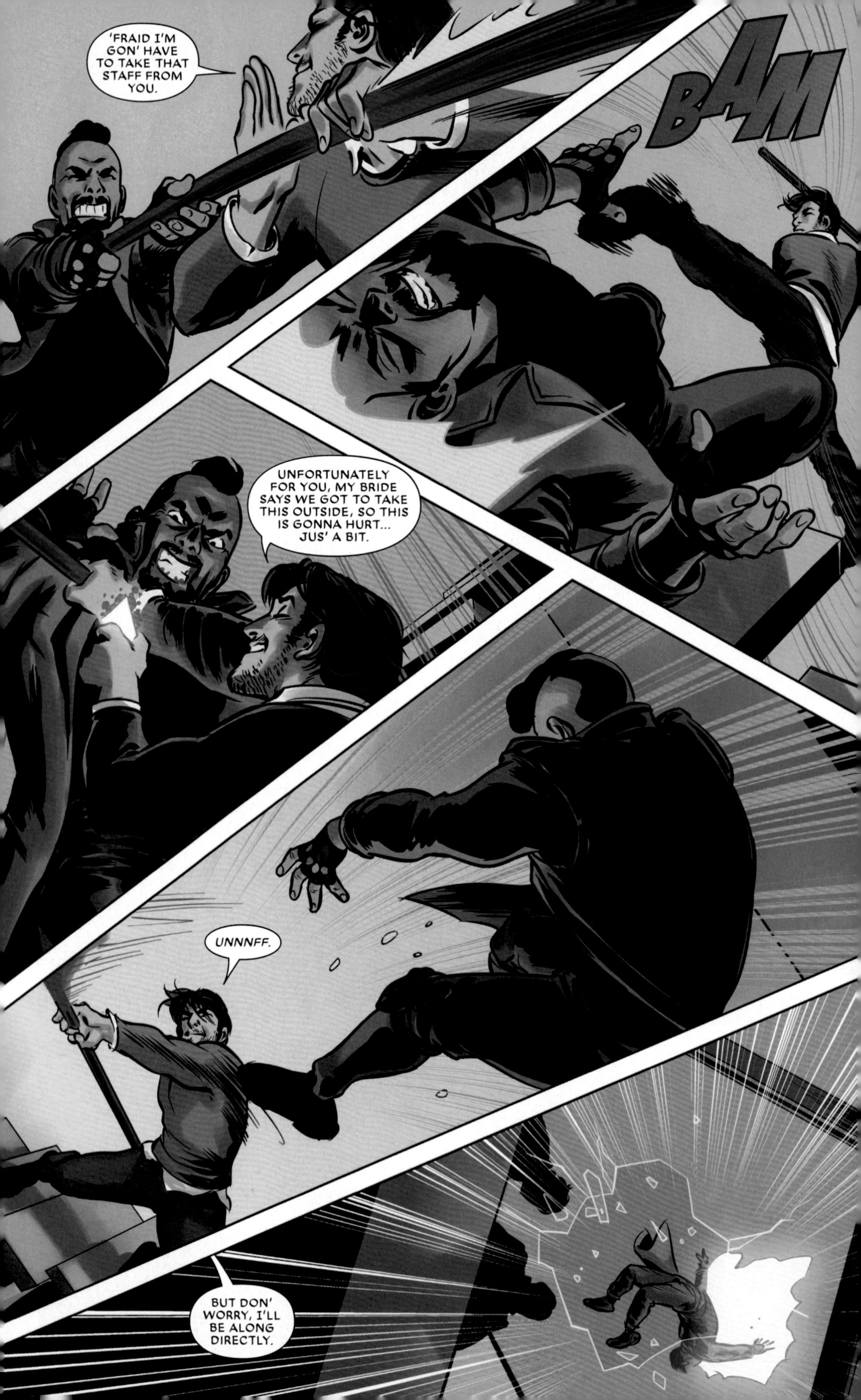
'FRAID I'M GON' HAVE TO TAKE THAT STAFF FROM YOU.
BAM
UNFORTUNATELY FOR YOU, MY BRIDE SAYS WE GOT TO TAKE THIS OUTSIDE, SO THIS IS GONNA HURT... JUS' A BIT.
UNNNFF.
BUT DON' WORRY, I'LL BE ALONG DIRECTLY.

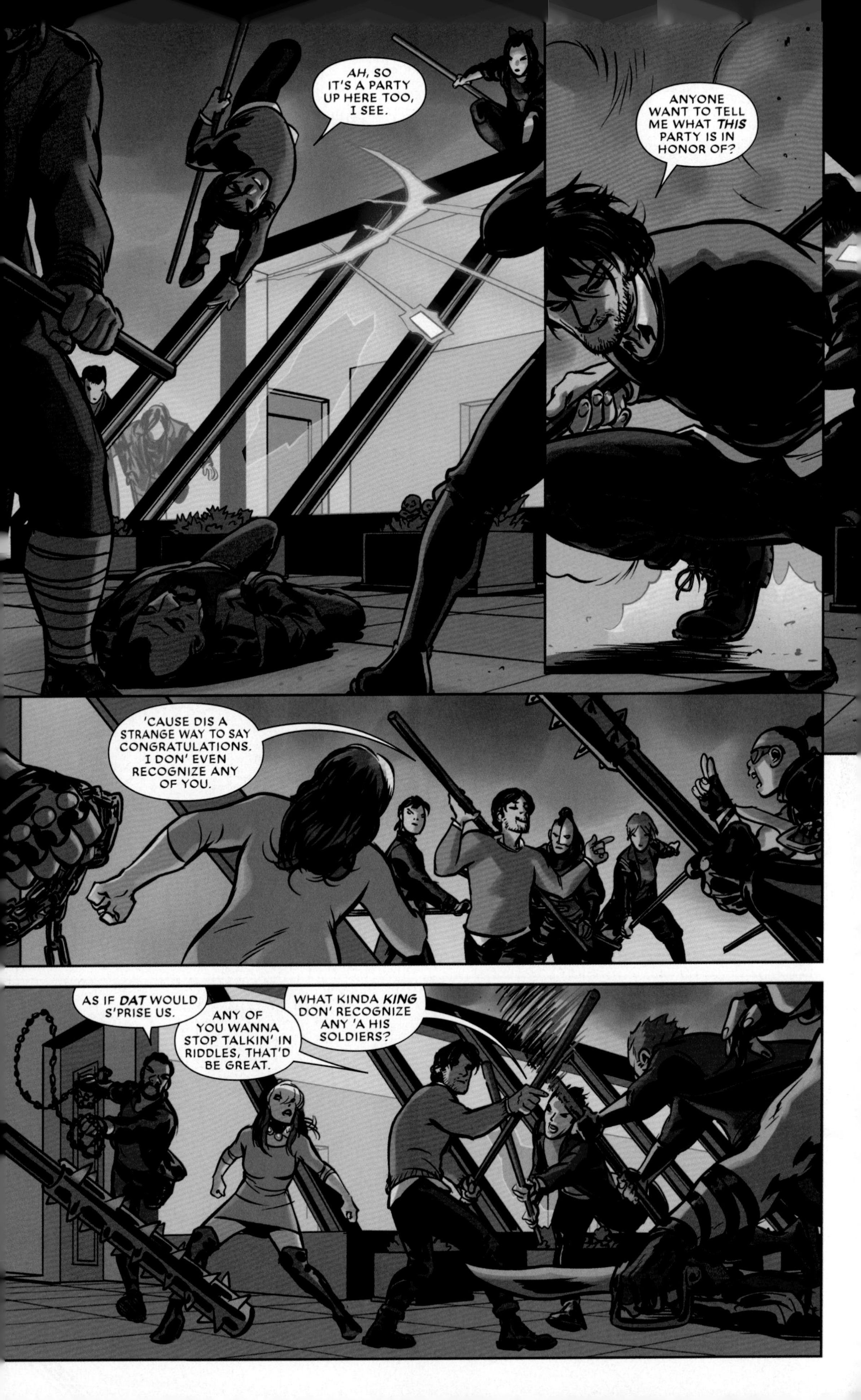
AH, SO IT'S A PARTY UP HERE TOO, I SEE.
ANYONE WANT TO TELL ME WHAT THIS PARTY IS IN HONOR OF?
'CAUSE DIS A STRANGE WAY TO SAY CONGRATULATIONS. I DON' EVEN RECOGNIZE ANY OF YOU.
AS IF DAT WOULD S'PRISE US.
ANY OF YOU WANNA STOP TALKIN' IN RIDDLES, THAT'D BE GREAT.
WHAT KINDA KING DON' RECOGNIZE ANY 'A HIS SOLDIERS?

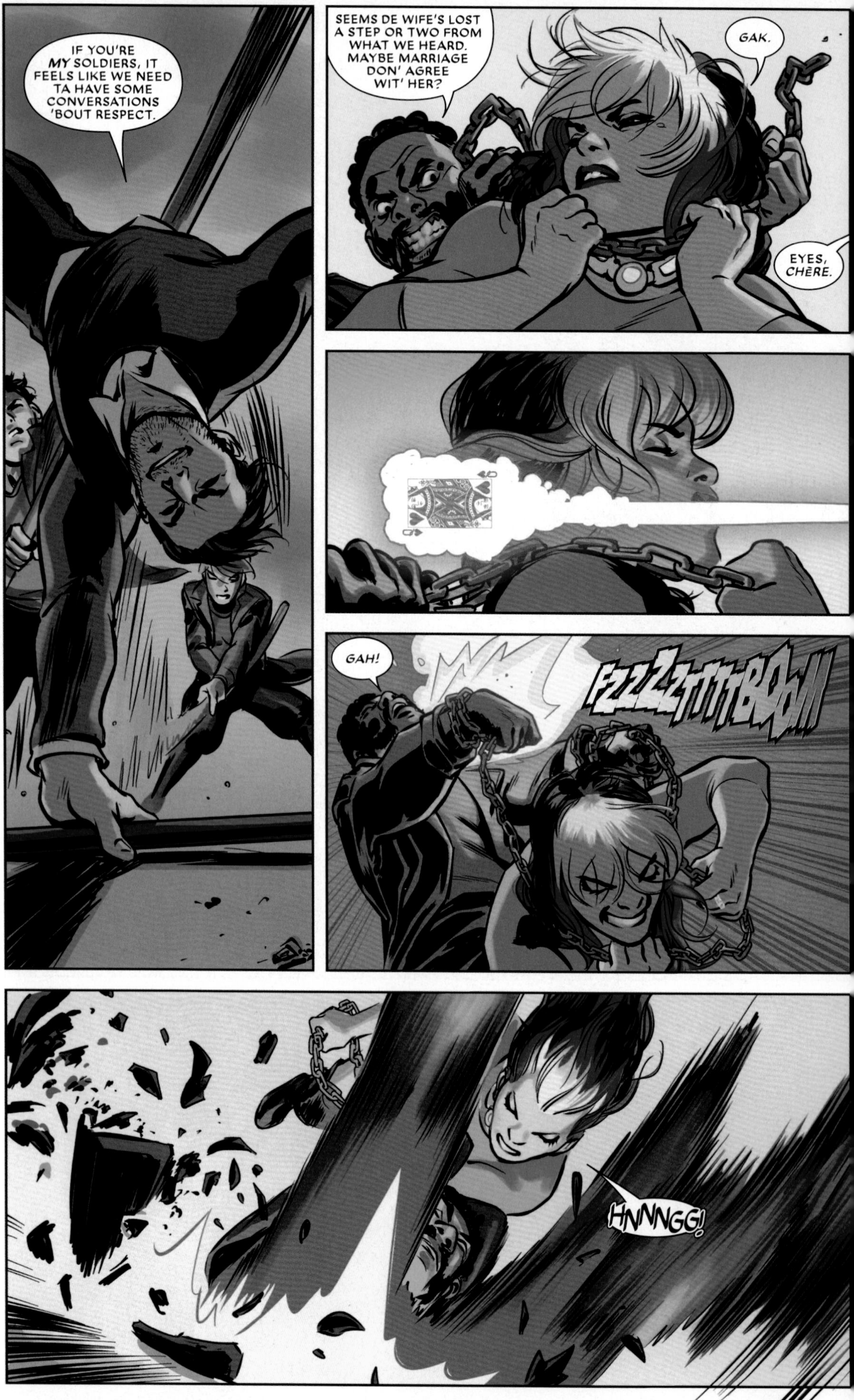
IF YOU'RE MY SOLDIERS, IT FEELS LIKE WE NEED TA HAVE SOME CONVERSATIONS 'BOUT RESPECT.
SEEMS DE WIFE'S LOST A STEP OR TWO FROM WHAT WE HEARD. MAYBE MARRIAGE DON' AGREE WIT' HER?
GAK.
EYES, CHÈRE.
GAH!
FZZZZTTTTBOOM
HNNNGG!

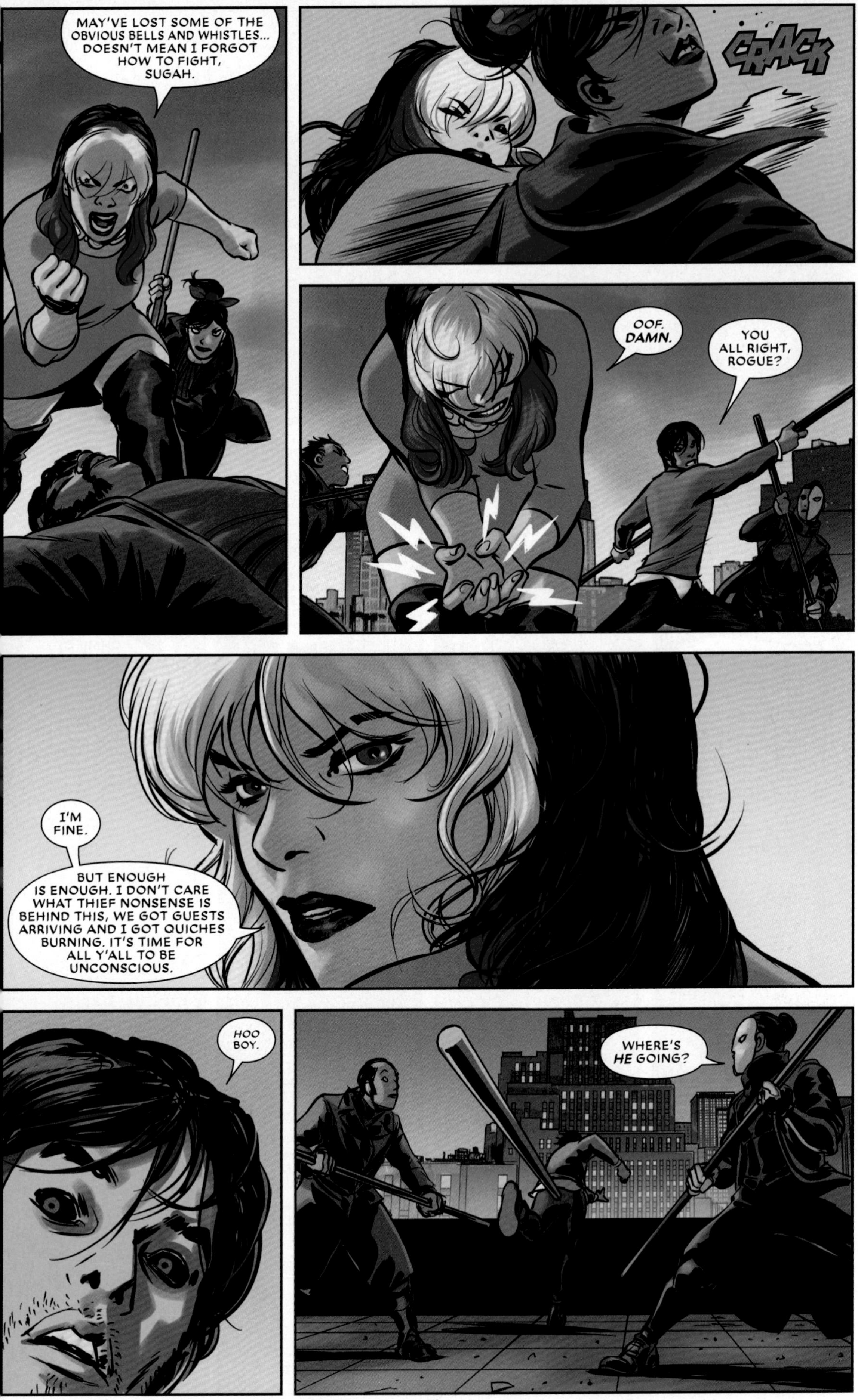
MAY'VE LOST SOME OF THE OBVIOUS BELLS AND WHISTLES... DOESN'T MEAN I FORGOT HOW TO FIGHT, SUGAH.
CRACK
OOF. DAMN.
YOU ALL RIGHT, ROGUE?
I'M FINE.
BUT ENOUGH IS ENOUGH. I DON'T CARE WHAT THIEF NONSENSE IS BEHIND THIS, WE GOT GUESTS ARRIVING AND I GOT QUICHES BURNING. IT'S TIME FOR ALL Y'ALL TO BE UNCONSCIOUS.
HOO BOY.
WHERE'S HE GOING?

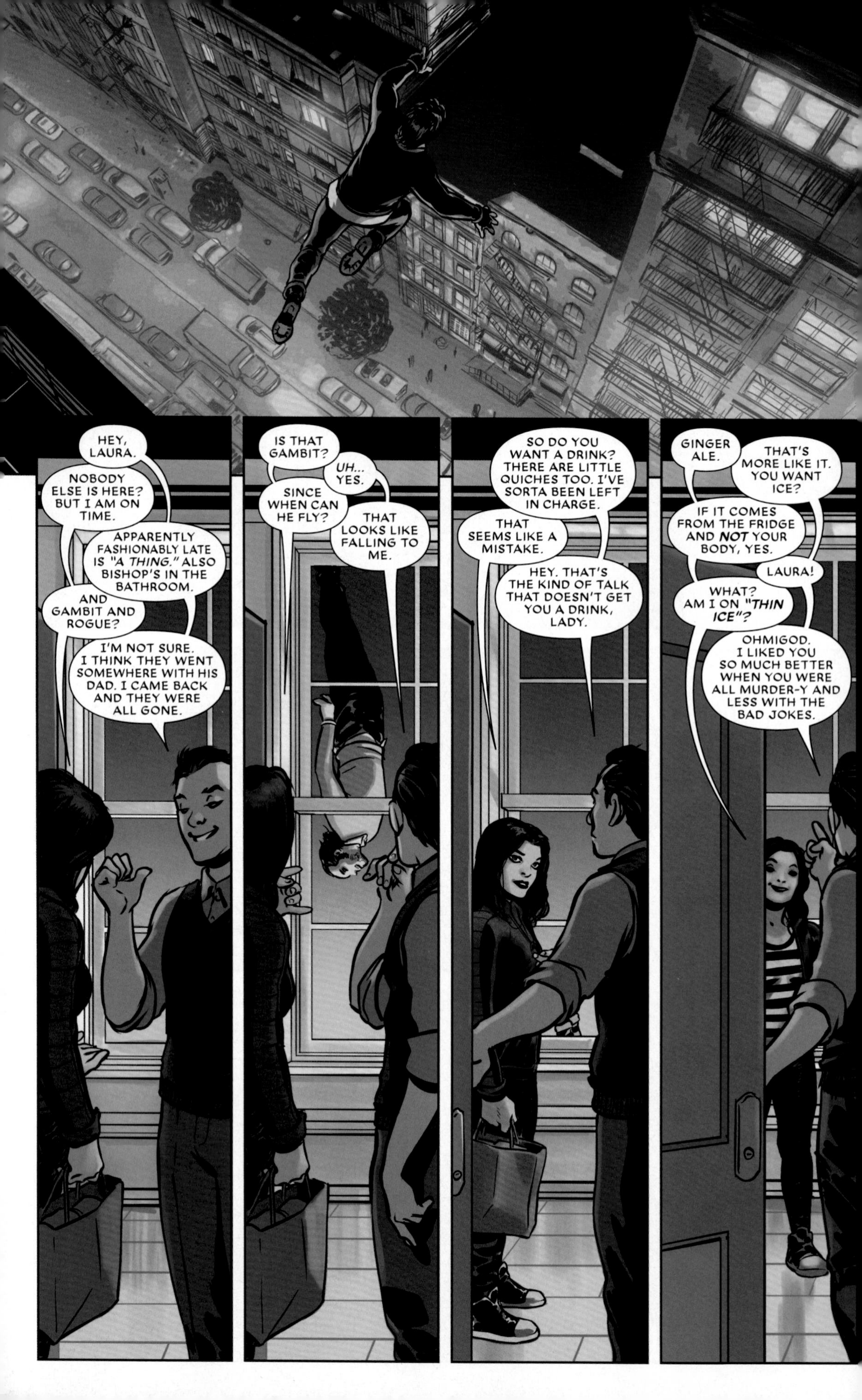
HEY, LAURA.
NOBODY ELSE IS HERE? BUT I AM ON TIME.
APPARENTLY FASHIONABLY LATE IS "A THING." ALSO BISHOP'S IN THE BATHROOM.
AND GAMBIT AND ROGUE?
I'M NOT SURE. I THINK THEY WENT SOMEWHERE WITH HIS DAD. I CAME BACK AND THEY WERE ALL GONE.
IS THAT GAMBIT?
UH... YES.
SINCE WHEN CAN HE FLY?
THAT LOOKS LIKE FALLING TO ME.
SO DO YOU WANT A DRINK? THERE ARE LITTLE QUICHES TOO. I'VE SORTA BEEN LEFT IN CHARGE.
THAT SEEMS LIKE A MISTAKE.
HEY. THAT'S THE KIND OF TALK THAT DOESN'T GET YOU A DRINK, LADY.
GINGER ALE.
THAT'S MORE LIKE IT. YOU WANT ICE?
IF IT COMES FROM THE FRIDGE AND NOT YOUR BODY, YES.
LAURA!
WHAT? AM I ON "THIN ICE"?
OHMIGOD. I LIKED YOU SO MUCH BETTER WHEN YOU WERE ALL MURDER-Y AND LESS WITH THE BAD JOKES.

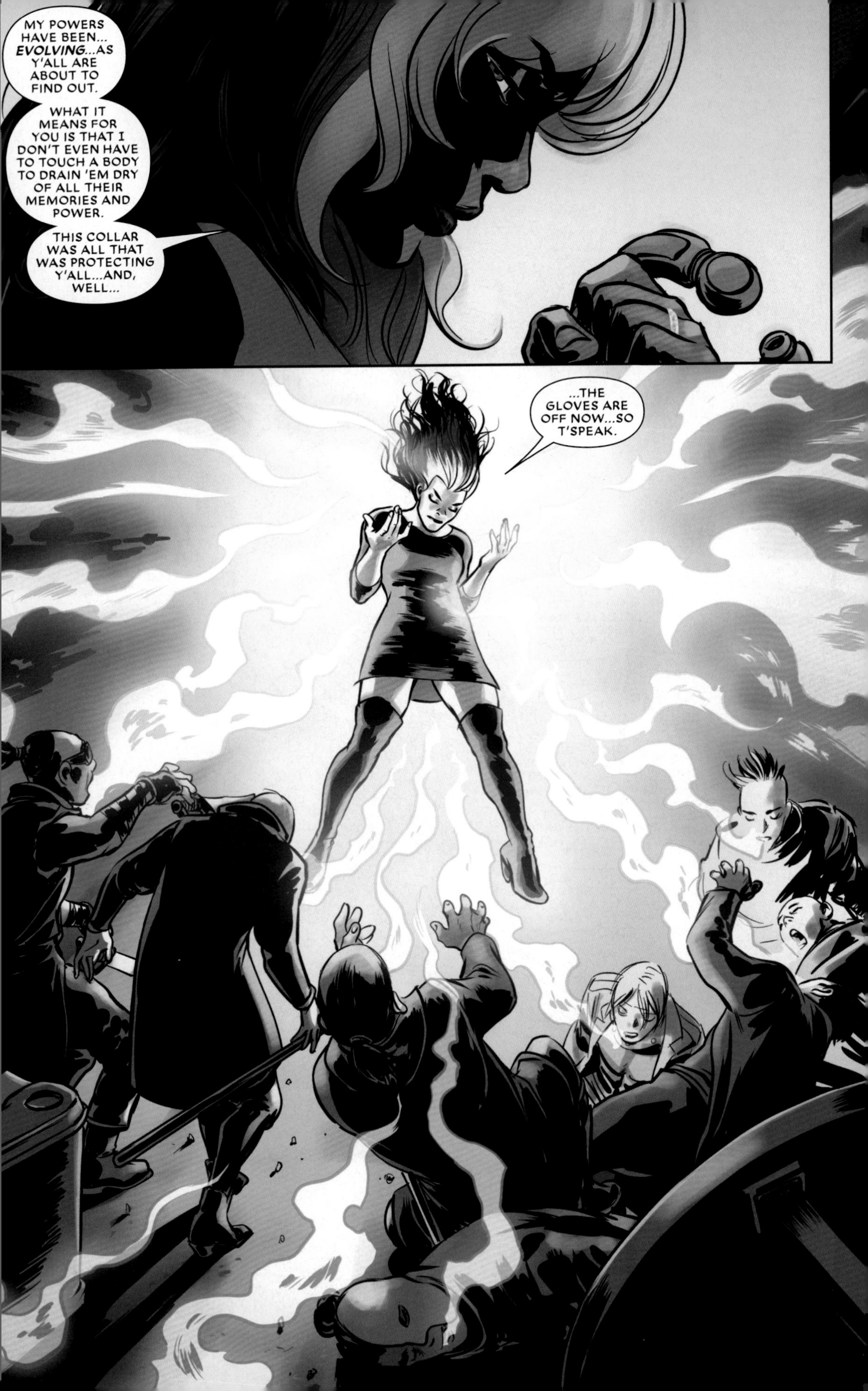

MY POWERS HAVE BEEN... *EVOLVING*...AS Y'ALL ARE ABOUT TO FIND OUT.
WHAT IT MEANS FOR YOU IS THAT I DON'T EVEN HAVE TO TOUCH A BODY TO DRAIN 'EM DRY OF ALL THEIR MEMORIES AND POWER.
THIS COLLAR WAS ALL THAT WAS PROTECTING Y'ALL...AND, WELL...
...THE GLOVES ARE OFF NOW...SO T'SPEAK.

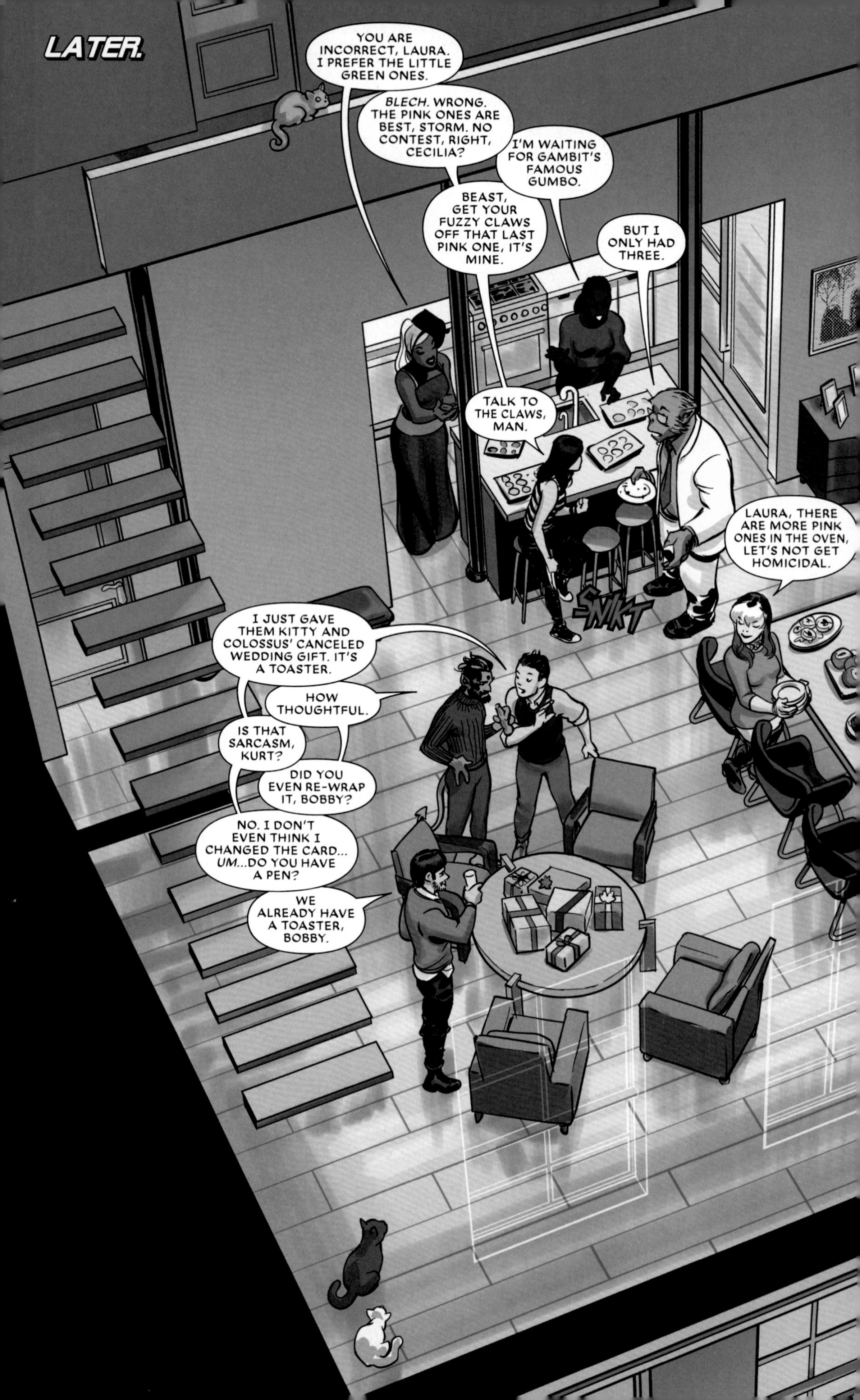
LATER.
YOU ARE INCORRECT, LAURA. I PREFER THE LITTLE GREEN ONES.
BLECH. WRONG. THE PINK ONES ARE BEST, STORM. NO CONTEST, RIGHT, CECILIA?
I'M WAITING FOR GAMBIT'S FAMOUS GUMBO.
BEAST, GET YOUR FUZZY CLAWS OFF THAT LAST PINK ONE, IT'S MINE.
BUT I ONLY HAD THREE.
TALK TO THE CLAWS, MAN.
SNIKT
LAURA, THERE ARE MORE PINK ONES IN THE OVEN, LET'S NOT GET HOMICIDAL.
I JUST GAVE THEM KITTY AND COLOSSUS' CANCELED WEDDING GIFT. IT'S A TOASTER.
HOW THOUGHTFUL.
IS THAT SARCASM, KURT?
DID YOU EVEN RE-WRAP IT, BOBBY?
NO. I DON'T EVEN THINK I CHANGED THE CARD... UM...DO YOU HAVE A PEN?
WE ALREADY HAVE A TOASTER, BOBBY.

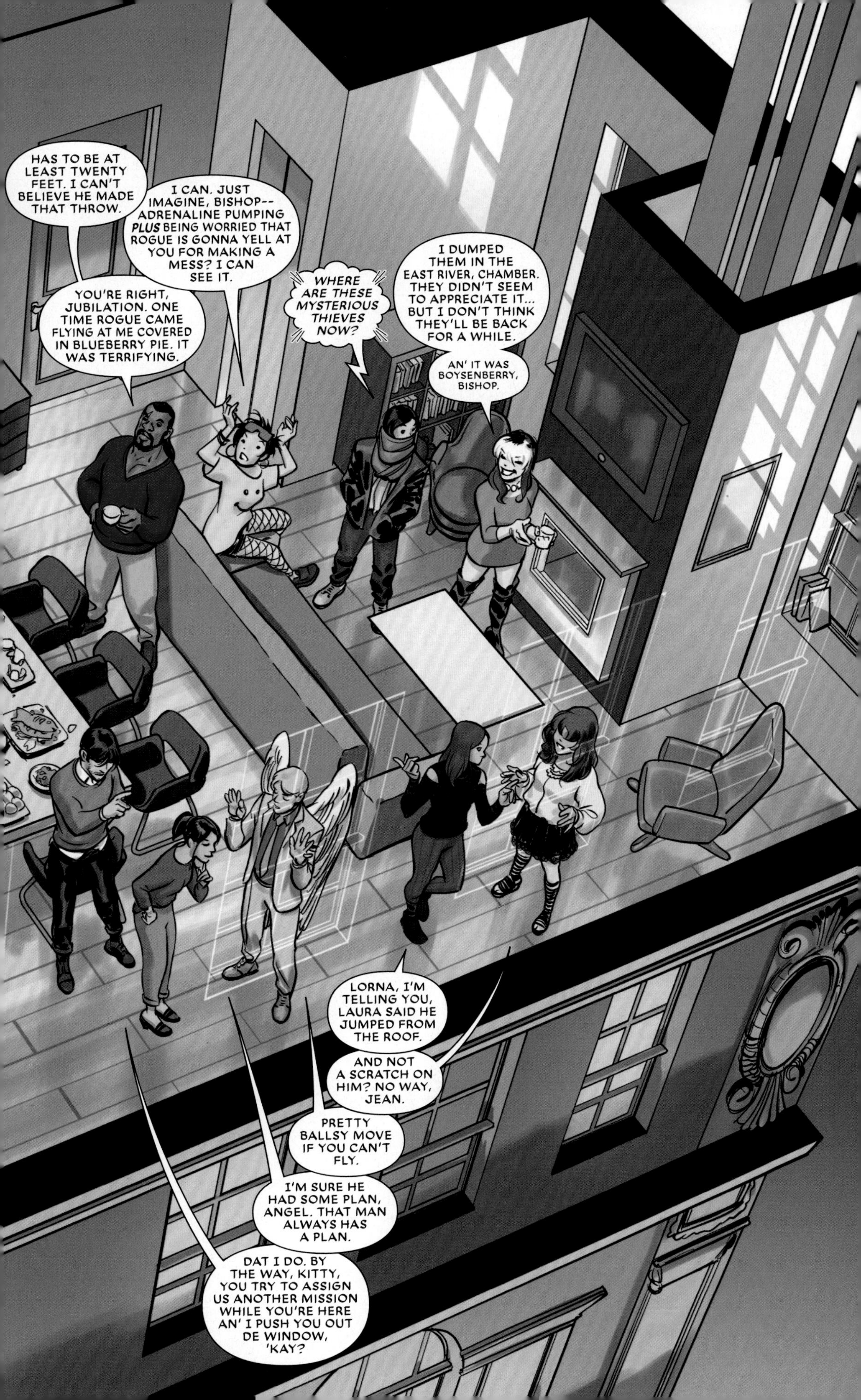
HAS TO BE AT LEAST TWENTY FEET. I CAN'T BELIEVE HE MADE THAT THROW.
I CAN. JUST IMAGINE, BISHOP-- ADRENALINE PUMPING PLUS BEING WORRIED THAT ROGUE IS GONNA YELL AT YOU FOR MAKING A MESS? I CAN SEE IT.
YOU'RE RIGHT, JUBILATION. ONE TIME ROGUE CAME FLYING AT ME COVERED IN BLUEBERRY PIE. IT WAS TERRIFYING.
WHERE ARE THESE MYSTERIOUS THIEVES NOW?
I DUMPED THEM IN THE EAST RIVER, CHAMBER. THEY DIDN'T SEEM TO APPRECIATE IT... BUT I DON'T THINK THEY'LL BE BACK FOR A WHILE.
AN' IT WAS BOYSENBERRY, BISHOP.
LORNA, I'M TELLING YOU, LAURA SAID HE JUMPED FROM THE ROOF.
AND NOT A SCRATCH ON HIM? NO WAY, JEAN.
PRETTY BALLSY MOVE IF YOU CAN'T FLY.
I'M SURE HE HAD SOME PLAN, ANGEL. THAT MAN ALWAYS HAS A PLAN.
DAT I DO. BY THE WAY, KITTY, YOU TRY TO ASSIGN US ANOTHER MISSION WHILE YOU'RE HERE AN' I PUSH YOU OUT DE WINDOW, 'KAY?

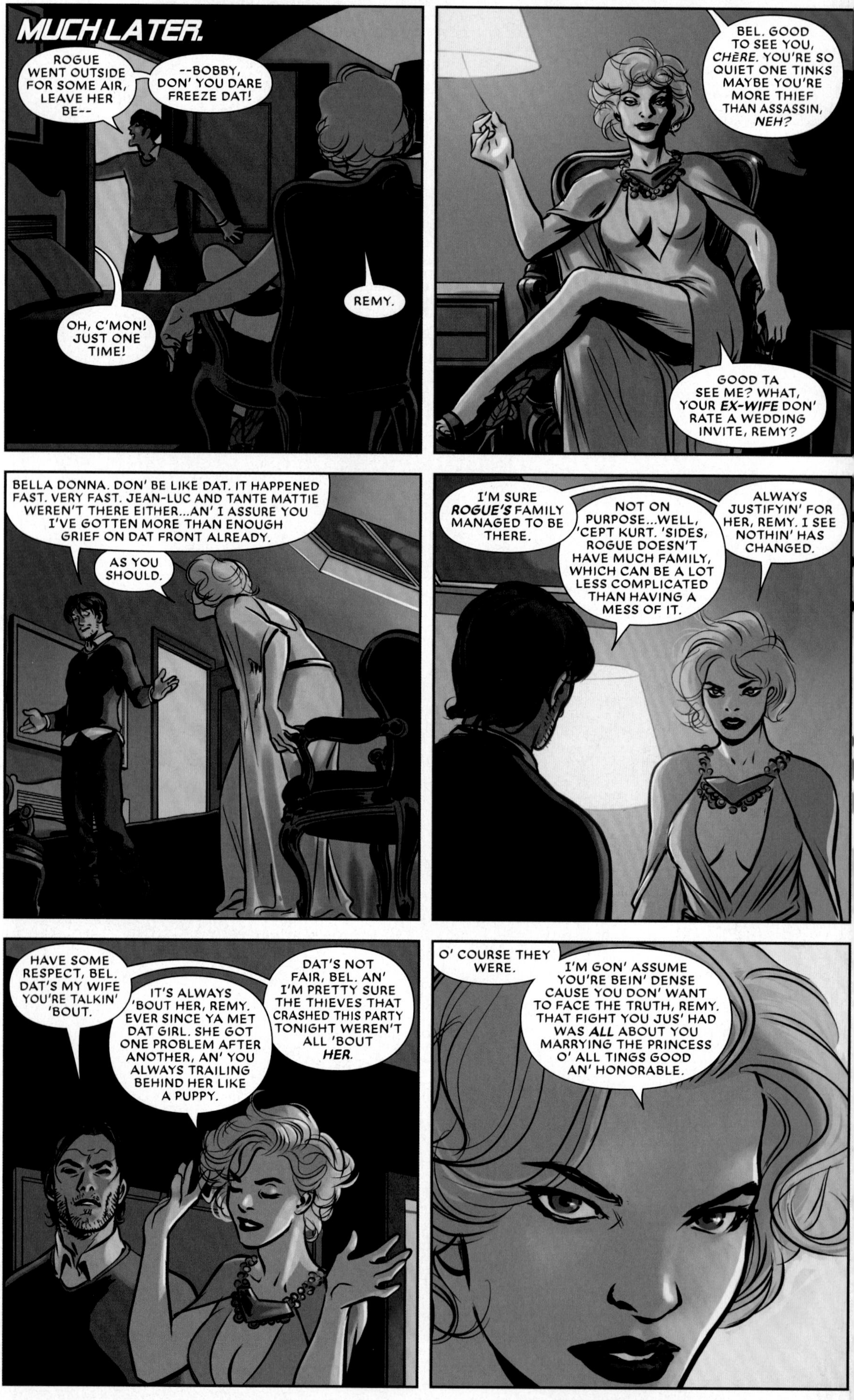
MUCH LATER.
ROGUE WENT OUTSIDE FOR SOME AIR, LEAVE HER BE--
--BOBBY, DON' YOU DARE FREEZE DAT!
OH, C'MON! JUST ONE TIME!
REMY.
BEL. GOOD TO SEE YOU, CHÈRE. YOU'RE SO QUIET ONE TINKS MAYBE YOU'RE MORE THIEF THAN ASSASSIN, NEH?
GOOD TA SEE ME? WHAT, YOUR EX-WIFE DON' RATE A WEDDING INVITE, REMY?
BELLA DONNA. DON' BE LIKE DAT. IT HAPPENED FAST. VERY FAST. JEAN-LUC AND TANTE MATTIE WEREN'T THERE EITHER...AN' I ASSURE YOU I'VE GOTTEN MORE THAN ENOUGH GRIEF ON DAT FRONT ALREADY.
AS YOU SHOULD.
I'M SURE ROGUE'S FAMILY MANAGED TO BE THERE.
NOT ON PURPOSE...WELL, 'CEPT KURT. 'SIDES, ROGUE DOESN'T HAVE MUCH FAMILY, WHICH CAN BE A LOT LESS COMPLICATED THAN HAVING A MESS OF IT.
ALWAYS JUSTIFYIN' FOR HER, REMY. I SEE NOTHIN' HAS CHANGED.
HAVE SOME RESPECT, BEL. DAT'S MY WIFE YOU'RE TALKIN' 'BOUT.
IT'S ALWAYS 'BOUT HER, REMY. EVER SINCE YA MET DAT GIRL. SHE GOT ONE PROBLEM AFTER ANOTHER, AN' YOU ALWAYS TRAILING BEHIND HER LIKE A PUPPY.
DAT'S NOT FAIR, BEL. AN' I'M PRETTY SURE THE THIEVES THAT CRASHED THIS PARTY TONIGHT WEREN'T ALL 'BOUT HER.
O' COURSE THEY WERE.
I'M GON' ASSUME YOU'RE BEIN' DENSE CAUSE YOU DON' WANT TO FACE THE TRUTH, REMY. THAT FIGHT YOU JUS' HAD WAS ALL ABOUT YOU MARRYING THE PRINCESS O' ALL TINGS GOOD AN' HONORABLE.

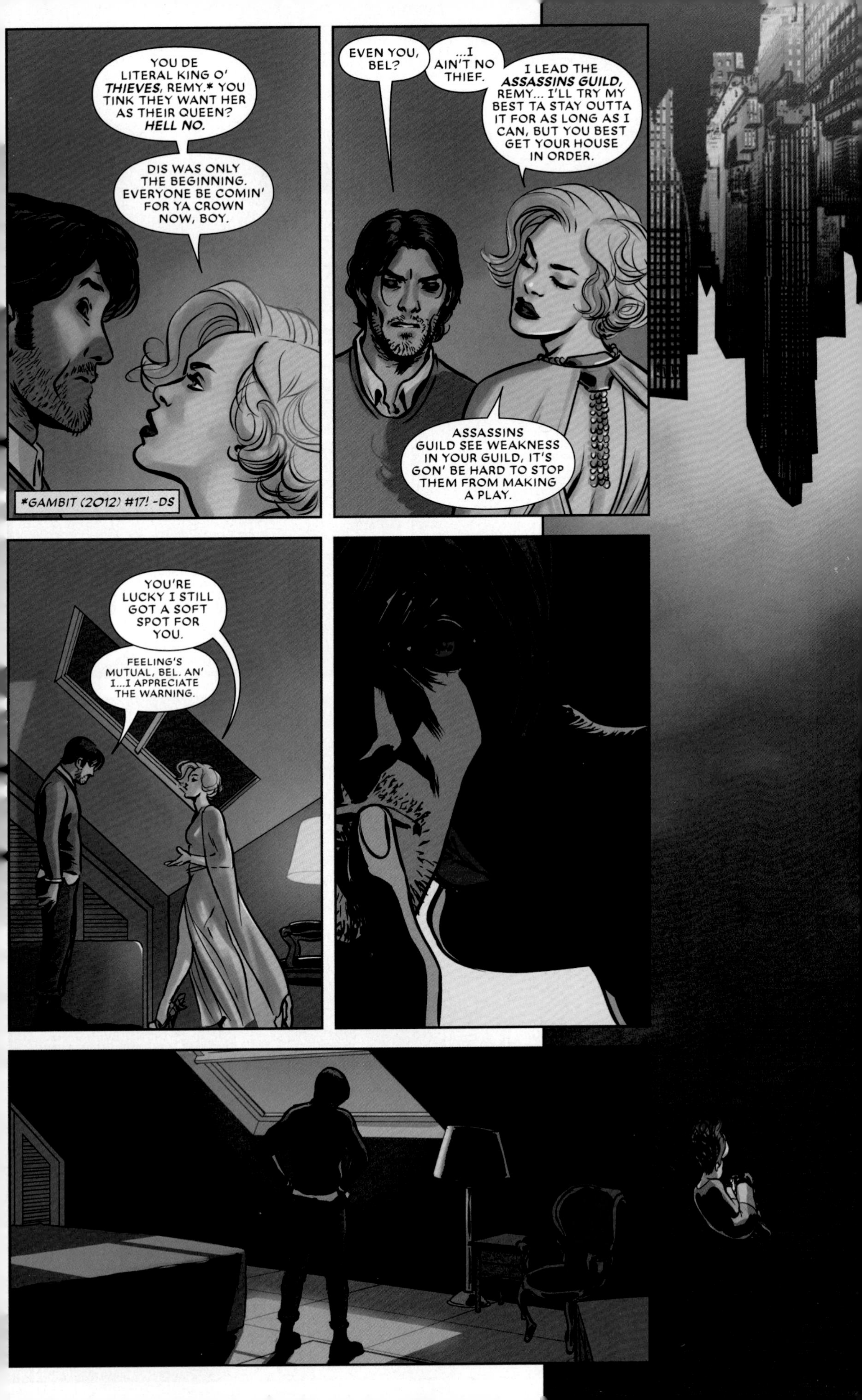

YOU DE LITERAL KING O' THIEVES, REMY.* YOU TINK THEY WANT HER AS THEIR QUEEN? HELL NO.
DIS WAS ONLY THE BEGINNING. EVERYONE BE COMIN' FOR YA CROWN NOW, BOY.
*GAMBIT (2012) #17! -DS
EVEN YOU, BEL?
...I AIN'T NO THIEF.
I LEAD THE ASSASSINS GUILD, REMY... I'LL TRY MY BEST TA STAY OUTTA IT FOR AS LONG AS I CAN, BUT YOU BEST GET YOUR HOUSE IN ORDER.
ASSASSINS GUILD SEE WEAKNESS IN YOUR GUILD, IT'S GON' BE HARD TO STOP THEM FROM MAKING A PLAY.
YOU'RE LUCKY I STILL GOT A SOFT SPOT FOR YOU.
FEELING'S MUTUAL, BEL. AN' I...I APPRECIATE THE WARNING.

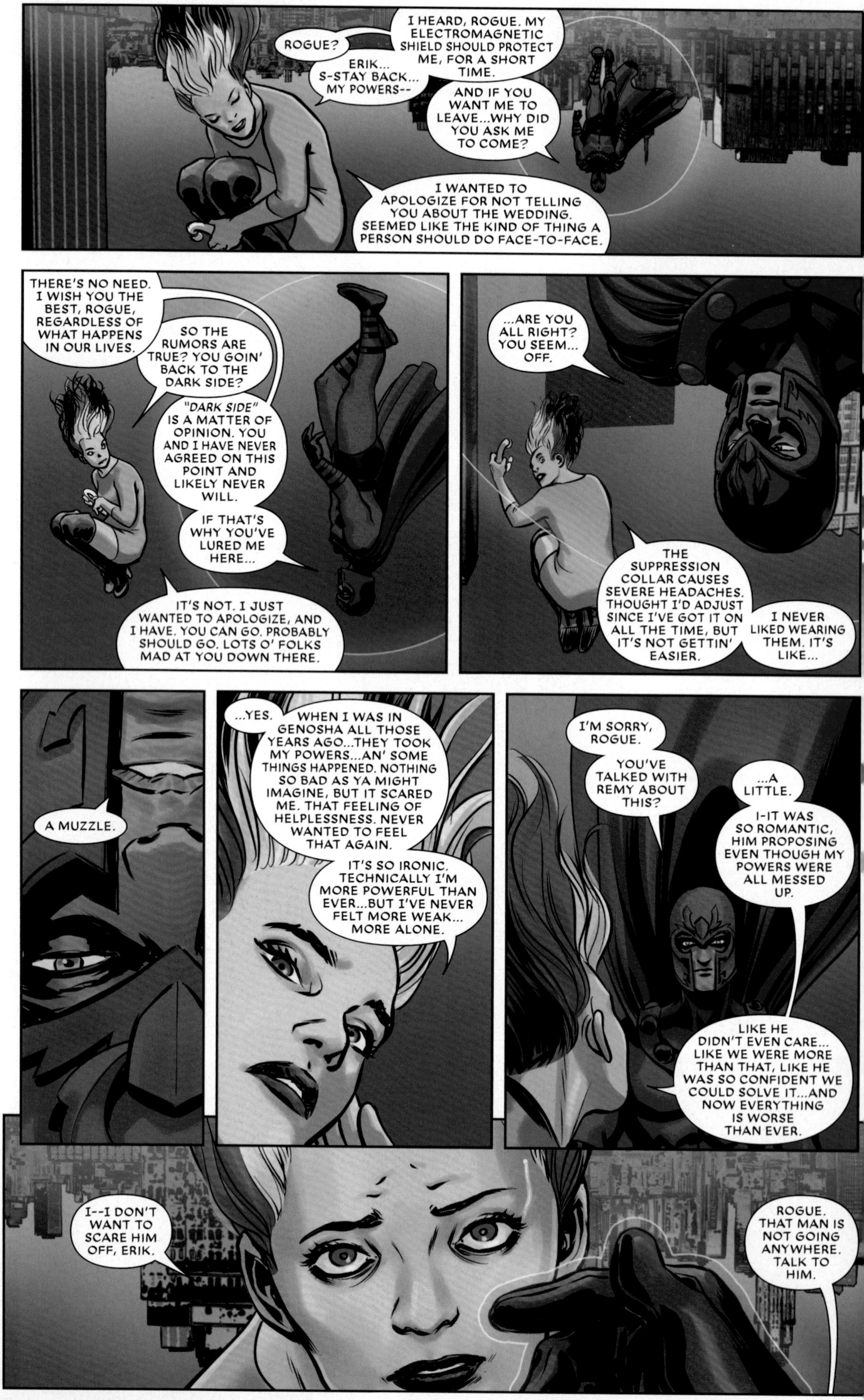
ROGUE?
I HEARD, ROGUE. MY ELECTROMAGNETIC SHIELD SHOULD PROTECT ME, FOR A SHORT TIME.
ERIK... S-STAY BACK... MY POWERS--
AND IF YOU WANT ME TO LEAVE...WHY DID YOU ASK ME TO COME?
I WANTED TO APOLOGIZE FOR NOT TELLING YOU ABOUT THE WEDDING. SEEMED LIKE THE KIND OF THING A PERSON SHOULD DO FACE-TO-FACE.
THERE'S NO NEED. I WISH YOU THE BEST, ROGUE, REGARDLESS OF WHAT HAPPENS IN OUR LIVES.
SO THE RUMORS ARE TRUE? YOU GOIN' BACK TO THE DARK SIDE?
"DARK SIDE" IS A MATTER OF OPINION. YOU AND I HAVE NEVER AGREED ON THIS POINT AND LIKELY NEVER WILL.
IF THAT'S WHY YOU'VE LURED ME HERE...
IT'S NOT. I JUST WANTED TO APOLOGIZE, AND I HAVE. YOU CAN GO. PROBABLY SHOULD GO. LOTS O' FOLKS MAD AT YOU DOWN THERE.
...ARE YOU ALL RIGHT? YOU SEEM... OFF.
THE SUPPRESSION COLLAR CAUSES SEVERE HEADACHES. THOUGHT I'D ADJUST SINCE I'VE GOT IT ON ALL THE TIME, BUT IT'S NOT GETTIN' EASIER.
I NEVER LIKED WEARING THEM. IT'S LIKE...
A MUZZLE.
...YES.
WHEN I WAS IN GENOSHA ALL THOSE YEARS AGO...THEY TOOK MY POWERS...AN' SOME THINGS HAPPENED. NOTHING SO BAD AS YA MIGHT IMAGINE, BUT IT SCARED ME. THAT FEELING OF HELPLESSNESS. NEVER WANTED TO FEEL THAT AGAIN.
IT'S SO IRONIC. TECHNICALLY I'M MORE POWERFUL THAN EVER...BUT I'VE NEVER FELT MORE WEAK... MORE ALONE.
I'M SORRY, ROGUE.
YOU'VE TALKED WITH REMY ABOUT THIS?
...A LITTLE.
I-IT WAS SO ROMANTIC, HIM PROPOSING EVEN THOUGH MY POWERS WERE ALL MESSED UP.
LIKE HE DIDN'T EVEN CARE... LIKE WE WERE MORE THAN THAT, LIKE HE WAS SO CONFIDENT WE COULD SOLVE IT...AND NOW EVERYTHING IS WORSE THAN EVER.
I--I DON'T WANT TO SCARE HIM OFF, ERIK.
ROGUE. THAT MAN IS NOT GOING ANYWHERE. TALK TO HIM.

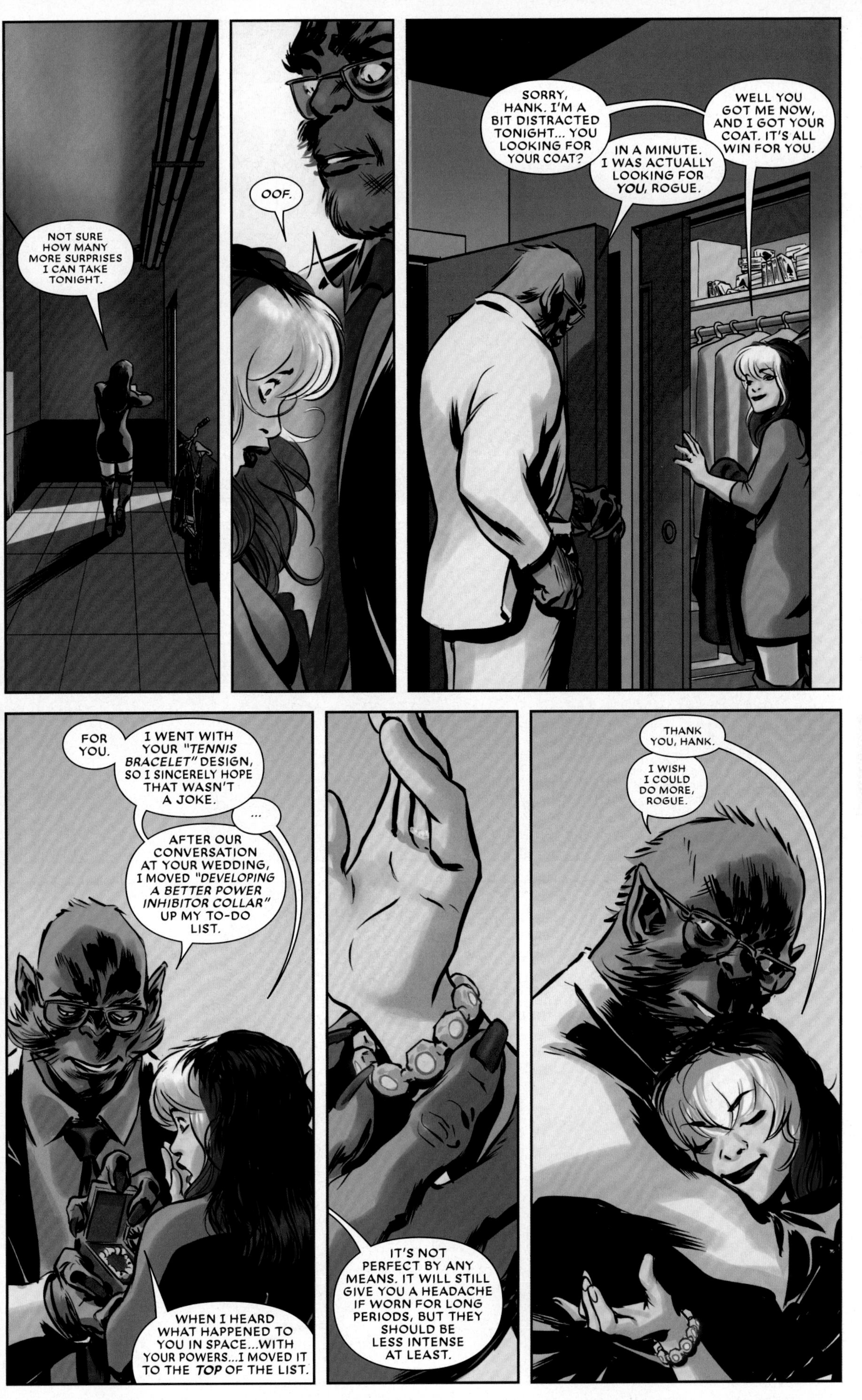
NOT SURE HOW MANY MORE SURPRISES I CAN TAKE TONIGHT.
OOF.
SORRY, HANK. I'M A BIT DISTRACTED TONIGHT... YOU LOOKING FOR YOUR COAT?
IN A MINUTE. I WAS ACTUALLY LOOKING FOR *YOU*, ROGUE.
WELL YOU GOT ME NOW, AND I GOT YOUR COAT. IT'S ALL WIN FOR YOU.
FOR YOU.
I WENT WITH YOUR "*TENNIS BRACELET*" DESIGN, SO I SINCERELY HOPE THAT WASN'T A JOKE.
...
AFTER OUR CONVERSATION AT YOUR WEDDING, I MOVED "*DEVELOPING A BETTER POWER INHIBITOR COLLAR*" UP MY TO-DO LIST.
WHEN I HEARD WHAT HAPPENED TO YOU IN SPACE...WITH YOUR POWERS...I MOVED IT TO THE *TOP* OF THE LIST.
IT'S NOT PERFECT BY ANY MEANS. IT WILL STILL GIVE YOU A HEADACHE IF WORN FOR LONG PERIODS, BUT THEY SHOULD BE LESS INTENSE AT LEAST.
THANK YOU, HANK.
I WISH I COULD DO MORE, ROGUE.

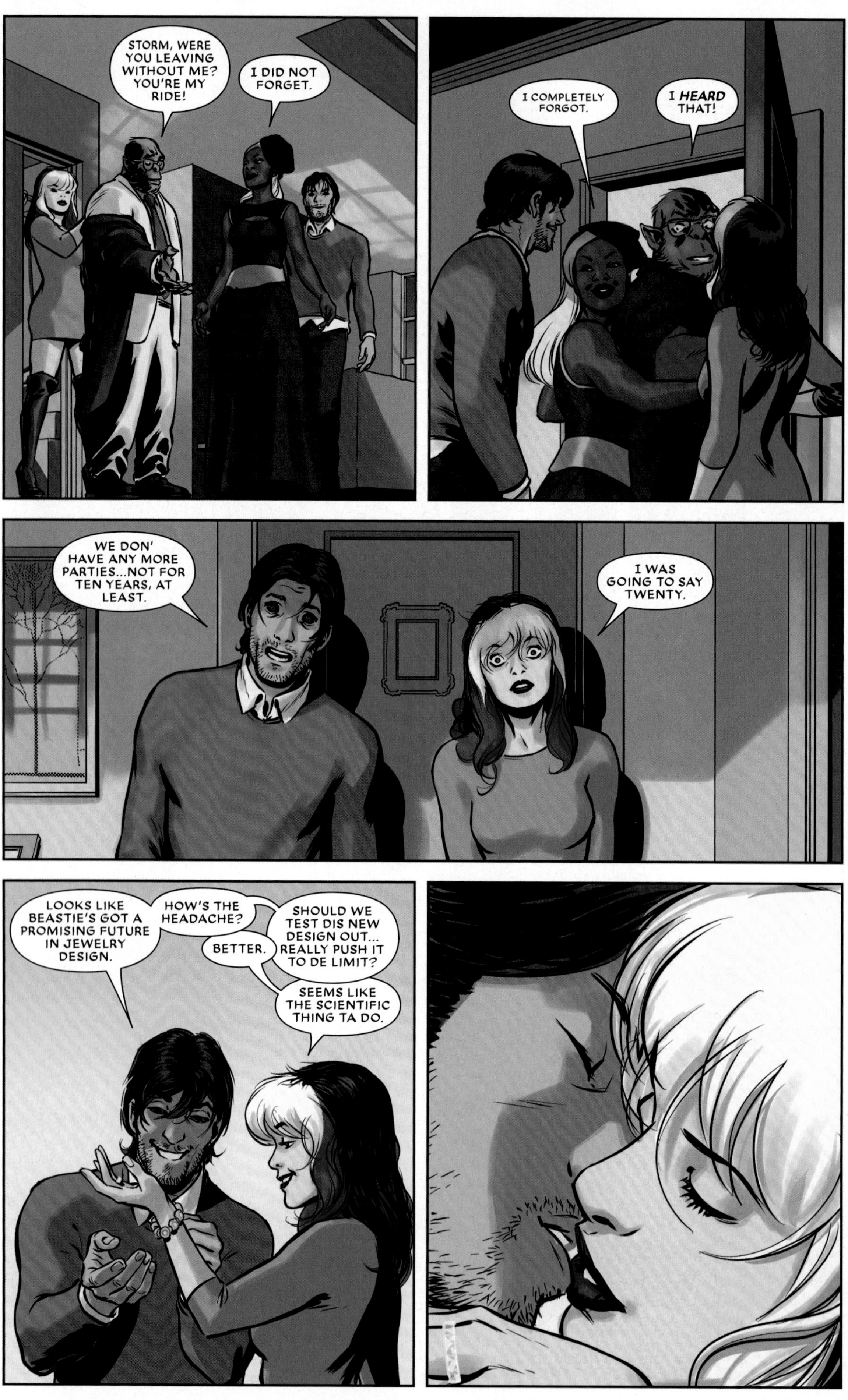
STORM, WERE YOU LEAVING WITHOUT ME? YOU'RE MY RIDE!
I DID NOT FORGET.
I COMPLETELY FORGOT.
I *HEARD* THAT!
WE DON' HAVE ANY MORE PARTIES...NOT FOR TEN YEARS, AT LEAST.
I WAS GOING TO SAY TWENTY.
LOOKS LIKE BEASTIE'S GOT A PROMISING FUTURE IN JEWELRY DESIGN.
HOW'S THE HEADACHE?
BETTER.
SHOULD WE TEST DIS NEW DESIGN OUT... REALLY PUSH IT TO DE LIMIT?
SEEMS LIKE THE SCIENTIFIC THING TA DO.

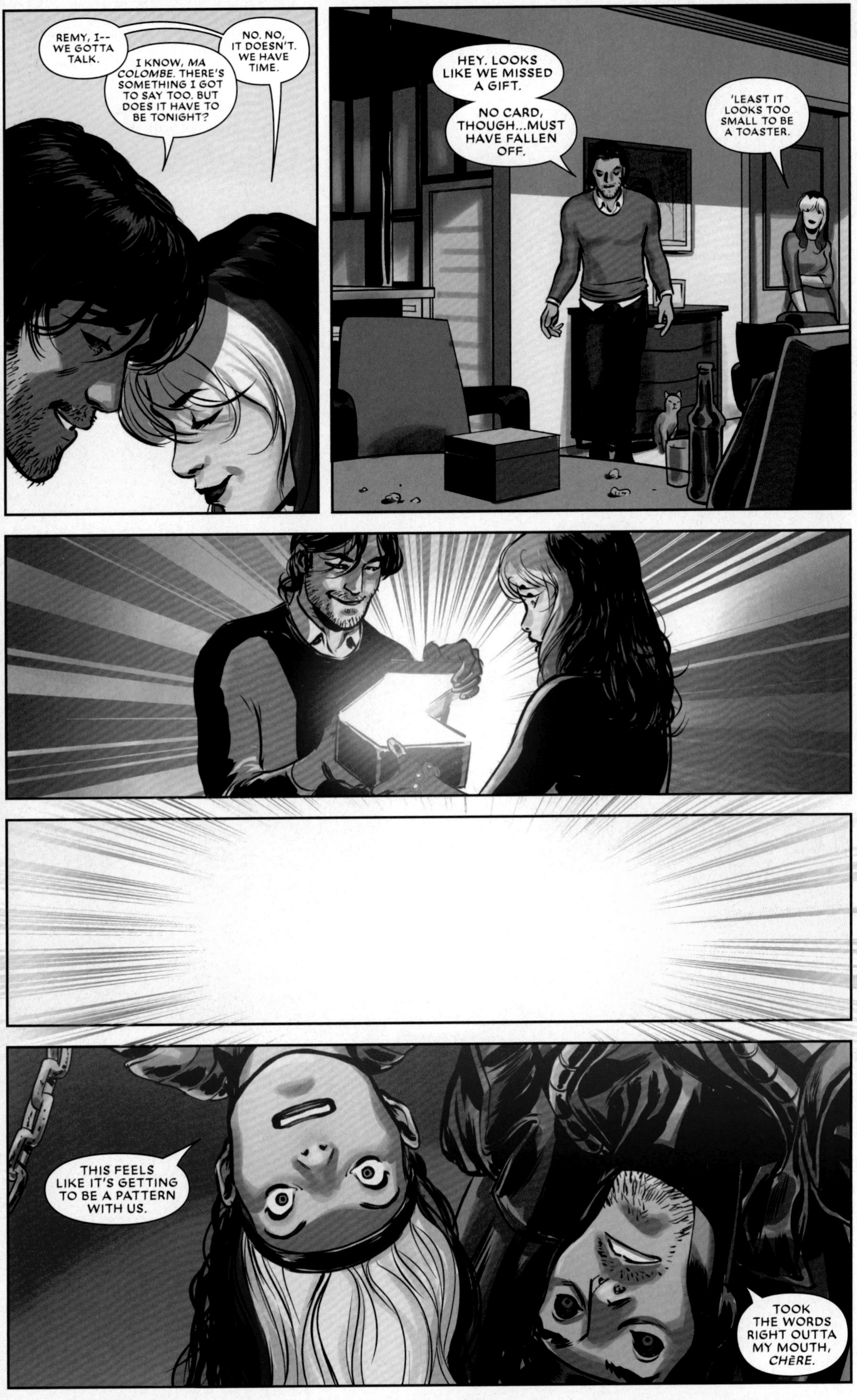
REMY, I-- WE GOTTA TALK.
I KNOW, *MA COLOMBE*. THERE'S SOMETHING I GOT TO SAY TOO. BUT DOES IT HAVE TO BE TONIGHT?
NO, NO, IT DOESN'T. WE HAVE TIME.
HEY. LOOKS LIKE WE MISSED A GIFT.
NO CARD, THOUGH...MUST HAVE FALLEN OFF.
'LEAST IT LOOKS TOO SMALL TO BE A TOASTER.
THIS FEELS LIKE IT'S GETTING TO BE A PATTERN WITH US.
TOOK THE WORDS RIGHT OUTTA MY MOUTH, *CHÈRE*.

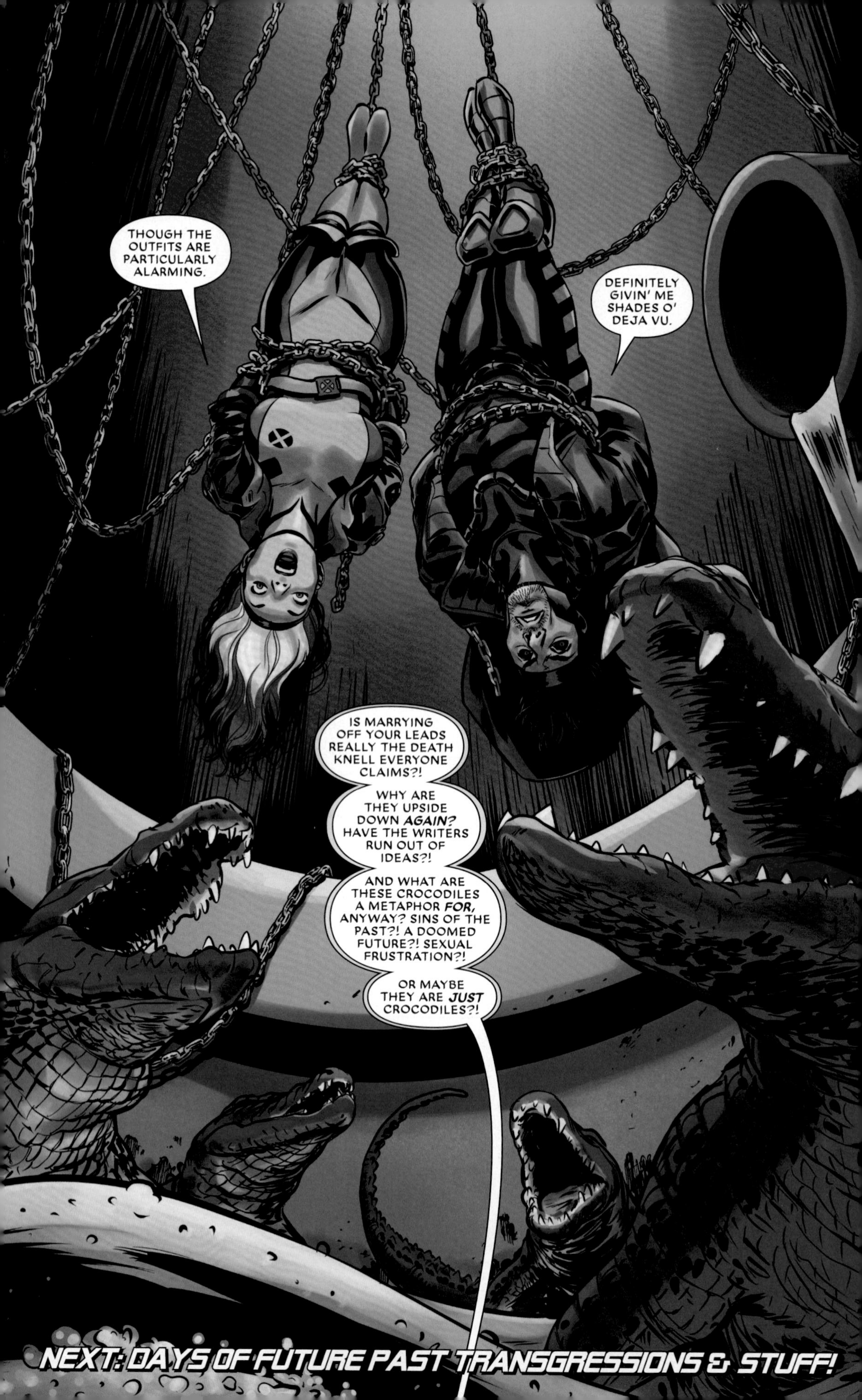
THOUGH THE OUTFITS ARE PARTICULARLY ALARMING.
DEFINITELY GIVIN' ME SHADES O' DEJA VU.
IS MARRYING OFF YOUR LEADS REALLY THE DEATH KNELL EVERYONE CLAIMS?!
WHY ARE THEY UPSIDE DOWN AGAIN? HAVE THE WRITERS RUN OUT OF IDEAS?!
AND WHAT ARE THESE CROCODILES A METAPHOR FOR, ANYWAY? SINS OF THE PAST?! A DOOMED FUTURE?! SEXUAL FRUSTRATION?!
OR MAYBE THEY ARE JUST CROCODILES?!
NEXT: DAYS OF FUTURE PAST TRANSGRESSIONS & STUFF!

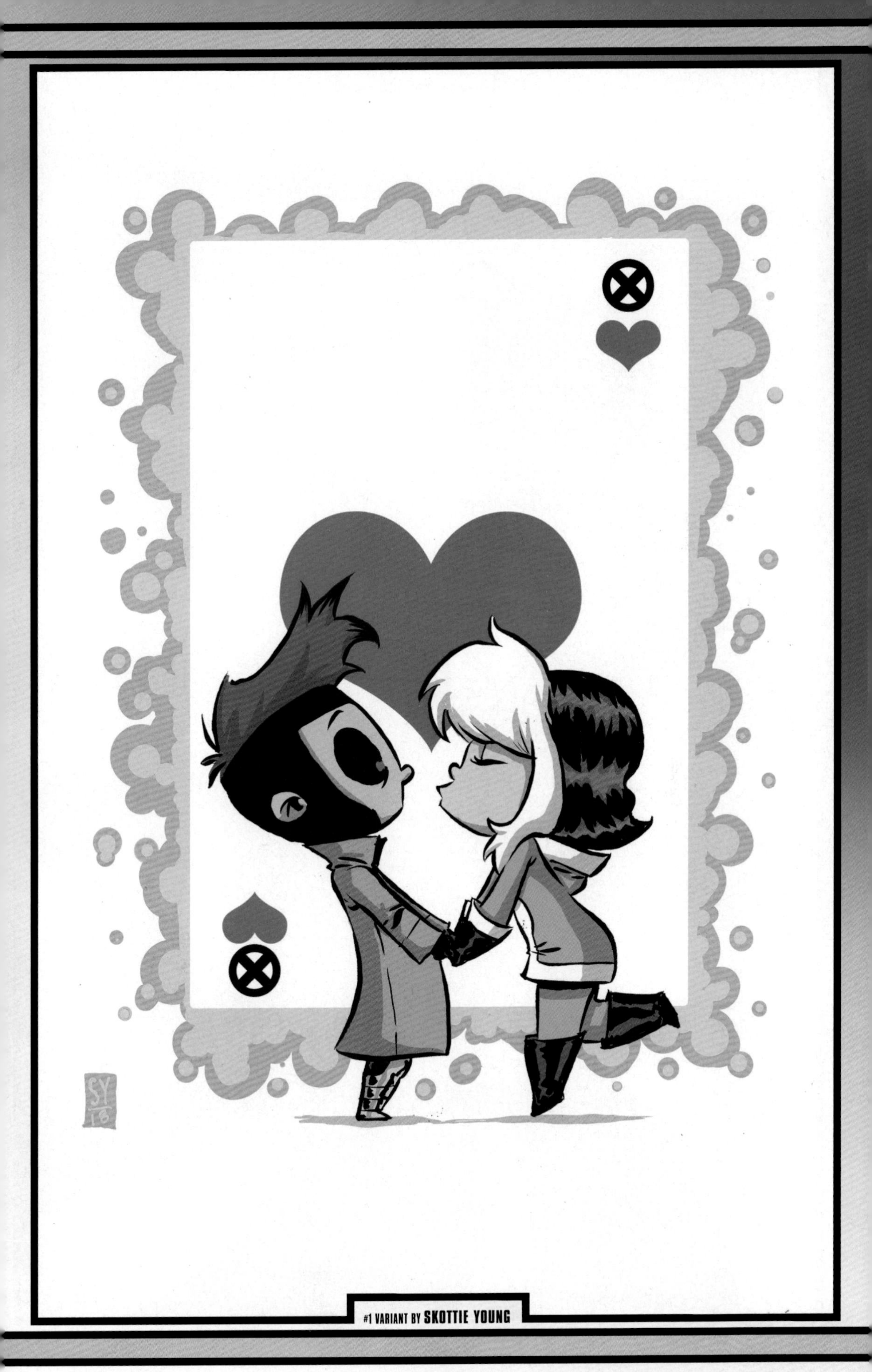
SY
13

#1 VARIANT BY SKOTTIE YOUNG

#2 VARIANT BY JEN BARTEL

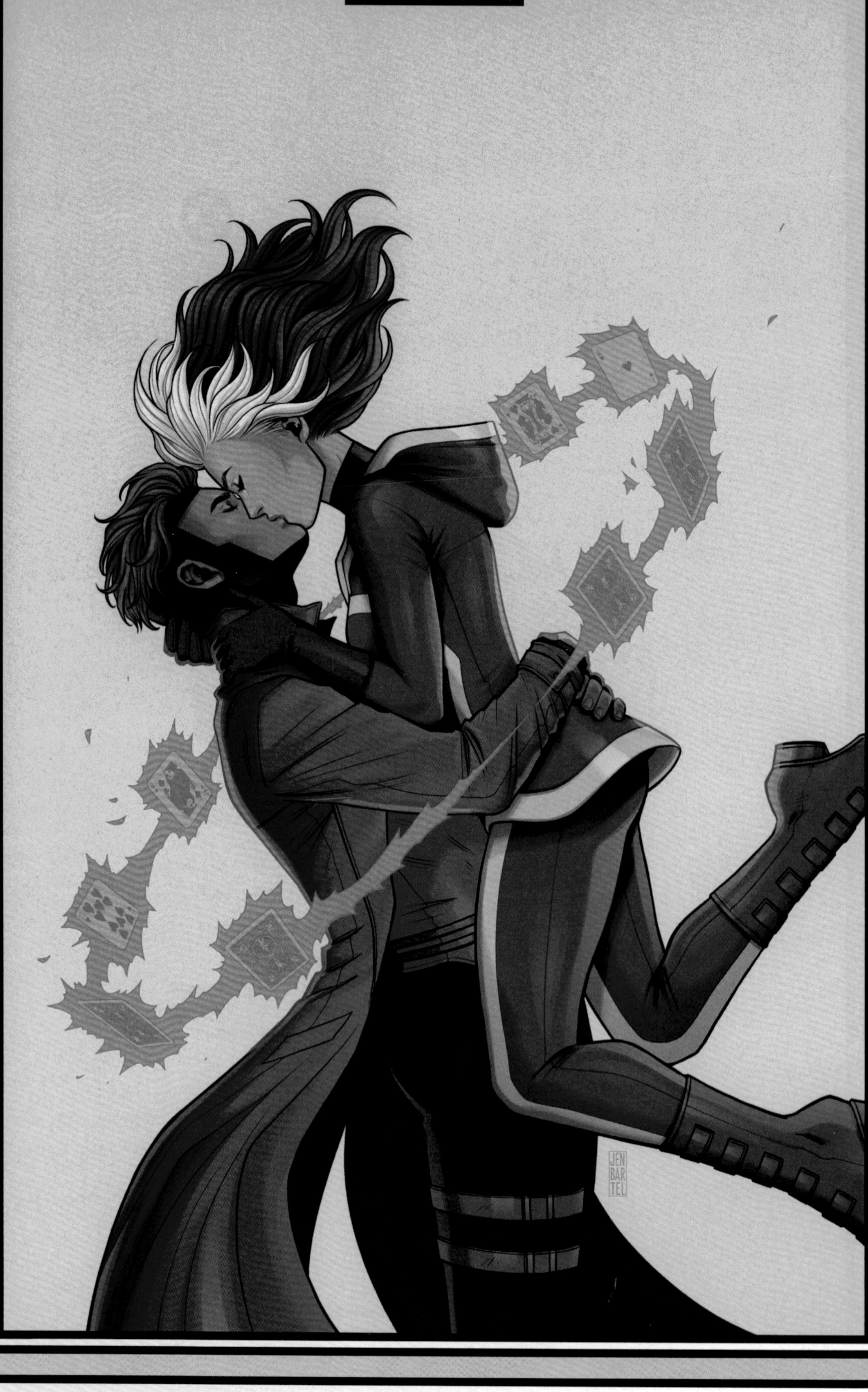
JEN BARTEL

#3 VARIANT BY PHIL NOTO

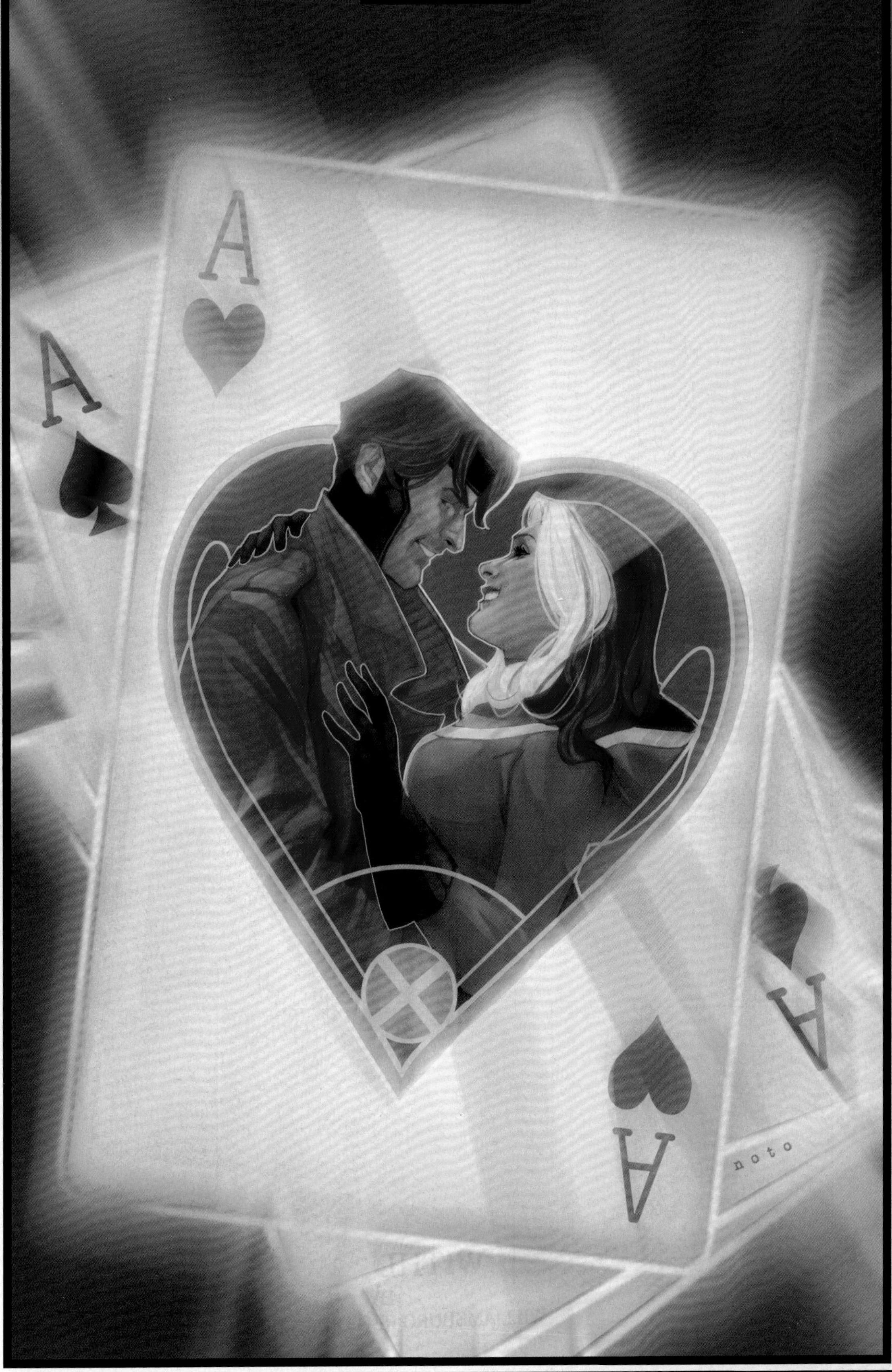

A
A
A
A
noto

#3, PAGE 3 ART PROCESS

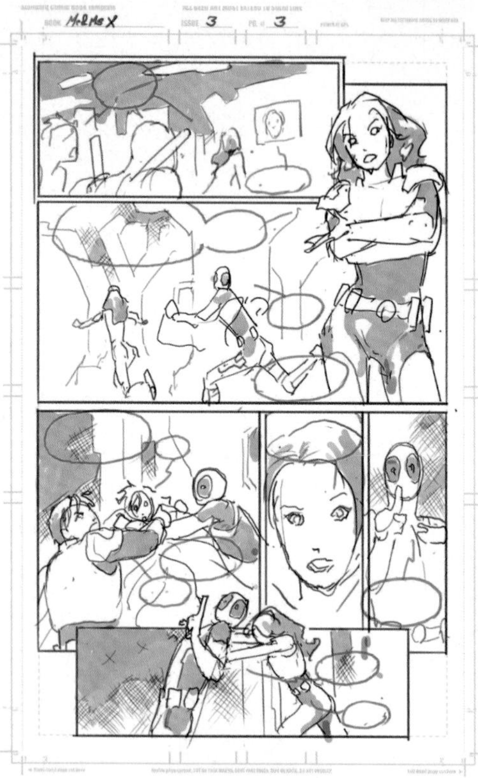

Mr&Ms X
3
3

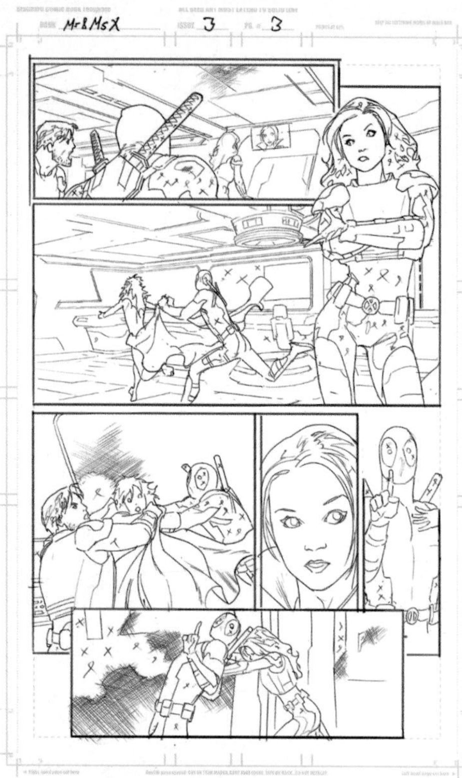

Mr&Ms X
3
3

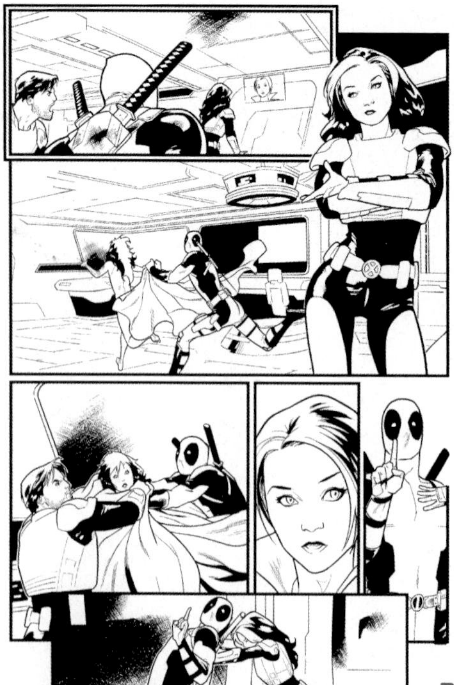

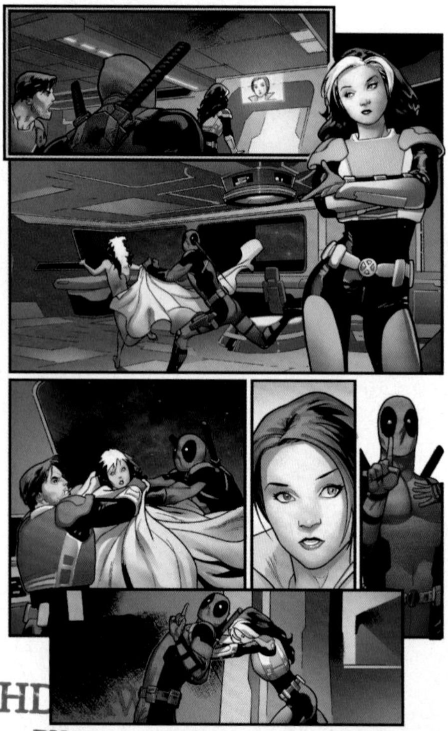